Electric and Hybrid Cars

Electric and Hybrid Cars

A History

CURTIS D. ANDERSON AND JUDY ANDERSON

McFarland & Company, Inc., Publishers
Jefferson, North Carolina, and London

Library of Congress Cataloguing-in-Publication Data

Anderson, Curtis D. (Curtis Darrel), 1947–
    Electric and hybrid cars : a history / Curtis D. Anderson and
Judy Anderson.
       p.   cm.
    Includes bibliographical references and index.

    ISBN 0-7864-1872-9 (illustrated case binding : 50# alkaline paper)

    1. Automobiles, Electric.   2. Hybrid electric cars.
I. Anderson, Judy, 1946– II. Title.
TL220.A53   2005
629.22'93 — dc22   2004013469

British Library cataloguing data are available

Cover images (top to bottom): Thomas Edison and a 1913 electric car,
the 2001 Toyota Prius electric/gas hybrid, and two Corbin Sparrow
zero-emission vehicles

Manufactured in the United States of America

McFarland & Company, Inc., Publishers
  Box 611, Jefferson, North Carolina 28640
    www.mcfarlandpub.com

To my mother and father, who always enjoyed a Sunday drive (C. D. A.)

Contents

Acronyms

ACEEE — American Council for an Energy Efficient Economy
AFV — Alternative Fuel Vehicle
ALABC — Advanced Lead-Acid Battery Consortium
AMC — American Motors Corporation
APS — Arizona Public Service
AT-PEZV — Advanced Technology Partial Zero Emission Vehicles
BEV — Battery Electric Vehicles
CaFCP — California Fuel Cell Partnership
CAFE — Corporate Average Fuel Economy
CARB — California Air Resources Board
CAUCA — Californians Against Utility Company Abuse
CFA — Central Facilities Area
CMA — California Manufacturers Association
CMAQ — Congestion Mitigation and Air Quality Program
CNG — Compressed Natural Gas
DOE — Department of Energy
EPA — Environmental Protection Agency
EPAct — Energy Policy Act (1992)
ERDA — Energy Research and Development Agency
ETA — Electric Transportation Applications
EV — Electric Vehicle
FCEV — Fuel Cell Electric Vehicles
FCV — Fuel Cell Vehicle
FOP — Field Operations Program
FTA — Federal Transit Act
GM — General Motors
HEV — Hybrid Electric Vehicle
ICE — Internal Combustion Engine
INEEL — Idaho National Engineering and Environmental Laboratory
ISTEA — Intermodal Surface Transportation Efficiency Act
LAW — League of American Wheelmen (1890)
LEV — Low Emission Vehicle

LEVP — Low Emission Vehicle Program
LiION — Lithium Ion (battery)
LNG — Liquefied Natural Gas
LPB — Lithium Polymer Battery
NELA — National Electric Lighting Association
NEV — Neighborhood Electric Vehicle
NREL — National Renewable Energy Laboratory
NiMH — Nickel Metal Hydride (battery)
OTEC — Ocean Thermal Energy Conversion
OWC — Oscillating Water Column
PEM — Proton Exchange Membrane
PEPCO — Potomac Electric Power Company
PNGV — Partnership for a New Generation of Vehicles
PZEV — Partial Zero Emission Vehicle
QVT — Qualified Vehicle Tester
RFG — Reformulated Gasoline
SCAT — Southern Coalition for Advanced Transportation
SCE — Southern California Edison
SULEV — Super Ultra Low Emission Vehicle
TEA-21 — Transportation Equity Act for the 21st Century (1998)
ULEV — Ultra Low Emission Vehicle
USABC — United States Advanced Battery Consortium
USCAR — United States Council for Automotive Research
USPS — United States Postal Service
VRDC — Vehicle Recycling Development Center
ZEV — Zero Emission Vehicle

Preface

The history of electric vehicles and hybrids reflects economic and social trends. The EV's popularity increases when fuel prices rise or when the public is concerned about environmental pollution.

This book chronicles the electric automobile's first century. It covers innovations in design, marketing strategy, government involvement and environmental issues that have shaped the electric car's evolution. It contains illustrations of batteries, fuel cells and chassis for the earlier models and photographs of both early and newer electric vehicles, with short descriptions of each. The book also considers developing technologies such as the Ballard fuel cell, the reappearance of hybrid vehicles and the various market forces that have shaped the industry. An annotated select bibliography and subject index are included for quick reference.

This work does not include mass transit vehicles, Neighborhood Electric Vehicles (NEVs), solar-powered vehicles or detailed explanations of the car's electrical systems. Nor does it explain the technical workings of the various fuel cells beyond the limits of a general reader's understanding. It is not meant to be a comprehensive history of electric vehicles. It is primarily concerned with United States history, with some references to the United Kingdom and Western European vehicle development. For a more detailed technical level of research, we suggest the reader begin with the works of Ernest Henry Wakefield, truly an expert in the field of electric motors and their applications in motoring.[1]

This is a glimpse for the curious, a shortcut for the busy executive enthusiast, a starting point for the student and a hint of the future based on the past for potential investors and consumers.

Introduction

The Birth of the Automobile Industry

The computer may soon lead in this category, but for the last one hundred years, the most ubiquitous item in America has been the automobile. It has captured our imagination. Even as the computer invades our environment, analogies to the automobile, like information superhighway, Infobahn and I-Way, hold fast to the culture of the automobile. Cars provide a security, freedom and comfort that are not found in mass transit or other public transportation. They are statements about ourselves. They affect all parts of our lives, and most importantly, where we live. The car created suburbia by providing the means to commute greater distances from home to work. In over one hundred years of inventions, such as the harnessing of electrical power, the telephone, radio, television and computers, none have affected our lives as much as the automobile.

At the turn of the 20th century, consumers shopping for motorized transportation were offered a choice of steam-powered, gasoline-powered internal combustion engines (ICEs) or electric vehicles (EVs). The marketplace was equally divided with no clear indication of which type would dominate. Steam-powered vehicles had speed and were less expensive, but required a long time to fire up and frequent stops for water. The ICEs were dirtier, more difficult to start and moderately more expensive, but could travel longer distances at a reasonable speed without stopping. EVs were clean and quiet, but slow and expensive. Each fought to be competitive in the open market in performance and price.

Electric and hybrid vehicles have a colorful past filled with ingenious inventions, patent wars and idealistic goals. Their designers strove to produce non-polluting, elegant, easy to maintain transportation for the motoring public. The advertising has reflected the woman's right to independence, appealed to the environmental cause, and frequently has a stylish flair that can bring a smile to fellow motorists.

As with many products, the most logical solution does not always capture the consumer's imagination. In early years, EVs held a competitive share of the market, holding their own against the popular steam and the faster, rumbling internal combustion engine automobiles. The prominence of electric vehicles at the Electrical Exhibition in Madison Square Garden in 1899 showed that the industry was well established. By 1904 one-third of all powered vehicles in New York, Chicago and Boston were electric. The advent of the electric starter, improved roads and the expansion of the road system in the second decade of the 20th century changed that equality. Autos with longer range, higher speed, and a refueling infrastructure (ICEs) had the market's attention. Since the 1920s, EVs have balanced on the edge of the market, becoming popular for brief periods during fuel shortages and environmental crises. Their alternate fuel source and non-polluting motor are popular until the crisis passes, then interest wanes.

Innovation resulted in many improvements and variety in the first EVs. The first horseless carriages were just that. The body design was similar to a horse drawn carriage with a battery, a motor and a means of steering added. Until about 1895 the wheels were the standard wooden spoke variety with solid rubber tires. The ride mimicked the rough jolting of the horse-drawn carriage subjecting both passengers and batteries to the bumps and ruts in the roads. Creative minds of the day saw a need for improving the ride. Pneumatic tires were introduced, smoothing out the ride and helping reduce the damage vibration caused to the batteries. The run from Paris to Frouville in the fall of 1905 that covered about 130 miles on one battery charge, and the 100-mile trek from Cleveland to Erie over ordinary country roads, some of sand, others with steep hills that taxed the battery charge, showed expanded potential for this auto that usually averaged 35 miles on a single charge. The spirit of winning also gave impetus to improving the speed of the electrics. In the first decade of the 1900s, electric autos were worthy opponents in auto racing. A. L. Riker won a 1908 race at Narragansett Park, Rhode Island, driving five miles in 11 minutes and 28 seconds. The best gasoline car finished over a mile behind. As for touring around the northeastern United States in 1909, some avid automobilists took electric vehicles on trips up to 1,500 miles. Such innovation put the EVs in a viable market position during its early years.

Competition, safety and a potential revenue source sparked local and state governments to pass laws and regulations for these new vehicles. Rules for right of way and speed, and registration payments for the new vehicles, appeared in the statutes, and lawsuits between horse-drawn and motorized vehicle owners hit the courts. All autos were assessed equally in the early decades, but by the 1920s the criterion for fees had changed. A vehicle's weight became a factor. Electrics, because of the extra weight from their onboard batteries, were charged a higher fee to cover wear and tear on the road's surface. Laws and regulations like the additional charge for weight gave electrics a slight disadvantage in the marketplace and a new source of financing for state and local governments.

Concern about the quality of life in the cities was prevalent at the turn of the 20th century. Horses, although hardworking and dependable for pulling wagons and cabs, did come with some drawbacks—manure cleanup on the city streets gave employment to many men. The electrics did not have the obnoxious smell and noise pollution of the ICE, and were considered a fine solution to the environmental problems caused by horses. Dirt and dust clouds along the roadways were still considered problems common to and created by each type of vehicle, but these would be addressed later as road surfaces improved. EVs garnered a reputation early in their history for being environmentally friendly.

Individual owners may have sparked their neighbors' and friends' interest to purchase their own electric vehicles, but the introduction and growth of the taxicab electric fleets gave the industry a core market. The electric taxicabs made their debut in New York City in 1896 and were being considered by other large cities as the ideal answer to the enormous problem of pollution by the horse drawn carriages. Henry Morris and Pedro

Columbia electric, 1902[1]

Salom (the Electrical Vehicle Company, New York) produced Electrobat electric taxicabs in 1896 and began their New York taxi service as a means for the average citizen to have the benefits of transportation without needing the expertise to maintain the vehicles. They claimed that selling individual vehicles to customers was impractical, "…because it would be impossible for them to send a skilled engineer out with every carriage they sold, and the average layman knows nothing about the electric business."[2] They believed the electric vehicle was too complicated and unreliable for lay operators and decided to create a transportation service company rather than an automobile sales company.[3] Morris and Salom were in the minority in this opinion. Most people of the day thought that the electric vehicles were so easy to drive and maintain that even a woman or child could operate one. Morris and Salom did prove the electric vehicle to be very effective in service as a taxi in competition with the horse-drawn cab.

> The judgment of the people is in the main favorable [and] is proved by the statement of the company that the cabs are in almost constant demand and that more will be put in service soon. For the enterprise they have shown in being the first to introduce [electric] motor cabs in the streets of New York this company is entitled to a great credit and will no doubt reap a commensurate profit.[4]

The *Horseless Age*'s author proved to be an accurate predictor. Electric cabs provided service to city dwellers for over a decade. The cabs proved to be reliable and sturdy.

> The first step away from the time-honored horse-drawn hack was the electric cab, a number of which were placed in service on the streets of New York City as early as 1899 [*sic*]. These cabs were naturally crude and cumbersome, but the majority of the original vehicles that were placed in service in New York more than ten years ago are still doing duty today [1910]. If a gasoline car of the "vintage" of 1899 were to be seen on the streets now, it would create a furore.[5]

By 1899 there were about sixty Electrobat II cabs in service, then produced by William C. Whitney. He envisioned a nationwide business. The vehicles would run about four hours, then be taken to a station, where the run-down batteries would be replaced by fresh batteries and the cab would be back on the street making money in a very short time.[6] An article in an 1899 *Scientific American* claimed,

> Undoubtedly the most important development in transportation has been the remarkable success of the [electric] automobile carriage in this country. The horse-

less cab has established itself as a thoroughly practical and popular means of travel with the general public in New York, while its high speed, its ease of control, its comparative noiselessness and its convenience for use in the city in place of a two-horse carriage is rendering it increasingly popular with the wealthier classes. The electric cabs of New York are standing the test of winter work, and, during the recent snowstorms, they ran under conditions which discouraged even horse [drawn] cabs.[7]

The Electrobats had become a mainstay for the emerging electric taxicab services. In 1902 New York Edison began a fleet with the delivery of one electric truck made by the Electric Vehicle Company. They purchased six more the following year and eventually expanded to fifty-three by 1906.[8]

The Association of Electrical Vehicle Manufacturers was formed in 1906 to promote electrics and provide a concerted effort to obtain better exhibition space for the machines in upcoming auto shows. Pope, Studebaker and Baker were on the board of directors. They felt at the time that "...the electric vehicle is destined to occupy a wider field of usefulness in the near future than in the past, due to the improvements constantly being made and the ability of electric cars to travel much longer distances than formerly on a single charge...."[9]

Colonel Pope, of the Pope Manufacturing Company, makers of the Columbia Motor Coaches,

> ...is of the opinion that in the present state of the art electricity — while not without its limitations, fulfills more of the necessary conditions of a successful motive power than the steam or gas engine.... The storage electric motor is clean, silent, free from vibrations, thoroughly reliable, easy of control, and produces no dirt or odor. While it is not so cheap in such mileage capacity as some other forms of motors, it is certainly not extravagant in proportion to the service rendered, and its capacity has been proved to be more than equal to the demand of the average city or country vehicle.[10]

Scientists researching electric current and its possible uses for the general population saw great promise for using electricity to power automobiles and commercial vehicles. Thomas Edison devoted efforts to a battery that ran direct current. From his laboratory in West Orange, New Jersey, he said the invention could be the key to cheaper, more efficient transportation. "In 15 years, more electricity will be sold for electric vehicles than for light." Nearly fifty companies produced electric cars between 1900 and 1910, when they were at their height of popularity. By 1912, more than 34,000 were registered.[11]

Dr. Charles P. Steinmetz, a contemporary electrical researcher with Thomas Edison, believed that for short hauls the electric truck would prove superior to the gasoline truck.

> Reductions in the cost of delivering merchandise would be distinctly a service to the public, for the merchant who effects such savings is usually able and eager to pass them on to his customers. One of the greatest evils in our economic system today is the high cost of distribution, and I am convinced that a greater use of the electric truck will mean a considerable decrease in the cost of distribution especially of food commodities. It has always seemed a surprising thing to me that electricity — the greatest driving power known — has not yet been given its full position in the transportation world. I do not think I exaggerate when I say that the use of electric motor trucks for short hauls will mean a savings of millions of dollars to the people of the country.[12]

In 1910 the *Cyclopedia of Automobile Engineering* introduced its volume three with a note of the specialized use for the electric automobile.

With the successful development of the gasoline car and its production on a large scale, it is more or less generally thought that the day of the electric vehicle had passed, and there are still many who are of this belief. It must be borne in mind, however, that the electric is a specialized type particularly well adapted for certain classes of service, and without an equal in its own field. The misconception regarding its status usually arises from the erroneous idea that the manufacturer of electric vehicles is attempting to compete with the make of gasoline cars. Despite the great and constantly increasing number of the latter, as well as the fact that the improvements on the score of reliability and silence have made them strong competitors in the electric's chosen field — town service — there will always be a constant demand for electric vehicles. Where pleasure driving is concerned, the electric is without a peer as a ladies' car, while its extreme simplicity and great economy in service give it a strong hold on the commercial field, in which the question of obtaining competent drivers militates against the gasoline type.[13]

Even with the efforts of the Association of Electric Vehicle Manufacturers and the optimism shown by Edison and his fellow researchers and developers, marketing the efficient city car proved difficult, but did meet with some success. Although the industry anticipated batteries being developed for greater distance between charges, their current product came with some drawbacks — short range and very few suitable recharging facilities. To stay competitive, sellers had to develop a better market strategy. Some chose to deal with the mileage problem "head on." Their strategy depicted the electric as safe, silent and free from offensive odors, smoke and grease, with roominess, comfort and luxurious equipment. They were also rugged, and the right vehicle — i.e. *their* product — could cover greater distances. One innovative Columbus agent gave a test drive for a customer, taking him about fifteen miles out of the city to farms where they ran over stubble fields and tall grass up to the axle. Then they returned to the city to climb a steep hill that had never before been ascended by an electric car. They made the climb and had traveled a total of seventy miles on the same charge in one day. The demonstration worked, and the car was purchased. Others touted the car's easy operation and maintenance. While the ability to operate the electric without the services of a chauffeur was definitely a strong advantage for the product, the advertising tactic seemed questionable since the upper levels of society, who were least likely to want to drive and maintain the vehicle themselves, were their primary market. In spite of its seeming contradiction, the marketing campaign was surprisingly successful. Members of society purchased the electrics for their city driving, and because they preferred to have others maintain the vehicles, convenient and numerous charging stations that could also provide minor overhauling tasks "sprang up." An expanded EV auto service industry began in a few of the larger cities.

Convenient, cost-effective charging stations beyond the major population centers had been an issue from the beginning for electrics. In 1895 a firm in London displayed a sign indicating it was prepared to charge "accumulators" of all sizes at any hour of the day or night. At the same time L'Energie Électrique in France painted a glowing picture of the future of electric vehicles, with charging stations being available at any of the 10,000 establishments that had electrical plants. By 1906 a battery exchange system had been developed in Hartford, Connecticut. A customer could purchase a vehicle without a battery and would then pay a flat fee for service and battery exchanging. The Philadelphia/Baltimore area, for example, had twenty-seven charging stations in 1910. In 1911, *Electrical World* wrote, "If a suitable automatic equipment can be installed in each private garage much will have been accomplished toward success. At present the high cost of most charging outfits stands in the way of their general use."[14]

A 1911 article in *Electrical World* examined a boom in the number of electric vehicles, recognizing them as a "vehicle of convenience, not ordinarily adapted to covering very long distances or running at very high speed, but immensely handy and workable within its limitations."[15] The cost for electricity to charge an electric vehicle was about five cents per kw hour in 1911. Electric car enthusiasts assumed that if a person thought this was too high a price, he could not afford to use electric energy. At the time, it was a competitive price with the horse or gasoline. With this in mind, proponents suggested emphasizing the electric's "cheapness, simplicity, economy and longevity."[16] They felt this had to be done to make a serious encroachment in the pleasure vehicle market, a market being taken over by the gasoline vehicles. By this time roads were improving, and distance became a swaying factor for many. "If charging stations could readily be found in every town where there is electric service, the use of electric pleasure cars on fairly long runs would become much more common than it is now."[17] At the 1914 Electric Vehicle Convention, Day Baker, treasurer and enthusiast, promoted his belief that electrics could be used for touring. He said he regularly made a trip from Boston to Providence, a distance of forty-six miles, in three hours. For this distance he did not need to recharge the batteries. For longer touring trips, infrastructure was a problem for an electric car. By 1914 the Lincoln Highway stretched from New York to San Francisco, but there were only fifty charging stations along the way, with only fourteen west of the Mississippi River. Even between New York and Chicago, there was one space of 123 miles between stations. There were no stations between Salt Lake City and Sacramento.[18] To make it through these areas, the driver had to arrange to have his vehicle either put on a railroad car or towed to the next city with a charging facility. This made it very difficult, if not impossible, for the average man to consider touring in his electric car. The adventure became more of a vocation than an avocation or vacation. By 1915 supporters were proclaiming that the increased use of electric vehicles would naturally be followed by an increase in the number of charging stations. EV enthusiasts' confidence was high, but the reality of finding a market balance between the number of EVs purchased and the availability of charging stations did not materialize. Potential EV buyers needed to see a convenient way of recharging the battery. To stimulate interest in providing charging stations, manufacturers needed to see a market. Fuel was not an issue with the ICE. Their owners continued to have an abundance of almost "free" fuel from the discovery of vast amounts of oil in Texas and exploration in other areas of the Northeastern United States and an abundance of liveries, farms and stations that willingly stocked the product. Electric grids were not in place to provide such convenience to the EV drivers to re-energize their autos. They remained hampered by limited recharging services.

The invention of the electric starter in 1912 dealt another hard blow to the competitiveness of the electric automobile. ICEs had been difficult and dangerous to crank start, making EVs the preferred model for the more timid and genteel. The invention made starting the ICEs easy and fast, taking away another of the electric's strong selling points. Even with this discovery, the marketplace might have absorbed the new competition for the electric city autos, if the roads between cities had remained rutted and difficult to traverse, but this was not to be the case. Roads improved. With its limited distance per battery charge, the EV was fast becoming a niche market.

By 1913, the general perception of electric vehicles was that they were not in competition with gasoline cars. They were meant for comfort, cleanliness, reliability and economy in making professional, business or social rounds, or for a daily commute to and from the office. Designer fashions clothed the driver and passengers as they ventured out for dinner and the theater or an afternoon of shopping. Suffragettes praised the independence the electrics gave women, the freedom to drive on their own. Great improvements in both the storage battery and in the body styles in the previous five years increased the range to about eighty miles on one charge. It was assumed that most people did not need to travel eighty miles a day, making that range sufficient. Careful, conservative driving at low speeds increased mileage and should satisfy any reasonable craving by the driver. Driving instruction suggested that one should drive at a steady rate and climbing hills at ten miles per hour to conserve the battery. The electrics were not advocated for cross-country touring, primarily because of the lack of charging stations, and "[e]lectrics are useless to speed maniacs; they are comfort vehicles giving legitimate speed for a reasonable running distance."[19] At the same time, gasoline vehicles were being written up in stories as "'racing' between towns, 'speeding' past cars leaving a cloud of dust, passing others so fast that the occupants could not recognize the faces in the other vehicles, buzzing, roaring and screaming through the air. Cars approaching at speed seemed to go by 'like meteors.'"[20] The EV and the ICE branched off to serve different market needs. The American love affair with gasoline-powered vehicles had begun. The EV as a personal vehicle of choice moved to an *aficionado* market. By 1915 supporters again proclaimed, as their counterparts had done ten and twenty years earlier, that the increased use of electric vehicles would naturally be followed by an increase in the number of charging stations. EV enthusiasts' confidence was high. "The progress in the electric passenger vehicle field during 1915 … has been greater standardization and factory economies in production, all of these making possible considerable price reduction in nearly every case."[21] The niche supporters continued to tout the benefits of EVs and lament the continued lack of infrastructure for providing power conveniently throughout the countryside, but the majority of the buyers moved to ICEs and have not returned to purchase the clean, quiet electrics.

The years from the late 1920s to the 1970s were a very lean time for the electric automobile. The Depression of the 1930s, followed by World War II, did not lend itself to daydreaming about or experimenting with alternative fuel vehicles. Very few articles concerning electric vehicles or alternative fuel vehicles even made it to the scientific publications. Emphasis was on patriotic involvement in the war effort. Countries on both sides of the war encouraged their citizens to do their part to support their troops. In Europe during World War II, a small scattering of electric car companies supplied small electrics for personal and commercial use to conserve gasoline for the war effort and as an alternative to gas rationing. In the economic prosperity after the war, very few people thought about saving energy. Oil and gasoline supplies were abundant and cheap; ICE cars got bigger and faster. Businessmen and "Sunday drivers" saw the potential for extended travel by automobile and looked to the ICE for range and speed. In 1956 President Eisenhower established the Interstate Highway System throughout the United States, linking roadways from state to state and simplifying driving for those enthralled with the wanderlust of touring. EV technology did not keep pace with the needs of the distance traveler in either speed or convenient charging station infrastructure. The electric vehicle did not make it back into the general public's eye again until public concern about air quality grew after mid-century.

Politics and legislation involving use, registration and licensing of automobiles have been a part of the world of electrics since their inception, but a political climate actually favoring the electric automobile may be argued to have started with the Clean Air Act of 1963. This Act has been amended and updated over the years. In 1975 Corporate Average Fuel Economy (CAFE) gasoline mileage standards were established for the ICE. The regulations passed by the California Air Resources Board (CARB) in 1990 depict the state-to-date of promoting electric vehicles. The rules forced manufacturers to sell a certain number of zero emission vehicles (battery only) in the state by 1998 or incur severe monetary penalties. Over the intervening years, CARB has been compelled to amend its strict regulations to include hybrid and alternative fuels vehicles, lower standards, and allow "trading" and "banking" EV credits to make it possible for manufacturers to comply. The modifications demonstrated that consumer demand and new technologies could not just be "created" by political mandates. CARB has changed its strategy over the years from "command and control" to a "partnership" strategy.[22] The public looked to technology for answers, and industry and government partnered to find a better battery.

Commenting on the research and development of new battery technologies in 1989, DeLuchi, Wang and Sperling add,

> The availability of an economical means of quickly recharging EVs, or the successful development of mechanically rechargeable batteries, may be the most critical factor in the future of EVs and could mean the difference between a minor and major role for EVs in transportation. Therefore, as R&D on powertrains and batteries continues, and the commercialization of advanced EVs draws near, R&D work on charging systems, and the cost and performance of batteries designed to accept very fast (20-minute) recharges, should commence. The development of a suitable infrastructure and the successful completion of advanced EV development programs will bring the electric vehicle dream much closer to reality.[23]

In a straight comparison of today's EVs and ICEs, the EV shows a number of practical advantages, but that advantage is narrowing as technological advances occur with ICEs and hybrids. The EVs do not have tailpipe emissions. They have about 70 percent fewer moving parts than an ICE. This means less maintenance — no oil changes, filter replacements or the necessary replacement of items such as fuel pumps, alternators, etc. EVs also pollute less, conserve energy and are cheaper to run, averaging about twice the distance on each dollar spent. The main disadvantages of electric cars continue to be their short range and high initial price. The advantage margin is narrowing. As EVs approach the performance levels, the speed and acceleration, of the ICE, more efficient, cleaner ICEs are getting closer to EVs in tailpipe emissions. Overall, the environmental advantage provided by EVs has been negated by the greater improvements in gasoline engines. Internal combustion engines are currently running very clean due to reformulated gasoline and computer-assisted combustion systems. CARB rules and restrictions that regulate the acceptable level of ICE pollution allowed are being relaxed, prolonging the advantage of the ICE. The environmental value gap between the ICE and the EVs is lessening. At the turn of the 21st century, even though electric vehicles come in many types, generating electricity from batteries, solar energy, fuel cells, biomass, etc., and hybrids combine the power of fossil fuels with electric energy created by on-board chargers, the technology stays just out of reach. The optimistic feeling about electric cars over the last century has always been that this time it will "catch on." Just as success seems inevitable, circumstances change.

The solution is always just around the corner, down the road, and all the other automotive metaphors, but the reality is that consumers want internal combustion engines and are not willing to change this conviction as long as they have the money to pay for the oil and gasoline to run them. The early 20th century brought inventions in motor and battery design that increased the range possible for an electric vehicle before it needed recharging. The electric automobile was a serious competitor to steam and internal combustion engines during the early 1900s. The new millennium offers a great opportunity for developing technology to advance the acceptance of alternative vehicles. Moore's Law concerning computers may soon be applied to battery and fuel cell technology. Hybrid vehicles are providing excellent mileage. Fuel cell and hybrid vehicles seem to be the best choice for the near future to answer the question of tailpipe emissions and pollution. This is an exciting time for developing new technologies to maintain a clean environment for the future. Improvements in utility power generators and advances in non-polluting fuels show a positive approach to transportation and energy. These solutions appear to be the realistic, sensible and necessary methodology needed today as they rely primarily on the marketplace (consumer demand) over the political (social awareness demand) as an approach to the problem. Time will tell.

The Competitors in the Early Years

The steam-powered vehicle was a viable competitor to electrics and ICEs in price and performance during the first quarter of the 20th century. Its main drawback was the time required to warm up and produce steam to begin locomotion. In 1906 a steam-powered vehicle set a land speed record of 127 mph. The steam cars were competitive in the early automobile market a little longer than the electrics and were still in production in the 1930s, in small quantities.

In 1899 the Stanley Steamer's success attracted the interest of John B. Walker, publisher of *Cosmopolitan* magazine, who wanted to buy the business. To dissuade him, the Stanleys named what they thought was a ridiculously high price — a quarter of a million dollars in cash. To their surprise Walker promptly paid it, and the Stanleys were temporarily out of the car business. The new owner changed the name to the Locomobile Company of America. The Stanleys were back to producing steamers in 1901.[25] Why did the steamer drop out? Quality versus quantity. Steam-powered cars were manufactured by a number of small manufacturers who were content to build a few hundred cars, while Henry Ford was thinking in the numbers of millions for his machines. Even the leading steam car manufacturer, the Stanley Motor Carriage Company, was primarily interested in providing cars to local markets and was more concerned with quality craftsmanship than volume and lower prices.

The environment, the infrastructure and market timing also played roles in the demise of the market for the steamers. Hoof-and-mouth disease broke out in 1914. To prevent the spread of the disease, most of the public water troughs were removed. Stanley Steamers were not designed with condensers to recycle

The GROUT STEAM CARRIAGE

Runs when you want it to for business or for pleasure.

GROUT BROS., ➻ ORANGE, MASS.

Grout Steam Carriage, 1902[24]

the water; owners were obliged to stop frequently to refill the boilers. Without the water troughs, the water was not readily available. The epidemic forced the Stanley company to rethink its design and develop a condensing system. It took two years at great expense, and with a definite drop in production, for the condenser to be integrated into the design. When the United States joined World War I in 1917, the government limited consumer goods production to one-half the average output over the previous three years. Since Stanley had been in a development phase and had built very few vehicles for market during that time, the limitation put Stanley at a major disadvantage. They needed volume to increase sales and visibility for their new product, but were limited by the government in how many vehicles they could produce and make available for the marketplace. When the war was over and Stanley was about to recover, it was hit by a third bit of bad luck — the 1920s recession. The Stanley did not recover.[26] Steam-powered vehicles disappeared around the time of the stock market crash of 1929 and the Great Depression and never found a way back to the marketplace to compete with the ICEs and EVs.

Names such as Ford, Studebaker, and Porsche produced internal combustion engine autos for the marketplace from its early years. Gasoline-powered automobiles became the market-shaping force over both electric and steam cars early in the 1900s for four reasons: (1) Better road systems connected many cities by the 1920s, promoting a need for longer-range vehicles. (2) In 1901 vast oil reserves were discovered in Texas. Gasoline was a waste by-product of the oil industry, which was in the business of producing kerosene for lamps. When the "Spindletop" oil gusher was brought in at Beaumont, Texas, the country's oil production doubled almost overnight. Fuel was cheap and readily available by 1905. An infrastructure of gasoline fuel stops began to appear. Cars could "fuel-up" at many convenient locations. General stores, shops and even liveries had a supply of gasoline cans on hand to fuel the new vehicles. The first gasoline station was built in 1913 by Chevron and they were widely present by 1920. Alternately, most service stations were not hooked up to an electrical grid at that time. (3) In 1912 a reliable easy-to-use electric starter for gasoline engines was introduced. ICEs in the early 1900s were difficult and dangerous to start — a chore for even an able-bodied man. If the engine backfired during the crank

Winton phaeton gasoline automobile, 1899[27]

start, the crank could spin backwards. Broken arms and other injuries were not uncommon. The technical advancement of the electric starter invented by Charles Kettering in 1912 made the option of starting not only electric cars but also ICEs open to the less-athletic women. (4) Henry Ford decided to mass-produce affordable gasoline-powered cars.[28] Henry Ford wanted to build cars for everyone, using mass production and interchangeable parts to streamline automobile maintenance. His method worked. He supplied large quantities of product at low prices. By 1912 electric roadsters were selling in the $1,750 to $3,000 range, while a gasoline car built by the new production processes sold for $650. By World War I, low-priced fuel and advanced technology gave a distinct advantage to the ICE, an advantage it has enjoyed through the turn of the 21st century.

The Battery

The battery, its reaction to heat and cold, its recharging capabilities and its weight are key to the success or failure of electric vehicles. The impact of its slow technological development when compared to improvements in the internal combustion engine cannot be minimized. It has been the main roadblock in the EV's fight for consumer market share. For the past 100 years, competition between the electric and the internal combustion vehicles has see-sawed. Just when confidence in EVs is rising and the electric seems to make a breakthrough, circumstances change and the ICE moves ahead. Whether it is in fuel infrastructure, technological advances or road infrastructure (including mud, hills, and cold weather), the electric finds itself at a disadvantage.

An editorial in the *Scientific American* in 1917 proclaimed that a new battery would be invented any day, which would change the entire look of cars and the infrastructure of the automobile. As in the past, the EV would continue to improve on the quality of the battery so that it could be a major viable competitor to the ICE. Nineteen eighteen also brought the promise of a breakthrough in battery technology that would benefit EVs. A 1918 article in the *Scientific American Supplement* proclaimed, "Though many adverse conditions and numerous objections that have to some extent been overcome, the electric vehicle for both pleasure and commercial applications has come to stay."[29] At the time a battery exchange system and a growing infrastructure of central recharging stations were developing, but battery performance continued to plague the EVs.

Cold weather and bad roads seriously tax the battery, affecting the mileage, amperage generated and battery life. Throughout the 20th century an answer to the problem of dealing with the climate and cold-weather performance eluded the inventors. In the 1990s fleet owners were reporting less range during the colder months. At the turn of the 21st century, federal regulations required climate control in all automobiles, both heating and cooling. Designing a battery that can generate the additional energy needed while withstanding the cold temperature without increasing weight or price continues to be a research dilemma. Manufacturers have tried to find solutions since the early years of EVs when the performance problem first surfaced. In 1918, the traveling distance (range) of the battery was noted as being less in winter than in summer — the colder the day, the greater the difference. During cold weather, the roads were also in poor condition, adding to the increased ampere-hours required from the battery per mile. Battery technology at the time was unable to meet the problem. Instead inventors concentrated efforts on two approaches to making the battery immune from the cold. One approach was to install the battery in a box that had the insulating characteristics of a Thermos bottle. The second was to use a small amount of energy from the battery itself (about 100 watts) to provide an electric heater to control the temperature around the battery. Neither proved effective for the marketplace. There was a general call at the time from conservationists asking for cooperation between the manufacturers and central-station companies to advance these improvements to make the electric vehicle a success. Such cooperation did not happen until almost a century later with the advent of partnerships, such as the U.S. Advanced Battery Consortium (USABC) and an increased emphasis on battery research and development.

In the 1950s, it was estimated that if as little as five million dollars per year were invested in research and development of a battery of high specific energy, light weight and low cost, the United States would have electric vehicles in 1990 that would be able to travel at fifty miles per hour for 150 miles on a single charge. Even if the money had been allocated, it is unlikely, based on the technological challenges still being examined, that the desired results would have been produced.

Since the 1960s, any electric car viable in the competitive marketplace has required subsidies from the government or the energy industry. This may change as the technology develops incrementally over the next few years, but battery technology has seen very little improvement over the last one hundred years and is still in need of a great breakthrough to move EVs into the industry mainstream.

For over one hundred ten years proponents of the electric vehicle have been predicting that it would take command of the marketplace soon. A technological breakthrough favoring EVs has been perpetually expected in "just a few years." The present technological buzz is the fuel cell, but fuel cells have been around longer than batteries. Will someone invent a new battery? This also has been predicted for over one hundred years. Based on past development patterns, it should not be expected. Consumer demand for a battery-only powered vehicle is still low. People just do not want to put up with the inconvenience of plugging in their cars. Hybrid vehicles and fuel-cell–powered vehicles hold promise as a bridge to achieve the California Air Resources Board's (CARB) requirements of a zero emission vehicle (ZEV). It is more likely that a hybrid vehicle will capture the market's interest as the next stage of development in saving fuel. The problem again is the cost. How long will automakers be willing to sell a car for $20,000 when it costs $41,000 to build? Historically, EVs have appeal during times of energy crises, such as World War I, World War II, the 1970s' oil shortage and when environmental and industry leaders create peaks of interest by calling attention to EVs as a solution to dependence on foreign oil, energy shortages and pollution problems. But overall, the electric vehicle industry is still struggling to become financially independent and a viable option in the consumer market. There is no conspiracy in the auto industry to prevent the electric vehicle from being built and sold. Automakers will sell any product that consumers want, and the first one to create such a car that captures the consumer's interest at a reasonable price can expect to enjoy striking profits.

Motor vehicles have been a fascination since the first motor was attached to a bicycle in 1881. They are used for work, for leisure, for prestige and for entertainment. Whether the power source is steam, gasoline internal combustion or electric current, cars are interwoven in the fabric of our society. They both drive and are shaped by the energy industry. Their style reflects individual personalities and their versatility echoes our functional needs in work and play. The automotive industry is at the heart of the way

American business works—mergers, acquisitions, patent fights, partnerships with government and the "bottom line."

As with the information revolution, the automotive industry is on the brink of upheaval. Triggered by environmental issues, interrupted oil supplies and a more affluent society, tighter restrictions for emission controls in some states and the success of Moore's Law in technology, manufacturers have again captured our fancy for revisiting electric and hybrid vehicles as possible solutions for these issues.

1   The Evolution of the Electric Vehicle

No one person can be credited for the invention of the automobile that you are driving today. It has developed bit-by-bit from the ideas, imagination, fantasy, and tinkering of hundreds of individuals through hundreds of years.[1]

The history of electric vehicles can be generally divided into three parts: the Early Years (1890–1929) with their Golden Age of dominance in the market from about 1895 to 1905; the Middle Years (1930–1989); and the Current Years (1990–present). In the Early Years, England and France were the first nations to experiment with electric vehicles, with the United States showing some interest in about 1895. The first electric vehicle may have been a converted Hillman Sociable tricycle created by M. Raffard in France in 1881. The first commercial application of EVs was a fleet of New York taxicabs in 1897. The general perception of the electric vehicle in 1899 was that it had many advantages over the gasoline-powered cars. It was clean, silent, free of vibrations, thoroughly reliable, easy to start and control (no shifting required) and produced no dirt or odor. The disadvantages were short range and high initial cost. It was not as cheap to run as other forms of automation and could only average about 18 miles per day, but this met the delivery needs of much of the population in the larger cities. Electric vehicles outsold all other types of cars in America in the years 1899 and 1900. The Middle Years brought a brief peak of interest in EVs due to gasoline shortages during World War II, the environmental concerns of the 1960s and oil shortages of the 1970s. The Current Years brought renewed interest in air quality and the impact that pollution from the internal combustion engine had on the environment, resulting in legislation such as the Clean Air Act of 1990, regulations put in effect by the California Air Resources Board (CARB) in 1990 and the Energy Act of 1992. The statutes encouraged research in EVs and re-energized the development of environmentally friendly vehicles. Each era of the EV touted the vehicle for its quiet, reliable, environmentally friendly advantages over its competitors.

Automobiles had a market in Europe earlier than in the United States. The first automobile to be put into production is thought to be the German one-cylinder, gasoline-powered three-wheeler Benz in 1885. Gottlieb Daimler put a four-wheel, gasoline-powered automobile into production in Stuttgart, Germany, in 1886. In 1890 the first American to build an electric vehicle was Andrew L. Riker. It was a tricycle (imported from England) with a motor attached that could deliver ⅙ horsepower and speed along at eight miles per hour with a range of about thirty miles. The United States did not have a production industry until 1896 when the Duryea brothers of Springfield, Massachusetts, produced thirteen matching "motor wagons."

In 1900 France led the world in car production and ownership. There were 5,600 automobiles in France; the support infrastructure shows a total of 3,939 stores for oil, gas, etc., and only 265 electric charging stations.[2] New York State had about 4,000 registered vehicles in 1903, 53 percent steam-powered (made primarily by the Locomobile Company), 27 percent gasoline-powered and 20 percent electric-powered. Automobile production was about to explode in the United States, but the ratio of support stations associated with gasoline and electric vehicles remained about the same as that of France in 1900.

> The electric car was the most conservative form of the automobile in that it bore the closest resemblance to the horse-drawn vehicle in both appearance and performance. Manufacturers of electric vehicles closely copied fashionable carriage forms. The Woods Motor Vehicle Company, a prominent early maker of electric cars, for example, hoped to supply hundreds of thousands of gentleman's private stables with fine carriages in all variety of styles rather than a creation of a machine which will transport a man from town to town, or on long country tours.[3]

The Automobile, an extensive two-volume treatise on steam, gasoline and electric cars and their parts, stated in 1905:

> It [the electric vehicle] is managed easily, is docile, has a noiseless motion, and the motor itself is mounted in a very simple manner. Over petrol cars it has the advantages of easier starting, greater cleanliness, and perhaps lower cost of upkeep. There is but little vibration with the electric automobile, no bad odour, and no consumption of energy whilst the car is stopped. The inconveniencies of electricity as automobile motive power are increase in dead weight carried, maintenance and renewal of accumulators ... and the loss of time in charging. These inconveniences are lessened greatly in cars for town work.[4]

Considering hybrid cars of the day, it states, "...it certainly seems that there is a big future before the petrol-electric car."[5]

The Automobile Club of America was incorporated in 1899 with the objective "to maintain a social club devoted to the spread of automobilism and to its development throughout the country; to arrange for through runs and encourage road contests of all kinds among owners of automobiles."[6]

The 1893 World's Columbian Exposition in Chicago (Chicago World's Fair), in addition to housing the world's first Ferris wheel, featured six electric automobiles. The only American entry was the Morrison electric surrey, built by William Morrison in Des Moines, Iowa, in 1892. It was a twelve-passenger open surrey wagon with twenty-four battery cells and a 4 hp motor. It could attain a speed of 14 mph. Charging time was estimated at ten hours. Steering was accomplished by rotating the wheel on a vertical steering apparatus and it was claimed to have been perfected "to such an extent that a light touch on the wheel will alter the course of the vehicle."[7] Morrison sold the electric automobile to the American Battery Company of Chicago. This is thought to be the first sale of an American automobile.[8]

Harold Sturges began building an electric surrey in 1895 fashioned on the model of Morrison's carriage. He removed the third seat to allow more room for batteries and claimed a range of seventy miles on a flat and even surface. Morrison and Sturges entered the vehicle in the *Chicago Times-Herald's* Chicago-to-Evanston race in 1895. It ran thirteen of the fifty-three miles in six inches of snow before running out of power. Duryea's gasoline-powered vehicle won the race.

Charles Jeantaud, a famous French carriage builder and inventor of complex gearing and differential systems, proclaimed in 1895, "The electric carriage has a future, and already in London there is a firm which displays a sign saying they are prepared to charge accumulators [batteries] of

William Morrison electric wagon, 1892[9]

all sizes at any hour of the day or night."[10] In that same year in France, he decided to develop his own vehicle to compete with the petroleum and steam carriages. He was looking for a smaller and lighter source of electricity and found it in the Fulmen accumulator. The accumulator (battery) consisted of lead plates and acid, as did other batteries of the day, but the weight was lessened by covering the plates with a perforated celluloid envelope. It was a non-conductor and was not attacked by acids. The box was sealed and watertight, and was resistant to shocks and bumps. Jeantaud used twenty-one of these elements in his carriage, enclosed in seven small boxes, each containing three accumulators. The accumulators were stowed away under the seat. On a level road, he managed a speed of thirteen miles per hour, while in hilly country the speed was reduced to about seven miles per hour.[11] By 1899 Jeantaud was the head of a fairly large carriage establishment that was producing some of the finest and best-known electric vehicles in Paris. He was one of the founders of the Automobile Club de France and was a leading member of the Civil Engineer's Society. He established a taxicab service for use in the city with vehicles that would carry two or three passengers. Jeantaud also experimented with a chain-drive system to drive the rear wheels, and different types of transmissions. One type had each rear wheel driven by a separate motor, with a large gear wheel affixed to the main axle. This eliminated the use of differential gearing and made the system less complicated. It was similar to the system developed by Krieger for his Electrolette machine. Jeantaud's motors primarily drove the front wheels and not the rear, which allowed for the vehicle to be steered in any direction without interfering with the working of the driving mechanism.[12] Differing speeds of 4, 8, 12 and 16 kilometers per hour were obtained, with a reverse speed of 4 kilometers per hour. The electric brakes were very efficient and were tested by a run down a steep grade at full speed. When given a signal to stop, the brakes were applied and the vehicle came to a full stop within a distance of eight meters. These brake tests were conducted by the Automobile Club de France. The Club also tested distance and speed. Jeantaud entered a number of his electric cabs and showed they could cover a distance of sixty kilometers in less than four hours, averaging fifteen kilometers per hour. The tests covered a ten-day period and a distance of over 6,000 kilometers. In a presentation to the Society of Civil Engineers of France, Jeantaud gave his opinion that the problem of city service could be solved by electric cabs and the competitive tests conducted by the Club proved it feasible.

In 1898 Charles Jeantaud convinced the Automobile Club de France to organize races. The race trials lasted nine days and the winners were Jeantaud and Krieger. The lone ICE Peugeot fared so badly one journalist declared, "The petroleum-spirit cab will never be a practicable proposition in large towns."[13] Jeantaud held the land speed record at the time of 39 mph, until rival Camille Jenatzy beat it with 41 mph. This rivalry led

The electric carriage of Charles Jeantaud

to a competition resulting in streamlined cars with bullet-shaped coachwork. Jeantaud's driver Chasseloup-Laubat set a record of 58 mph, which was again beaten by Jenatzy on April 29, 1899, when he reached a speed of 65.8 mph.[14] Deciding to take another tactic to find greater speed to win races, Jeantaud switched to a hybrid gasoline-electric vehicle, as did Austrians Ludwig Lohner and Ferdinand Porsche.

The first Lohner-Porsche debuted at the Paris Exposition in 1900. "Dr. Ferdinand Porsche (1875–1952), although not the first with hybrid electric vehicles, probably carried the concept furthest of early pioneers at the turn of the century and later."[15] He was an employee at the Lohner's Electric Vehicle Company in 1898, when his employer, Mr. Lohner, boasted to the press: "He is very young, but he is a man with a big career before him. You will hear of him again."[16] Porsche helped develop a hub-mounted drive system that eliminated a transmission by mounting the electric motors on the front wheels. The hybrid automobile was not cost effective for production and Porsche turned to gasoline-powered vehicles.

In America in the 1880s carriage-building was considered an art. The invention of the horseless carriage as a new form of self-propelling machine was less impressive than the production of the fine artistic carriages that would surround the mere electrics and mechanics of the vehicle. The Woods Motor Vehicle Company (1898), founded by Clinton E. Woods and also known as the American Electric Vehicle Company, was an excellent example of that art. It produced eight different models. Many had side lantern electric lights, electric lights in the interior and even electric foot warmers. The company devoted its efforts to fine coachbuilding in a variety of styles. They claimed they could work easily with electricians and mechanics. They did make one exception for adaptation: they could not accommodate rubber tires. For the 1915 season, the company completely remodeled its line of electric vehicles. They used a new type of spring suspension, improved

Lohner-Porsche electric coupe, 1899[17]

brakes and replaced the bevel gears with a worm-drive system. The new body style also included headlamps that were set into the body. The motor was suspended by a ball joint mechanism to prevent jarring. The Anheuser-Busch Brewing Company owned a fleet of fifty Woods electric delivery wagons for transporting beer. By 1916 interest in electric vehicles began to fade. In response, Woods began development of a hybrid (gasoline-electric) car.

Another electric vehicle that concentrated on the tradition of coachbuilding was the 1895 Holtzer-Cabot. It was promoted for its comfort, simplicity and ease of operation. Powered by forty-four chloride cell batteries, it had a three-speed transmission operated by a lever near the steering shaft and had a top speed of fifteen miles per hour. Part of the coachbuilding process involved applying many layers of acid proof paint to prevent damage in the event of a battery cell's breaking.

From their inception electrics had difficulty with distance and battery recharging. Racing and popular journals of the time brought the problem to the public's attention, and solutions appeared on a limited scale. One of the first organized automobile races in the United States took place in Chicago in 1895. Very few electrics competed; the batteries did not have enough storage capacity and the race course did not have charging stations. By 1900 the *Scientific American* noted that an important aid in popularizing the electric car would be to have central station owners provide their plants with the necessary apparatus to charge the carriage, for the convenience of drivers traveling in unknown territory. A new feature at the time in New York was the charging "hydrant." It was being perfected by a prominent electric company and consisted of a coin-operated mechanism with a wattmeter, voltmeter, rheostat, switch and terminals. After the driver deposited the necessary coins he could draw upon it for a certain number of watt-hours. It was assumed that the general adoption of this type of device would greatly enhance the use of electric automobiles. Prices for charging current for the storage batteries varied over a considerable range, depending on the locality and the differing conditions contributing to

Woods' Victoria hansom cab, 1899[18]

varying daily loads of electric use. The novelty of the service also added cost to the product. The average price was about two and one-half cents per kilowatt-hour. The greatest financial problem facing the central station operators was the relation between the cost of installation and the possible return on that investment. The start-up cost at the time was high. It was the chicken-and-egg situation again, with the prediction of more electric cars demanding more charging stations and more charging stations causing a higher demand for electric cars. EV supporters like H. M. Maxim were confident that the industry could meet the challenge. In one article he said, "It does not seem to me to be an exaggeration to say that the [electric] horseless carriage builder now offers the solution of this vexed problem."[19] Researchers and entrepreneurs continued work on battery design and charging possibilities to improve the EV powerplant.

Electrics were especially useful in commerce, where they were efficient and practical work vehicles for the cities. Fleets were less affected by the need for charging stations. The company garages maintained the units and the distance "cabbies" traveled was well within the electric's range. Electric taxicabs became a thriving business in the larger cities on both sides of the Atlantic. On August 19, 1897, W. H. Preece inaugurated an electric taxicab service in London to compete with the hackney carriages. Thirteen cabs were ready for use and the company expected to have twenty-five more cabs available in the near future. The "cabbies" were very enthusiastic about the new vehicles and were undergoing instruction in managing switches and steering. The motor was a three horsepower Johnson-Lundell with a variety of speeds and a range of about thirty-five miles. The storage batteries were hung on springs beneath the vehicle and could be recharged in place or taken to a supply station and exchanged for fresh batteries by using hydraulic lifts.

Henry Morris and Pedro Salom built one of the first American electric cars and called it the Electrobat. They took the suffix "bat" from a Greek word meaning "to go." Morris was a mechanical engineer and Salom was an electrical engineer when they formed a partnership in 1894 and called it the Electric Carriage and Wagon Company. They were ahead of their time with the concept of offering several different models of their product simultaneously, giving the consumer a choice within the same company. They were also one of the first to make electric vehicles for commercial use. Morris and Salom thought electric taxis would be cheaper to operate than horse-drawn cabs. They produced Electrobat taxis for New York City from 1896 to 1898. In August 1897 they wrote a letter to the editor of the *Horseless Age* indicating the success of their taxi business. It showed a total mileage for the previous six months of 14,459 miles with 4,765 passengers being carried. They wrote, "While we do not care to publish the actual receipts and expenditures for contracting the service, we would say that the results have been so satisfactory as to warrant the organization of a new company with a large capital stock for the purpose of manufacturing and operating electric motor vehicles of all styles, and that the construction of 100 additional electric hansoms will be begun within the next thirty days."[20] Their brougham featured a new concept known as the "Tracteur" principle that consisted of mounting the motors, gears and batteries on the front part of the body. This allowed for standard carriage construction of the body built on the same line as those intended to be drawn by horses. The motors were mounted on the axle and would swing radially about it. The average speed was six miles per hour with a range of about thirty-six miles. In 1898 Morris and Salom sold their Electrobat Company to Isaac L. Rice who expanded the service to 200 taxis by the end of the year and renamed it the Electric Vehicle Company.

As with many entrepreneurs of the era, Rice took advantage of trusts and mergers. He went on to create the Electric Boat Company in Groton, Connecticut. The company then became part of the Lead Trust, a very powerful monopoly directed by William Whitney. Whitney initially ordered the construction of 200 taxis from Colonel Albert A. Pope, and then increased the order to 1,600. In 1899 Col. Pope's Columbia Automobile Company acquired the factory and by 1900 both Pope and Riker Electric Motor Company's automobile division had become part of the Electric Vehicle Company. In 1900 the Storage Battery Company gave Electric the right to use storage batteries on vehicles around the country and agreed to sell batteries and machinery to them at all times at a rate of 15 percent below the market price. The Electric Vehicle Company was sued in 1901 for illegal dividends payment and the directors of the company were held responsible and were directed to repay $800,000. This did not stop the business from thriving.

In 1895 the Pope Manufacturing Company of Hartford, Connecticut, a well-known bicycle manufacturer, decided to enter the horseless carriage field. Pope was one of the first companies to take another approach to producing EVs— it produced electric vehicles, not merely coaches with electrics. The company began experimenting without regard to expense and by 1897 produced the Columbia Motor Carriage. The electric motor was powered by four sets of batteries consisting of forty-four cells, and produced about two horsepower. Unlike its competitor Woods, Columbia saw great advantage to pneumatic tires. It was this vehicle's most exceptional feature. The Columbia's wheels were fitted with heavy rubber pneumatic tires that could travel 3,500 miles before needing to be replaced and were considered practically unpuncturable. The carriage had a range of thirty miles at a maximum speed of 15 mph. The company claimed this range could be increased if "the roads are good and free from mud." It promoted the electric vehicle as being very economical since charging the batteries cost about fifty cents, which corre-

sponded to a cost of about a cent a mile to operate. In a testing session on May 13, 1897, the scientific press found that the carriage was as easy to handle as "guiding the gentlest horse," even by those totally unfamiliar with a horseless carriage.[21] The company did not ignore fine coachbuilding. Its top-of-the-line 1899 brougham offered a fine oak wood frame with a mirror-like lacquer finish, a satin roof and goatskin upholstery. Standard equipment included a hand mirror, electric reading lamps and a small clock. It also had a meter on the dashboard

The Columbia Motor Carriage, 1897[23]

that allowed the "coachman" to read the condition of the batteries. The first brougham was made for a prominent physician in New York City and was shown there in the Electrical Exhibition in 1899. This model sold for $5,000 and only the wealthy could afford it.[22] The Electric Vehicle Company absorbed Pope's Columbia Electric Company in 1898.

By 1902 the company was producing a hybrid (electric-gasoline) vehicle.

Another gasoline/electric hybrid appeared in the Third Annual Automobile and Cycle Show in Paris in 1901. It was designed by Camille Jenatzy and carried an electric motor and a gasoline engine, which could work independently or in combination. The gasoline engine could be coupled to a small dynamo and used to charge a battery of accumulators. This would also charge the batteries when going down grades. The 1902 Jenatzy cab and delivery car had two motors, each geared to drive a rear wheel. The single controller was replaced by a rheostat with a handle that allowed ten different speeds. The forty-four battery cells were split between front and rear boxes to balance the body.

The Columbia hybrid vehicle, 1902[24]

The City and Suburban electric car company produced electric and hybrid cars from about 1901 to 1905. They made many styles, from a light and cheap runabout to the graceful victoria shown here. The larger hybrid (gasoline-electric) car was experimental, but was ascribed to be a good performer for its day. It was a four-seat double phaeton with a chassis consisting of two frames. The upper frame (the chassis itself) was mounted on double elliptical springs on the lower tubular framework consisting of front and rear axles connected by a tubular span. The electric motors were mounted on the tubular rear axle and drove the rear wheels with a pinion gearing system. This gearing system worked in combination with the brakes. When the control pedal under the driver's seat was depressed, the first movement cut off the current; if it was depressed further, the brakes would engage. The gasoline engine was a twin-cylinder five-horsepower Daimler set in front. It charged the batteries on flat roads. The battery would supply power to the vehicle when climbing hills, or it could provide a range of up to twenty miles on a flat surface without using the gasoline engine.

The Milde electric car company produced a variety of body styles from about 1901 to 1906. The electric motor was enclosed in a case to protect it from dirt, but was said to be readily disassembled for access to the parts. The forty-two battery cells weighed in at 1,014 pounds and transmitted the power via pinion gears to the rear wheels. The controller was operated by a handle, and provided nine forward speeds ranging from one to eighteen

Jenatzy cab, 1902[25]

miles per hour, and three reverse speeds. Milde made a gasoline-electric hybrid four-seat car in 1904 that weighed about the same as its electric car and was capable of a range of 400 miles. It incorporated a de Dion-Bouton nine-horsepower gasoline engine housed under the driver's seat. This would charge the batteries, which would come into use when climbing hills or when the gasoline engine was stopped for short distances through traffic.[27]

Another early hybrid gasoline-electric vehicle was the Munson Electric Motor Company of LaPorte, Indiana. It used a two-cylinder gasoline engine in conjunction with a dynamo and flywheel. The controller could be used to connect the batteries in series or parallel and the car had a total of four speeds, but two of these speeds involved running the gasoline engine at half power, resulting in an unsatisfactory outcome in the speed produced.[28]

W. C. Bersey manufactured open motorized horseless carriages and electric buses and cabs from 1895 to 1900 in England. The Bersey carriage was the focal point of the 1896 auto show in South Kensington, London. A highlight of the company's history came in 1917 when

City and Suburban electric victoria, 1902[26]

the Prince of Wales rode in a Bersey cab. The carriages were powered by two motors and contained an unusual feature for an electric car — a clutch. "Three of these carriages ran in the London-Brighton Emancipation Run in November 1896, though it was widely rumoured that they completed the journey by train. This was finally confirmed by Walter Bersey in a speech to the Veteran Car Club in 1935."[29] Bersey is best remembered for building taxis between 1897 and 1900. Bersey's "Hummingbirds" began operating on the London streets in late 1897. These cabs, owned by the London Electrical Cab Company, had removable battery packs to make recharging easier, Mulliner bodies supplied by the Great Horseless Carriage Company, and 3½ hp Lundell motors. Reliability was a problem for this design. A larger package was also supplied by the Gloucester Railway Carriage & Waggon Company. Breakdowns were frequent and cost of batteries was high. The company closed in 1899. Bersey switched to selling gasoline-powered cars.

Ransom E. Olds of Lansing, Michigan, built his first steam-powered automobile in 1892 and a gasoline-powered vehicle in 1897. He began producing electric automobiles in 1898. Olds was the only manufacturer to offer all three types of powered vehicles until he finally decided to pursue the gasoline Oldsmobile in about 1900. In 1904 Olds was approached by his head of engineering, Henry Leland, with a lighter, more powerful engine that could improve the runabout. To the dismay of his backer, Samuel Smith, Olds refused to use the new engine. Smith forced Ransom Olds out of the company. Olds went on to found the Reo Motor Car Company, and Oldsmobile went on without him. Henry Leland took his motor elsewhere to power the world's first Cadillac.

In 1897 M. A. Darracq displayed his electric coupe in the Salon du Cycle show in Paris. It was possibly the first vehicle to use a regenerative braking system. When the brakes were applied, the kinetic energy was converted to electrical energy to charge the battery. It had a steel tube chassis, hard rubber tires on wooden wheels and forty Fulmen batteries weighing 800 pounds. It could reach a speed of six miles per hour and had a range of about thirty miles.

The Riker Electric Motor Company of Brooklyn, New York, built a four-wheel one-person vehicle in 1895. It was as sparse in design as a bicycle and it may have been the first vehicle to be equipped with wire spoked wheels. In 1897 Riker drove a Victoria model six hundred miles around New York City at a cost of $10.35, averaging 1.7 cents per mile. Riker also saw economic possibilities in the hansom taxi market. By 1899 he designed and produced a Demi-Coach cab with the driver positioned at the rear of the passenger compartment, giving the occupants a free and unobstructed view of the road. Half of the batteries were stored in the front box-like compartment and the other half under the driver's seat. This gave the taxi a well-balanced and symmetrical appearance. It was elegantly upholstered and had a full glass front with an electric light on the roof and exterior lamps. Instruments attached to the back of the vehicle and in front of the driver included a voltmeter and ammeter. It could carry four passengers and travel twenty-five miles on one charge at about ten miles per hour.[30]

The Riker Electric Vehicle Company expanded by opening a new plant at Elizabethport, New Jersey. The facility was equipped to make every part of the vehicle. In 1899 Riker produced a surrey, a delivery wagon and a brougham with a system of electric motors and a controller stored under the front and rear seats. "The Riker system" was considered to be one of the new ideas of the time. The design fitted a large number of storage batteries into a small space. It was seen as a portent of things to come and projected a confidence that expected improvements would continue to produce greater

Riker Electric Demi-Coach, 1899[31]

efficiency for the electric car. The system used forty-four Willard storage cells (batteries) approximately 3×5×9 inches in configuration. The system could be modified to produce different energy exchanges. Each battery was compactly placed so that either only a few cells would operate at one time, or the batteries would operate in parallel, or in series, or with the direction of the current reversed. The car approached 15 mph on a level road. Instead of having a steering wheel, the driver guided it by a vertical steering shaft. In 1896 a Riker Electric car decisively defeated a Duryea (ICE) at the first auto race in the United States on a race track at Narragansett Park, Rhode Island.[32] In December 1900, Riker merged with the Electric Vehicle Company, maker of the Pope-Columbia, and thereafter only electric trucks were made under the Riker name.[33] That did not stop Riker from racing his electric automobiles. The Long Island Automobile Club ran one-mile straightaway races in 1901 featuring one electric vehicle (Riker), eight gasoline-powered and six steam-powered vehicles. The vehicles were stripped of all unnecessary equipment leaving only a frame and a seat. Mr. Riker had a man riding behind him clinging to the frame. Henri Fournier set the new one-mile land speed record with a time of 51.5 seconds. A. L. Riker's electric finished with a respectable 1 minute 3 second run for third place. Fifty thousand people watched and occasionally some fans wandered onto the course as there was very little supervision by the club, but miraculously no one was hurt. After the race, A. L. Riker switched to producing gasoline-powered cars. He became vice-

The Electric Surrey constructed on the "Riker System" showing details of working parts[34]

president of the Locomobile Company of America in 1902 and was influential in replacing its steam-powered cars with gasoline cars.

The 1900 Waverley used a braking system, based on a bi-directional controller concept that charged the batteries as the driver was applying the brakes. It incorporated a recharging motor for its electric car. By continuing to run the motor downhill instead of immediately applying the brakes, the motor continued to increase in speed "until the counter electromotive force of the armature equals that of the battery, which would be 80 volts with the controller on the third position or notch. At this point the motor will take no current and … if the speed increases … will generate a current in the opposite direction."[35] The inventor claimed this process would provide from 20 to 40 percent greater distance than the conventional wound motor. The Waverley had a unique feature of a rear-facing front seat and a steering lever in the center of the back seat, which would allow the driver to converse face-to-face with the passengers. In 1904 Waverley merged with Pope's American Electric Vehicle Company. The company became Pope-Waverley in 1908. Pope sold the company in 1908 to a group of executives who renamed it simply the Waverley and introduced a front end resembling a gasoline-powered car as a new design feature.

The 1914 Waverley electric brougham incorporated many new design principles including rounded corners on the body. It also featured larger windows for a wider range of vision and a spacious "four chair" seating arrangement with maximum "knee, shoulder and elbow room."[37] The construction of the body included the use of new lightweight aluminum in the roof and panels. A standard forty-two-cell battery gave a range of about seventy-five miles. At a slightly higher cost the purchaser could have an option of the new Edison or Ironclad Exide battery installed. The battery boxes were located at the front and rear and were covered with sloping decks that rounded off to present grace-ful lines. The battery compartments were lined with acid-proof material to prevent any damage to the paint should the liquid be spilled. Other unique features of this brougham included a trussed hardwood beam frame, five quarter-elliptic springs front and rear and a double set of expanding brakes. The standard color was black with blue panels, but the company offered to paint the vehicle to suit the demands of the customer. With luxuri-ous bodywork and leather upholstery, the model 109 sold for $3,150.[38]

The Electromobile, made in Britain from 1902 to 1920, was one of the best-known electric vehicles in England. The British & Foreign Electric Vehicle Company was founded in 1900 and sold a Krieger under the name Powerful. They changed their name to the British Electromobile Company in 1902 and began to assemble vehi-cles with parts from different sources. The chassis was from Greenwood & Batley in Leeds, bod-ies were obtained from the Gloucester Railway Carriage & Waggon Company, which also sup-plied Bersey, and motors from France. In about 1905 they offered a "for-hire" leasing service in which a brougham could be hired, includ-ing maintenance and free charging, for £325 per year. Chauffeur ser-vices were extra. "In 1908, a fleet of 20 taxicabs went into service in London, some still being on the streets in the 1920s."[39]

Pope-Waverley surrey, 1908[36]

The first horse-less carriage for Studebaker was a light runabout built along buggy lines. It had leather fenders, bar-lever steering, chain drive and a leather dashboard. The advertisement claimed "Reliable Brake Control ... with All Machines equipped with Two Brakes." The Stude-baker brothers of Fort Wayne, Indi-ana, were the largest

Studebaker Electric ad, 1902[40]

wagon makers in the United States by 1895 and became interested in supplying the federal government with wagons for the Spanish-American War (1898–1902). They also wanted to supply the Army with electric vehicles, but were slow in developing the complete product. Their first electric appeared in 1902. By 1904, electric production ceased and the company moved to producing gasoline vehicles.

In 1903 Thomas A. Russell produced an electric two-passenger Ivanhoe runabout, called the "Thoroughly Canadian Car," in a Younge Street plant in Toronto. Production of the electric car only lasted two years. Then Russell turned his attention to gasoline-powered vehicles and began making a two-cylinder Model A.

De Dion-Bouton produced an electric car in France in 1904 that featured a large, slow-speed four-pole motor, mounted in a position occupied by the gearshift in a gasoline car. This was a simple arrangement to provide for speed changes, but added to the overall weight of the vehicle. The motor was completely enclosed in an aluminum casing with inspection openings near the brushes and incorporated a direct drive to the rear axle by means of a bevel gear. The steering mechanism and thick treaded tires copied the design and construction of contemporary gasoline vehicles.

The Babcock Electric Carriage Company (1903 to 1912) of Buffalo, New York, promoted safety and comfort in its vehicles. They advertised the vehicles as having "sufficient speed, besides greater mileage than is required in city or suburban riding." Founder Frank A. Babcock claimed a world record for range when he drove a runabout 100 miles from New York to Philadelphia in 1906 on a single charge. The actual distance to Philadelphia was 105 miles. The car consumed the last kilowatt of electricity a half-mile from the Camden city limits and was towed the remaining five miles to the ferry, but the record had been set. It had a top speed of 30 mph and claimed to be able to climb any hill at better than 20 mph. In 1911 Babcock maintained an electric garage at 66th St. & Euclid in Cleveland, Ohio, for the convenience of electric car owners "who wish to leave their cars downtown while attending business or the theater."[41] A special inspection service, provided as part of the manufacturer's guarantee, was furnished free for the first year and included batteries being charged, inspection and adjustment of chains and minor repairs being made "at the great convenience to electric owners."[42] The service could be extended after the first year by a payment of $2 monthly. Frank Babcock merged his company with the Clark Motor Company, changed the name to the Buffalo Electric Vehicle Company and continued production until 1915. Attempts were made to increase sales by designing the body to look similar to a gasoline-powered car, but the company went out of business in 1915. Their model 6 victoria sold for $1,700.

In 1908 Henry Ford introduced the first Model T at a price of $850. The gasoline-powered "Tin Lizzie" was his idea of a universal car. Ford kept reducing the price of the car

Babcock Electric coupe, 1912[44]

STANDARD OF EXCELLENCE

Model 6 Victoria, Price $1700

HAS BEEN ATTAINED IN

Babcock Electrics

These cars combine all the elements of safety and comfort with sufficient speed, besides greater mileage than is required in City or Suburban riding.

The popularity of the BABCOCKS is the best proof of their merit.

"When you build right, IT IS right and works right."—Babcock.

FIVE MODELS. WRITE FOR CATALOGUE

Babcock Electric Carriage Co., Builders

234 West Utica Street, Buffalo, N. Y.

New York Branch, 1591 Broadway, Corner 48th Street
Chicago Branch, 1328-30 Michigan Av.

Babcock advertisement, 1908[43]

until it reached $265 in 1923. In 1914, Clara Ford, Henry's wife, bought a Detroit Electric car for herself, claiming Henry's cars were too noisy.

By 1911 electric auto manufacturers were experiencing increased competition from the Fords and other ICEs. They decided to combine forces to enhance market share. A 1911 article in *Electrical World* reported:

> Each Wednesday noon, all representatives of electric vehicle manufacturers located in the Boston district gather at the Edison Building for a pleasant social hour, after which, under the oversight of the chairman elected each week, a large number of imparted topics in connection with development of electric vehicles in the district are discussed. It is inspiring to see these competitive interests putting their shoulders to the wheel with the single object of advancing the industry. Reference was also made to recent decision of the Boston Electric Company to replace all its gasoline and horse-drawn vehicles by electrically driven machines. On Memorial Day, an electric vehicle parade occurred in Boston in contrast to the annual work-horse procession, sixty two electric vehicles being in line.[45]

Thomas Edison made moving pictures of the parade. The movies were used by W. C. Baker in his lectures to promote electric vehicle transportation in the New England territory.

Another well-known and successful company from 1905 to 1923 was the Rauch & Lang Carriage Company of Cleveland, Ohio. The firm produced in quantity compared

Rauch & Lang, 1923[46]

to most and offered a variety of open and closed vehicle models. In 1916, they merged with the Baker Electric Company to become Baker, Rauch & Lang.

The Columbus Buggy Company of Columbus, Ohio, had been a prominent maker of horse-drawn vehicles since the 1860s. It entered the electric automobile market in 1903 with a folding top runabout and added a station wagon, surrey and coupe in 1906. Columbus began making gasoline vehicles in 1907. The company was sold in 1915.

The Hupp-Yeats electric vehicle was promoted as a "town car designed and built for the twentieth century" with a low-slung construction that was easy to enter or exit. It claimed to be safe and graceful without the dangerous tendency to skid or swerve that the high-ride electrics had. They used Westinghouse motors and attained a range of 75 to 90 miles on one charge. The auto was first manufactured by the R.C.H. Corporation from 1911 to 1912. The Hupp-Yeats Electric Car Company took it to a level of high fashion from 1912 to 1919. In 1915 the company introduced three models, replaced a bevel drive axle with a worm drive and reduced the price to $1,500. Hupp-Yeats offered a unique feature for the buyer. The purchase price included, as part of the standard equipment, a Lincoln (motor generator type) electric battery charger. This was a good selling point aimed at reducing the customer's anxiety about the additional investment in maintenance and charging. In 1919, when interest in the electric car was waning, the Hupp-Yeats was discontinued.

Although the concept of the gasoline-electric hybrid auto had been used with some success in the late 1800s by Jeantaud, Porsche and others, it was only marginally used. The Hybrid Electric Vehicle (HEV) concept came to wider public view in November 1905. H. Piper filed a patent to produce a vehicle with an electric motor augmented by a gasoline motor for greater performance. The patent was not issued for three and one-half years and by that time the internal combustion engine achieved better performance. The use of the HEV concept disappeared except for a few companies, like Galt, soon after 1910 and was not looked at again seriously until the oil shortages of the early 1970s. There are two types of hybrid vehicles, series and parallel. In the series, a gasoline engine generates power to drive an electric motor. In parallel, the two systems are distinct and separate, being able to propel the vehicle independently or together.

The Galt Motor Company was founded in 1909 and produced a series hybrid vehicle in 1914 called the Galt Gas Electric. It was one of the early Canadian entries into the efficient hybrid market. The auto was powered by a small gasoline engine, which turned a Westinghouse generator to produce electricity. The electricity powered the motor and charged the batteries. It had five speeds forward and three in reverse, was reported to get seventy miles per gallon and have a top speed of 30 mph. Traveling on battery power

Columbus Electric coupe, 1912[47]

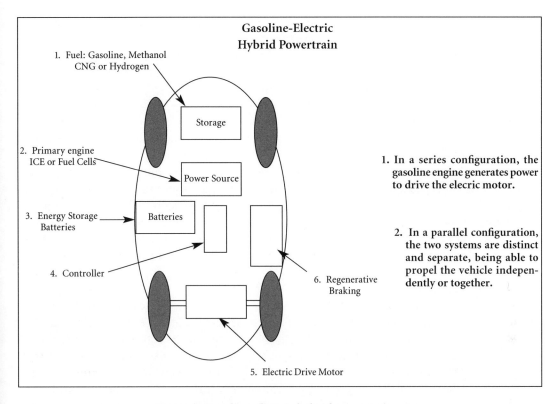

Gasoline-Electric Hybrid Powertrain

1. Fuel: Gasoline, Methanol CNG or Hydrogen

Storage

2. Primary engine ICE or Fuel Cells

Power Source

3. Energy Storage Batteries

Batteries

4. Controller

6. Regenerative Braking

5. Electric Drive Motor

1. In a series configuration, the gasoline engine generates power to drive the elecric motor.

2. In a parallel configuration, the two systems are distinct and separate, being able to propel the vehicle independently or together.

Figure 1: Gasoline-electric hybrid powertrain

only, the Galt could tour 15–20 miles, reducing the risk of being stranded without gasoline. As an added feature the Galt's front headlight was coupled to the steering gear and turned with the front wheels. This car did not sell well, possibly because the 30 mph speed was no match for the gasoline-powered competition.

The Flanders Electric Company of Pontiac, Michigan, produced a three-horsepower electric vehicle in 1914 with a worm drive to the rear wheels and a horizontal steering controller lever on the left side.

By 1913 the Electric Vehicle Association of America was working overtime to promote their product. The Association was formed with twenty-nine charter members in 1911 and had grown to 885 members by 1913. The members included seventeen electric vehicle makers, fifty-six central charging stations and ten manufacturers of accessories. Its promotion campaign targeted every aspect of the industry. It vigorously encouraged central station managers to open more stations for more electric cars. It persuaded the managers to lower their rates. It also approached insurance companies to lower rates so that the rates for electrics were about one-half that of gasoline vehicles. It promoted standardization of parts for electrics and had practically succeeded in standardizing the charging plug. It called for a standard speed limit and recommended a standard sign for battery charging stations. The Association also called for the establishment of electric garages to more rapidly advance the introduction of electric cars. The Association worked to bring about cooperation among the manufacturers, the central station owners, the battery trade and others in a nationwide advertising campaign for the benefit of the electric vehicle.

The National Electric Lighting Association (NELA) conducted a survey of seventy-five central station representatives and discovered that the electric vehicle as an off-peak revenue producer was not yet fully appreciated by many central stations. By 1914 there were approximately 1,500 electric vehicles in the New England area of the northeastern United States. The committee recommended the purchase of at least one electric vehicle by each central station of any size, membership in the national organization and the introduction of charging equipment into their facilities. "The day is at hand when the companies will be forced by the public to give the electric vehicle its proper service and when the companies themselves will have to use this class of equipment or become hopelessly out of date."[48]

The "dual-powered" car was a 1916 attempt at making a commercially viable hybrid vehicle. It was capable of running on either electricity or gasoline or both simultaneously. On electric power alone, the vehicle could speed up to 20 mph. Adding the gasoline power increased the speed to 30 mph. Running the gasoline engine "now and then" would be sufficient to recharge the batteries. The power plant consisted of a small gasoline motor and an electric motor generator combined into one unit. The movement of a lever on the steering wheel connected the gasoline motor to the electric motor generator, which transmitted power through the armature shaft of the electric motor and the propeller shaft directly to the rear axle. As the lever was moved forward it caused the car to be operated more and more on gas. With a variation of another lever on the steering wheel, the battery could be charged or used for the electric motor. It was promoted as having 40 percent greater speed than electric vehicles of the time and was simple, efficient and had more power. It was not competitive with its gasoline powered counterpart.

The Baker Motor Vehicle Co. of Cleveland, Ohio, was an industry leader from 1899 to 1916. The company offered fifteen different models of EVs. The earliest Bakers sold for $850 and one of the first customers was Thomas Edison. Other famous owners of Bakers were Mrs. William Howard Taft, the King of Siam and "Diamond Jim" Brady. In 1905

The dual-power car, 1916[49]

annual production reached 400 vehicles and doubled to 800 the following year, making Baker the largest producer of electric vehicles in the world.[50] In 1910 company advertising claimed, "It outsells all other Electrics because it outclasses them. More than three times as many Baker Electrics are sold each year than any other make." Baker supplied fleets of Baker Electric trucks to over 200 companies in 1912. In 1911 Baker maintained a charging garage at 71st Street in Cleveland, Ohio. The garage had facilities for charging 66 vehicles simultaneously and providing care for 100 automobiles. "The front of the building is given over to sales offices for the Baker ... while above these are high-class bachelor apartments."[51] Baker introduced a two-passenger roadster model in 1914 featuring a very sleek body style, high speed, and a steering wheel instead of a lever. By 1915 Baker acquired the R. M. Owen Company, maker of the Owen Magnetic car. After this acquisition, production was divided: the chassis was built in the Baker factory and the body was made by Rauch & Lang. Also in 1915, Baker and its competitor Woods each switched from a straight bevel drive train to worm drive, providing quieter operation and fewer gear reductions between the motor and the rear axle. The 1915 Baker models sported two head lamps, colonial side lamps and rear quarter interior lamps that lit automatically when the right-hand door was opened. Simplicity and reliability were the watchwords used to promote the Baker as the "standard" of the industry. Walter C. Baker referred to his vehicles as "The Aristocrat of Motordom." The company claimed to produce the most efficient, simplest-to-operate vehicle, with the fewest parts and fewer adjustments than others. This advertisement goes so far as to say it is an "automobile without a repair bill." While the company maintained its vehicles were the safest and simplest to operate and the cheapest to maintain, it did admit they were not the cheapest to buy. The initial cost factor again was a deterrent in a time when few people had the extra money to spend on such an extravagance. Baker tinkered with a gasoline-electric hybrid for a short time, but decided it was too cumbersome. The Baker electrics were discontinued in 1916. Walter Baker moved on to form a successful electric forklift truck business.

The Owen Magnetic Company, founded by brothers Raymond and Ralph Owen, began producing a gasoline-electric hybrid car in 1914 featuring an electric transmission that replaced the clutch, gears, starter motor and magneto. It was known as the "Car of a Thousand Speeds." The Baker, Rauch & Lang Company acquired the Owen Magnetic in 1915 and production was moved from New York City to Cleveland, Ohio. Baker produced the chassis, while Rauch & Lang produced the body. Famous owners included operatic tenors John McCormack and Enrico Caruso.[53] The price kept rising ($6,500 in 1918) while sales were falling, and in 1919 Baker discontinued production of the Owen. The company was acquired by J. L. Crown, who continued production on a small scale until 1921 under the name of Crown Magnetic.[54]

The Beardsley Electric Car Company of Los Angeles, California, marketed three models in 1915, a victoria, a brougham and a roadster. The brougham sold for $3,000 and the roadster for $2,600. They all had the same chassis and used wire wheels exclusively.

The Columbian Electric Car Company of Detroit, Michigan, began in 1915 and offered three models. The first was a very low-priced two-passenger roadster listing at $950, the second a three-passenger coupelet selling for $1,250, and the third a four-passenger brougham listing at $1,450. All employed the same chassis and the standard body color was dark blue with silver-gray trim.[55]

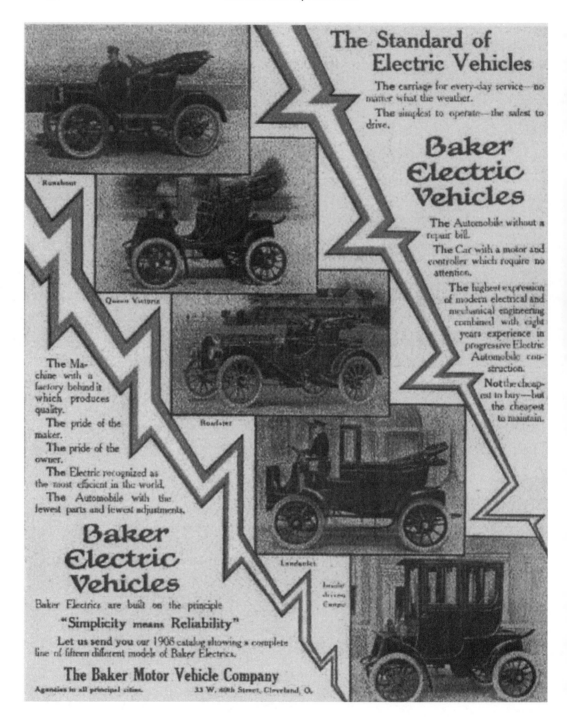

Baker advertisement, 1908. Showing 5 of its 15 models[52]

The Storms Electric Car Company, founded by William E. Storms, formerly of the Anderson Electric Car Company, was another 1915 start-up. He produced two low-priced models, a coupe for $950 and a roadster for $750. They were shorter than most, with a wheelbase of only 90 in. and had large 44 in. tires. The motor was located in the center of the chassis to create a direct drive by a shaft to bevel gears in a tubular full floating rear axle. Two sets of brakes were operated by a pedal.

The Century Electric Car Company of Detroit, Michigan, manufactured electric vehicles from 1911 to 1915 in cooperation with Westinghouse. The motor was geared directly to the rear axle. The company offered only one model in 1915. It was the first to incorporate an underslung frame and came with a choice of solid or pneumatic tires.[56] The company went bankrupt in 1915.

The Grinnell Electric Company, founded by Ira and C. A. Grinnell, produced electric cars and enjoyed moderately successful sales from 1912 to 1915. In 1915, they offered a dual-drive model with a set of control levers operated from either the front or rear seats and selling for $3,400. As interest in electric vehicles faded, the Grinnell brothers changed their entire business strategy to move from a loss in automobile sales to a profit by establishing a chain of piano and music stores in Detroit.

In 1916 the Walker Vehicle Company produced a product line termed the "Edison models" designed specifically for use with the new G-Type Edison battery. The new battery provided increased power with reduced weight. The models included a five-passenger car, a four-passenger car and a sleek cabriolet roadster. The rear seat of the roadster was wide enough to carry three passengers and an auxiliary folding seat would carry a fourth person. The car body design avoided sharp angles and a new crowned fender design gave it a sleek look. Aluminum was used exclusively for all parts exposed to the weather. Luxury items in the interior included dome lights, reading lamps, arm rests, arm slings, a concealed toilet vanity case and smoking set, a clock and dash instruments. The chassis was a one-unit rigid frame thought to be well-adapted to the solid tires. The construction included better

The Century Electric, 1915[57]

Grinnell Electric coupe, 1912[58]

lubrication of the steering gear and a worm-bevel gear axle drive similar to that used in the Chicago electrics. Cooler winter weather took its toll on the battery performance in the electrics, but the new batteries included in the package were claimed to be less affected by temperature changes than other batteries. To promote sales, Walker offered a battery exchange system and lowered prices from an average of $2,600 to $1,985. If a buyer wanted the battery exchange system, the new list price would go up another $270. The purchaser could "rent a complete battery service at a minimum charge per month."[59] This service covered the entire maintenance and repair expenses incident to the hardest wear and tear on the battery. The service would cover the maintenance expense whether the car was driven fifty or one thousand miles a month and if the battery wore out, it was replaced with a fresh one.

The most successful company in the electric vehicle field was the Detroit Electric Car Company, in production from 1907 to 1939. It produced one of the most popular electric cars in the United States. The popularity was due in part to a false front end resembling the radiator of a car with a gasoline engine. The company started as the Anderson Carriage Co. in 1907, then became the Anderson Electric Car Co. in 1911 and finally the Detroit Electric Car Co. from 1919 to 1939. The Detroit electric in 1915 featured a new beveled worm gear drive and large expanding brakes. Window glass was fitted into the bodies mounted on thick rubber, with a dovetailed channel to prevent rainwater from entering the interior. They offered six different models. To encourage sales, the company dramatically lowered the prices of various models from $600 to $725 bringing the average selling price down to about $2,000. The Anderson Electric Car Company produced a four-passenger model Detroit in 1917 that featured windows operated by a patented window lifter. In the warm summer, the car could be converted to an open-air vehicle with a permanent roof. While the basic body design changed little over the years, in 1930 Detroit offered an option of a body supplied by either Dodge or Willys. Production gradually declined from a high of 4,669 vehicles in 1914 to "by-order-only" in the later stage of the company. During its thirty-five years in business, it produced over 35,000 vehicles, far more than any other electric car company.

Detroit Electric 2-seater, 1912[60]

The Milburn Wagon Company, founded in 1848 in Toledo, Ohio, was another of the more successful electric carmakers of the time, producing thousands of vehicles from 1914 to 1922. In 1909 they leased part of their wagon plant to the Ohio Electric Car Company. When Ohio moved to its own factory in 1911, Milburn's directors became interested in electric vehicles and began production in September 1914. Milburn produced a variety of coupes and roadsters and a delivery van. They used aluminum, hammered by hand, to produce arched fenders and sweeping curves in the body style. The craftsmanship of the bodywork was excellent, reflecting the Milburn Company's concern for the coachbuilding business. In 1915 they introduced a battery swapout system with the batteries on rollers that allowed the owner to roll out the discharged batteries and roll in the charged ones. President Wilson's Secret Service staff used Milburns. General Motors (GM) bought the Milburn factory in February 1923 and proceeded to make Buicks. Milburns may have been produced on a "custom-order" basis as late as 1927.

Detroit Electric roadster Model 46, 1915[61]

Detroit Electric coupe, 1917[62]

In 1917 electric vehicles in general were thriving in the commercial vehicle industry. The electric truck was being used in over one hundred types of industries, some having been in use for about ten years. Express companies, department stores, breweries, bakeries, central stations, laundries and warehouses were the major users of electric car fleets. The fleet managers began gathering data on their performance and were pleased with the results. Fire departments in particular held great appreciation for the electrics and converted from horse-drawn vehicles to EVs. Horses sometimes balked near fires and the gasoline engine was considered too flammable. The Camden, New Jersey, Fire Department modernized its entire fleet in 1917 and made a thorough investigation with rigid tests. The results showed the new fleet had a quick get-away, the ability to negotiate crowded streets easily and to readily climb hills. They were easy for anyone to operate, economical and generally had good reliability. The city council was so impressed that they ordered a charging apparatus for each fire station. Many other cities, including Philadelphia, Pennsylvania, Brooklyn, New York, Grand Rapids, Michigan and Akron, Ohio, followed suit. Police departments and most hospitals in large cities with ambulance service were increasingly using electric vehicles.

The war in Europe materially added to the development of the electric vehicle. In

Milburn coupe, 1915[63]

the United States, as well as Germany, France and England, electric vehicle fleets began to be used for street cleaning and sweeping and garbage collection. In England when gasoline cars were commandeered for the war effort, many merchants began experimenting with electric vehicles. England had a nearly inexhaustible supply of coal to produce electricity, one of the few items it did not have to import. In the three years following the beginning of the war, England increased its electric truck sector from 150 to over 1,000. Electric vehicle use expanded in England by 400 percent during the war. By 1917, Birmingham district had twenty-two charging stations in the area and seven stations in the city. Growth was expected to continue after the war. Germany was mining an abundance of coal in occupied France to provide cheap electricity. It was using the electricity to power railroads and troop transport trucks to support the war effort. Italy was generating cheap electricity using waterfalls as a source of water power to supply the energy needed for large numbers of electric vehicles. The market for EVs was plentiful, and the United States auto manufacturers came forward to meet the demand. In 1917 the United States became a major exporter, delivering electric vehicles to South America, Norway, China and England. During this era, a solution for recharging also seemed within reach. A battery exchange system had been developed four years earlier for taxicabs and was being used in most large American cities and in Berlin. Under the new system the charging station owned the battery, leased it to the customer at a fixed rate, and charged the customer per mile instead of selling electric current for charging a battery by the kilowatt-hour. The batteries could be exchanged in a few minutes and showed a possibility of unlimited mileage.[65] It was expected that studies conducted by qualified engineers, in the analysis of transportation after the war, would show the electric vehicles were the most efficient mode of transport. The future of electrics looked bright.

James H. McGraw, president of the McGraw-Hill Company, presented a paper to the Electric Vehicle Section meeting in June 1918. In it he stated, "The supply of electricity for the big developments to come in cheapening the cost of handling goods in terminals and warehouses, and in cutting the cost of deliveries on our city streets, is worth the attention of every central station."[66]

Cheap electricity, gasoline shortages, improved battery recharging post–World War I (1918) had all the elements for marketing electric vehicles, and the United States auto industry was poised to deliver. European and Scandinavian factories needed time to refurbish and rebuild. The U.S. auto factories had expanded production to meet demand during the war. In the United States alone there were an estimated 50,000 electric vehicles,

Milburn ad, 1916[64]

10,000 of them in Chicago. Now the U.S. auto industry was the only source for supplying large quantities of autos quickly to the war-torn recovering nations. The Central Palace Auto Show in New York in 1918 had four electric companies as exhibitors. The show drew several representatives from Scandinavia, Europe, South America and Japan who were prepared to place contracts for large orders of passenger motor vehicles. Demand for electric vehicles was exceptionally high. A Norwegian representative ordered one hundred Rauch & Lang broughams for $3,000 each, with arrangement to buy forty more within two weeks. Norway and Sweden were producing abundant and cheap electricity using their water power systems. With electricity plentiful in Norway, the representative expected to sell the cars as soon as they had been shipped. Rauch & Lang, Ohio, Milburn and Detroit Electrics all exhibited at the show. Rauch & Lang sold ten new taxicabs to Japan. Milburn featured a model with a long hood holding the batteries and a radiator to mimic the appearance of the high-powered gasoline vehicles. Studebaker had an exhibit, but did not feature any electric models at the time. The volume purchased gave indications that the interest in electrics would continue after the war, but even with the postwar interest, they did not regain the popularity they had seen ten years earlier.

Harry E. Dey in Jersey City created a revolutionary vehicle in an attempt to revive the electric automobile in 1919. It was a hybrid billed as having its own portable charging plant — a three-horsepower air-cooled gasoline engine to charge the two-horsepower electric motor. The gasoline engine could be removed and used as a stationary charging unit for charging a separate battery or house lighting. Of its many new features, the motor combined a rotating armature with field magnets connecting to a driving wheel by way of reduction gears. This eliminated the expense and weight of a differential gear. The construction of the vehicle included a number of tapered slip rings and was called the "nutless" car as so few were used. The chassis was made of wood and the commonly used elliptical spring suspension was replaced by air springs. The construction consisted of a helical spring inside a cylinder providing for the static load, while the air would take up all the shocks. If an air leak occurred, the spring would bring the load back to normal position and the air would return. Many other points of the construction reduced the overall weight of the car. The battery was carried underneath the floor of the chassis housed in truss rods. This permitted more room for passengers and luggage. The battery could be lowered to the floor of the garage, or, by lifting a trap door in the floor of the car, water could be added to the battery. The "nutless" lightweight revolutionary new vehicle never made it to mass production.

The stock market crash of 1929 and the beginning of a ten-year global depression virtually ended the production of the electric automobile in the United States and crippled companies in England and Europe. Dozens of major companies went bankrupt with the Detroit Electric Car Company surviving until 1939 and Studebaker and Willys surviving in the United States beyond that. Electric car production was not seen again in the United States until World War II when fuel shortages caused consumers to find an alternative to gasoline vehicles.

The renaissance of electric vehicles had begun in Great Britain about five years before the war. They were being used primarily for delivery service such as coal, bread and milk. There were about 1,400 electric vehicles in Great Britain in 1933 and by 1940 the number had grown to 6,500. By 1939, due to the war, milk delivery had been shortened from two rounds a day to one. This created an opportunity for marketing larger electric vehicles to meet the delivery need. Attempts at producing EVs with a larger capacity resulted in the same problems earlier manufacturers had had. The battery was not robust enough to handle the added weight of battery and larger vehicle. The battery, used under these conditions, had a guaranteed life span of only two years. It was hoped that a newer, lighter battery would soon be invented and produced, but the prospects looked bleak.

By 1940, England and Germany were in the midst of war. Every gallon of gasoline saved was important to the war effort on both sides. Germany had already taken advantage of the use of electric vehicles and had promoted their use by making them tax-exempt. They had over 27,000 EVs in service. Their postal service alone had more electrics in operation than the total number of electrics operated in England. Some in England realized that if electric vehicles could replace even more gasoline-powered cars in the transport of everyday items such as milk and bread deliveries, it might free up an estimated 70 million gallons of gasoline each year that could be redirected to military needs. To promote the move from gas to electrics, a strong marketing campaign closely resembling the advertising points used thirty-five years earlier was put into place. Several advantages of the electric car were pointed out. The long life of the electric vehicle would conserve natural resources. The cheaper operation of the electric vehicle would keep transport costs down and reduce the cost-of-living increases and the risk of inflation. The sales pitch to English customers was that they must be made to realize that the electric car was not intended to be a direct competitor to the gasoline car. It would provide reliable transportation and reach a cruising speed of twenty miles per hour with a range of about fifty miles per day. The buyer should think of the electric as the perfect purchase for transport and delivery vehicles. Hills were not a problem. Even the hilly districts of Sheffield and Bristol already had over three hundred Morrison vehicles operated by the Co-operative Society. Advocates pointed out that slight hills gave somewhat increased mileage to the electrics compared to traveling on flat roads as the batteries could be recharged when going down hills. Advocates of the electric vehicles campaigned that they were not more expensive to purchase when taking into account the expense of gasoline being four times the price of electricity. Another selling point was the lack of maintenance. Simplicity and efficiency were a keynote point that had made the electrics a favorite vehicle for unskilled or even careless drivers since the beginning of the century. There were fewer components to get out of order and thus less likely to break down. The main problem was to pay attention to topping off the battery. With fewer components to maintain, the electric cars could expect a longer life span. Gasoline-driven vehicles were expected to have a life span of about five years, while electric cars were averaging ten years and sometimes up to thirty years. It was anticipated that increased demand would bring about an increase in mass production. A few manufacturers were involved in what they called semi–mass production of electric vehicles in Great Britain in 1940 to meet the limited demand.

Other countries also looked for alternative fuel possibilities to serve the civilians' needs for transportation to carry out their business and meet family and travel requirements. In addition to the British, European and Japanese civilians began exploring alternate energy possibilities; many turned to the electric vehicle. Manufacturers made efforts to meet the demand, including:

- The Bleichert Transportanlagen company of Leipzig, Germany, manufactured two-seat electric vehicles from 1936 to 1939.
- The Electrolette was a two-seat light electric vehicle manufactured in France from 1941 to 1943. It was powered by a single 1.5-hp motor and attained a speed of 20 mph. Only a few hundred vehicles were produced.
- The French Faure was produced from 1941 to 1947.
- The Netherlands produced the Story (1940–1941), a three-wheeled electric that attained a top speed of 18 mph with a range of 60 km.
- The French Stela (1941–1948) was a four-door vehicle used by private citizens. They also provided transport for government officials and served as taxis.
- The C.G.E. was a two-seat vehicle produced in France from 1941 to 1948 by the Compagnie Générale Électrique of Paris.
- The Dauphin (1941–1942) was another Paris example of a four-door two-seat electric vehicle.
- The Paris-Rhone (1942–1944) was a tiny three-wheeler car with a 2 hp electric motor driving the rear wheels.
- The Partridge-Wilson Company of England produced electric vehicles from 1935 to 1954 in small numbers (perhaps fifty) with a top speed of 27 mph and a range of forty miles.

All of these vehicles were mildly successful during World War II due to the shortage and rationing of gasoline. When the war was over and gasoline became more available the marques vanished, with only a few continuing into the 1950s.

The Tama Electric Motorcar Company of Tokyo produced a popular electric car from 1949 to 1951, a time of severe gasoline shortages in Japan. It had a range of 125 miles and a speed of 35 mph. In 1952 when gasoline became more readily available, the company began making gasoline-powered cars and changed its name to Prince.

The hybrid Symetric (Arbel) was produced in Paris from 1951 to 1953, and again from 1957 to 1958, when it incorporated plastic bodywork. It featured a four-cylinder engine to power four electric motors, one for each wheel, following the early design of cars like the 1901 Krieger. Many options were offered, including Electric-Drive transmission, Thermogum suspension, phosphorescent bumpers and a choice of powerplants that included a Genestatom nuclear reactor. "The Arbel quickly disappeared in a haze of unpaid debts."[67]

An unusual vehicle at an unusual time was the Electronic, made in 1955 by the Electronic Motor Car Company of Salt Lake City, Utah. It was a hybrid sports car powered by a small gasoline engine with an electric motor attached to the rear axle. The company had an outrageous idea for the time of setting up a system of radio transmitters coast-to-coast that would relay electronic signals to a receiver in the car. The signal was to be converted into electricity to charge the batteries.[68]

Environmental concerns again spiked interest in EVs in the 1960s, but the 1960s' electric vehicle production was confined to small experimental types such as the Peel (1962–1966), a small three-wheeler with a fiberglass body, and the Marketour (1965) intended for short shopping trips. In 1960 the American Motor Company (AMC) experimented with a hybrid vehicle in collaboration with the battery maker, Sonotone Corporation. It featured nickel-cadmium batteries charged by a small gasoline engine. The companies regarded it as the wrong direction to take as it still emitted gasoline exhaust fumes.

Possibly the most successful electric car of the '60s was the Enfield 8000, produced in London, England, as a two-door, four-seat car that claimed a range of 90 km and a speed of 60 km/hr. It had a steel tube-frame chassis and rack and pinion steering. The eight-horsepower motor was powered by eight twelve-volt batteries. Only 106 cars were made and the price was too high for most private buyers. The Electricity Council of England promoted the practicality of electric cars by purchasing seventy of the Enfields to be used by the electric utility companies.

Next to the Enfield, the Electracation (1976–1980) was the only serious electric car produced in England in the 1970s. It had a fiberglass body and a 7.5 hp Lansing-Bagnall electric motor. Three models included a town coupe, a van and a rickshaw with a soft top. "There were a number of appearances at international motor shows and the famous sports car maker AC was lined up to make up to 2,400 cars per year, but nothing came of the plan."[70]

During the same time, the Battronic Truck Company of England delivered electric trucks to the Potomac Edison Company in the United States for fleet use. The Battronic had a range of sixty-two miles and a speed of about 25 mph with a payload of 2,500 pounds. General Electric worked with Battronic from 1973 to 1983 developing passenger buses and fleet vans for the utility industry. By 1977 gasoline in the United Kingdom cost twice as much as in the United States and England had about 70,000 electric vehicles being

Enfield 8000, 1969[69]

used to deliver milk, mail and other products or to provide transportation in some type of service capacity.

In 1966 GMC experimented with an Electrovan, a GMC Handivan converted to a fuel-cell-powered vehicle. It contained a very dangerous combination of fuels that included tanks of pure hydrogen and oxygen behind the back seat and hot potassium hydroxide running through pipes beneath the floor. The safety factors included a hydrogen shut-off switch in the glove compartment and a large knife switch to kill the power. It was destined to travel just a few "well-chosen miles."[71]

Ford produced a small number of electric city-cars in 1967 called the Ford Comuta. It had four batteries and two electric traction motors and had a very limited range.

In 1972 AMC produced a concept car called the Electrosport, a conversion of a Hornet to an electric vehicle. Two other examples of independent manufacturers in the mid–1970s electric car arena were the Sebring Vanguard CitiCar and the Elcar 2000. They were both very small two-seater wedge-shaped vehicles not much larger than a golf cart with only about 3.5 hp. Sebring Vanguard was the only American firm at the time producing electric passenger cars on an assembly line. The CitiCar had a top speed of thirty-eight miles per hour and a range of about forty miles. It was not allowed on limited access highways. *Consumer Reports* judged both the Elcar 2000 and the CitiCar as "Not Acceptable" in their 1976 review. During testing, the cars showed a number of safety and operating problems. At one point in testing, the CitiCar's brakes failed. Production was stopped in 1977.

Nissan of Japan experimented with concept and prototype vehicles in the 1970s, producing the EV4P, powered by a lead-acid battery. It also made a variation of a battery-battery hybrid vehicle known as the EV4H, which combined lead-acid batteries with zinc-air batteries. It claimed a range of 250 to 490 km on a charge and a top speed of 85 km/h.

In Australia, in the late 1970s experimenters produced the Investigator Mk II, a battery-powered electric based on a Fiat 127 body. It had a top speed of 75 km/h with a range of 60–80 km.

The Marathon Electric Car Company of St. Leonard, Quebec, Canada, produced more than six hundred battery-powered vehicles by 1978. The Marathon C-360 van was a six-wheeler. The body was lightweight foam-core aluminum. The company closed its doors in 1980. By the 1980s, Canadians, such as the Ballard Company in Vancouver, were concentrating on fuel cells. In 2001 the *Canadian Driver* magazine and Web site focused on the Toyota Prius, Honda Insight and Daimler-Chrysler hybrid trucks for potential marketability.

The Elcar, built by Zagato of Italy, was a two-door, two-seater light electric car. It had a fiberglass body shaped like the Fiat 124. About 500 were produced in the mid–1970s. It had a range of sixty miles and a top speed of 45 mph. Fiat itself began experimenting with electric vehicles in the 1970s. Some of its products were the two-seat X1/23, the 900 Evan, the Iveco Daily van, and in 1990 a twenty-two-passenger electric minibus.

The General Engines Company of Sewell, New Jersey, produced the 1980 Electro-Sport, a full-scale replica of a 1929 Mercedes-Benz roadster. It had a range of fifty miles and a top speed of 50 mph. It was powered by twelve 6-volt golf cart batteries that weighed sixty-two pounds.

The CityCom is a popular city commuter German vehicle built from 1987 to date with a range of thirty miles at 30 mph.

Ford developed the Ecostar utility van in the early 1990s. Its top speed is 75 mph and it has a range of 80–100 miles and regenerative braking. If the driver maintains a constant speed of 25 mph, the range can be extended to 200 miles. Gasoline-powered vehicles tend to creep forward when put in drive; EVs do not. To help in the transition from ICE to electrics, Ford built an electronic "creep" into the Ecostar to satisfy the disconcerted traditional ICE drivers.[72] The Ecostar was considered an R&D vehicle, and while about one hundred were produced and delivered to Southern California Edison and Detroit Edison fleets to monitor their performance in the controlled fleet environment, they were never sold commercially. Ford was also in the process of developing a natural gas pickup truck for fleet use.

Ford introduced its TH!NK City car in Norway. The TH!NK is a sub-compact battery-powered vehicle designed for urban transportation. It provides acceleration of 0–30 in seven seconds and has a range of fifty-three miles. Although the response in Norway was positive, Ford executives believe there is only a limited customer demand for battery-electric vehicles and plans to focus its resources on hybrid and fuel cell technology. Ford is working on a battery-fuel cell vehicle to be released in 2004 called the Escape Hybrid.

General Motors has been experimenting with EVs throughout the last decades of the 20th century, primarily making prototypes. The Impact (universally acknowledged as badly named) was introduced as a prototype in 1990 and became the predecessor of the EV1. The Impact was capable of 0–60 in eight seconds, could top 100 mph and travel 120 miles on one charge. The bad news, as usual, was the battery pack — it would only last 25,000 miles and cost $1,500 to replace. Many advanced technologies contributed to the introduction of the General Motors EV1 in 1996. In order to help extend the limited range of the all-electric vehicle, GM designed the car to minimize weight, power consumption and drag. They used molded plastic body panels filled with hollow glass beads and supported by cast aluminum. The body shape had a drag coefficient of only 0.19.[73] Part of the development of the EV1 bodywork and efficient ride came from experiments with GM's Ultralite vehicle in 1992. The prototype vehicle was a four-door design that incorporated a high tech carbon fiber body that weighed only 1,400 pounds. The biggest drawback of carbon fiber is the price — ranging from $40 to $150 per pound versus about $2 per pound for plastic and forty cents per pound for steel. It could go from 0–60 in nine seconds. The inductive type Magne-Charge charging system used a plastic paddle at the end of the charger's cord which was inserted into the front fascia of the car. The system could be used in the rain; GM claimed water could run over the paddle without damage. This type of system was selected for safety and was the only charger to be approved by Underwriters Laboratory.[74] The car was offered for lease only. GM wanted select customers who were "green" minded, had an annual income over $125,000, and wanted to use the EV1 as a second car. By 1997 disappointing sales of the EV1 forced GM to lower the monthly lease payment by 25 percent from $530 to $399. The 176 people who had already leased the cars were given the same lower rate. The new rate also included the $50 per month cost previously paid for a home charging station.

In the late 1990s Ford developed its Ranger pickup with a range of about 65 miles and a top speed of 75 mph. GM added the Chevrolet S-10 pickup to its product line. Honda offered its EV Plus sedan and Chrysler presented its EPIC minivan. Honda's EV Plus was discontinued in 1999. The Chrysler EPIC is being used for demonstrations and fleet service. All of these vehicles were equipped with nickel metal hydride (NiMH) batteries. Nissan announced in 1998 it would provide its Altra EV station wagons to California fleets, equipped with lithium–ion batteries. Ford's Ranger EV pickup and Toyota's RAV4 EV are very popular fleet vehicles and are also available to the general public.

The Corbin Sparrow, of Hollister, California, is a one-seat three-wheel electric zero emissions vehicle that was introduced in 1999. The company was co-founded by Mike and Tom Corbin, who began researching the Sparrow in 1996. As of 2001, Corbin had sold 200 Sparrows and a waiting list of over 1,000 orders. The Sparrow is rechargeable in three hours at a 220-volt outlet or six hours at a 110-volt outlet and travels at 50 mph for a range of 50 miles on one charge. It does the quarter mile in fifteen seconds reaching 95 mph. The company suffered from lawsuits and financial problems and filed for bankruptcy in 2003.

The Honda Insight, available in the United States in 1999 is an Ultra Low Emission Vehicle (ULEV) hybrid with a compact electric motor. Regenerative braking recharges the NiMH batteries. It boasts a drag coefficient of 0.25. The gasoline engine is the primary source of propulsion with the electric motor assisting when additional power is needed. Honda began producing the natural gas Civic GX in 1998. The engine was similar to the 1.7 liter, four-cylinder gasoline engine of the traditional Civic with small modifications made to run on natural gas. It has a range of 200 miles and was sold primarily for fleet use. The Nissan Sentra CA (Clean Air) was the first vehicle to receive Partial Zero Emission Vehicle (PZEV) credits from CARB. It has also qualified as a Super Ultra Low Emission Vehicle (SU-LEV). GM's Precept is a hybrid vehicle with an electric motor driving the front wheels and a lean-burning gasoline motor driving the rear wheels. GM's Triax is unique in that it has three propulsion options: all-wheel-drive electric, all-wheel-drive hybrid electric or two-wheel-drive internal combustion.

Corbin Sparrow, 2000[75]

GM Precept[76]

GM's Chevrolet Triax[77]

In July 2000 GM introduced a prototype fuel cell vehicle called the HydroGen 1 that produces about sixty percent more power than its predecessor. Up to two-thirds of the energy generated by the fuel cell is transferred to the wheels, about four times as much as in a gasoline vehicle. GM was predicting at the time to be competitive in the showrooms by 2004.[78]

In November 2000 Daimler/Chrysler unveiled its Necar 5 fuel cell vehicle powered by methanol. The fuel cell stack is 50 percent more efficient than the previous model Necar 3 and the Necar 5 can reach speeds up to one-hundred miles per hour. Daimler/Chrysler spokesmen admit the fuel cell is still in the development stage, but feel they can be competitive with the ICE in a few years.

In November 2000 Volkswagen introduced the Bora HyMotion, known as the Jetta in the United States. It contains a fuel cell engine that runs on liquid hydrogen with the only by-product being water vapor. The hydrogen storage tank has a capacity of fifty liters, equal to twelve liters of gasoline for a range of about 350 kilometers.

In 2001 the U.S. Army announced plans to develop a hybrid diesel-electric truck, based on the Dodge Ram. The diesel motor will power the vehicle with added acceleration supplied by the electric motor, or it can run for a short range on electric power only.

At the Detroit Motor Show in January 2002, General Motors introduced its prototype fuel cell vehicle called Autonomy. The new fuel cell stack is only fifteen cm thick. The x-by wire computer control systems are held in a six-inch skateboard structure that attaches to four wheels. The Autonomy features this unusual chassis with four attach-ment points for different body styles. The bodies can be manufactured and sold sepa-rately. They include a choice of standard sedan, coupe, pick-up truck or sport-utility styles. High cost keeps the prototype from moving to the current marketplace.

In May 2002 Toyota introduced its all-electric RAV4 EV to the public, available in California only. It had been road-tested for four years within Toyota's fleet division. Cal-ifornia incentives include a rebate of up to $8,000 over a three-year period, driving in the carpooling lane, even if there are no passengers aboard, and parking in desirable spaces designated for electric vehicles only.

Auto racing has served as a proving ground for new technology in the past, but has not played a major role in the development of the more current electric vehicles. Nine-teen ninety-six saw the beginning of several all-electric races such as the Solar & Elec-tric 500 at the Phoenix Firebird International Raceway and the EV Grand Prix in Virginia. The entries tended to come from educational institutions. The public response was min-imal.

A poll taken in December 2000 showed 71 percent of Americans would probably not buy an electric or hybrid vehicle if they were only available at a price higher than most new cars.

Only one car rental company is offering a hybrid in its fleet. Budget rents the Honda Insight in Phoenix, and the Toyota RAV4 EV and GM's EV1 in Los Angeles. The response of customers has been positive, and once familiar with the car, repeat customers are fre-quent.[79]

Throughout their first century, electric vehicles have proved to be reliable, clean, low-maintenance transportation. Their manufacturers have created coaches for the style-conscious, improved the auto's speed and mileage, and risen to the challenge of devel-oping a more environmentally friendly vehicle. Their market has gone from a popular choice to an alternate in times of fuel shortage, and the best choice for an environmen-tally friendly mode of transportation.

2 Politics

"Why should we be mandated to build a product that no one wants to buy?"[1]

How do governments influence industry and vice versa? Since the first steam road locomotive (automobile) began using public roadways, the automotive industry has been affected by laws and regulations. Today, the transportation sector of the U.S. economy is a major energy consumer. Automotive technology developers tend to look at government as one of many groups they need to deal with, along with utilities, the oil industry and the automotive industry. Of these various factors, only government has the official role of shaping civic duties of citizenship. Government becomes involved for the public interest when citizen groups wish to promote specific products for the public good or industries need assistance in research and development costs in search of products that have political potential.

In *Future Drive*, Daniel Sperling discusses the need to invoke creative technologies to produce environmentally benign automobiles, and government's role in encouraging development and sale of the technology through tax incentives, fees and credits.

> The answer is founded on technical fixes. Technical fixes preserve the fundamental attractions of vehicle travel — mobility, convenience and privacy — while requiring few behavioral changes. They support rather than subvert travelers' wishes and needs. Given the shortcoming of travel reduction strategies, and the huge promise of new technologies, the focus of any effort to create a more environmentally benign transportation system should be technological innovation.
>
> The public strongly prefers this approach to restrictions on their behavior. In a 1991 survey conducted in the Los Angeles area, over half the respondents (57 percent) expressed willingness to purchase an alternative fuel vehicle as a response to air pollution problems, compared with only 17 percent who were willing to carpool, 16 percent who would use mass transit and 6 percent who would walk or bicycle.[2]

Like many safety features on cars, such as the seat belt and the air bag, legislation for electric vehicles is being driven without consideration for manufacturing costs or demand. Advocates think that legislation will help advance the electric cars, but is it the most effective way to promote the product? While environmental concerns and legislation can provoke public awareness, new technology is needed to make the autos succeed in the marketplace. New batteries, fuel cells and hybrid vehicles need to be in place, alongside the improved internal combustion engines to meet the government regulations, or the regulations will need to be adjusted.

Through laws, regulations, subsidies, tax incentives, research support and purchasing, federal and state governments assist and promote research and provide markets for alternate energy vehicles. Governments have a direct effect on the technological research and development. The Ballard Fuel Cell Company, for example, is succeeding partially due to the market created because manufacturers needed to meet the low emissions standards regulations initiated by the California Air Resources Board (CARB). Partnerships formed between government agencies and private industries allow each to benefit from the discoveries made in the national labs and the testing available through the consumer marketplace. During the last one hundred years government alliances have sustained the development of electric vehicles that have not succeeded through market forces alone.

The United States imports billions of gallons of oil each year. It is estimated that 10,000 fuel cell vehicles running on hydrogen (the most abundant element in the universe) would save seven million gallons of gasoline each year and if fuel cell cars occupied ten percent of the market share, the United States could reduce oil imports by 130 million barrels per year.[3] Unfortunately, most analysts predict this type of fuel cell engine is about ten years down the road if left up to competitive consumer market demand. Government intervention in the form of tax rebates and subsidies for technology innovators is one way of possibly speeding up this development. President George W. Bush announced in mid–2002 that his administration is backing the development of fuel cells.

Early Laws and Litigation

In the United States, patents had an early impact on which automobiles would be successful in the marketplace. At the turn of the 20th century, great industrialists like Rockefeller, Morgan, and Carnegie, and financiers like William C. Whitney, were using trusts to further their interests by controlling prices and protecting patent rights. They combined business interests of groups of companies by turning over their management to a single board of directors. These trusts followed two designs, each having the capability of creating a monopoly in the marketplace, curbing competition. The horizontal type brought together and controlled companies with a similar product. The vertical type controlled the production from raw materials to finished product. Patent rights held by each company on each model were owned by the trust. Financiers P. A. B. Widener and William C. Whitney saw the potential for profit in automobiles, electric taxis in particular, and put together the State Trust Company, later called the Lead Cab Trust. This trust included trolley franchise holders, lead-acid battery manufacturers and electric vehicle companies.

George B. Selden, a Rochester, New York, lawyer, had seen the future success of the internal combustion engine, and on November 5, 1895, he was granted patent no. 549,160 for any automobile concept using a two-stroke internal combustion engine. The Electric Vehicle Company, as part of the Lead Cab Trust, bought the rights to the Selden Patent in 1899 for $10,000 (Mr. Selden retained the rights to one-fifth of any royalties gained from the patent). Each ICE manufacturer was obliged to secure a license and pay royalties to the Lead Cab Trust in order to use an internal combustion engine. Under the Selden patent, early autos would display a plaque on the engine indicating that they had legitimate rights to use that engine structure. The Lead Cab Trust saw this as an opportunity to profit from the rising popularity of the internal combustion engine, as individuals and small businesses making cars started to dot the landscape, and as a hedge to develop electric vehicles by preventing the development of gasoline vehicles should they prove superior.

The first lawsuit concerning the Selden patent was against the Winton Motor Carriage Company in 1900 when the company attempted to sell ICEs without first purchasing a license. Winton settled out of court in 1903.

Henry Ford was offered a Selden patent license in 1902 and refused it. In 1903 the Electric Vehicle Company and the Lead Trust sued Ford, and for eight years the case was in the courts.

Ford eventually won the case because the court ruled the Selden patent was valid only for the two-stroke (Brayton principle) engine and not for the four-stroke (Otto principle) engine. This important decision allowed internal combustion engine auto manufacturers to develop their products unhampered by royalty payments. The Electric Vehicle Company suffered greatly financially and in 1908 Pope abandoned electrics to make internal combustion engines. This court decision lessened the control the trusts had on early auto development.

Other early laws and court cases were concerned with speed, competition with the horse and accidents on public roads. It was generally agreed that the public wanted protection against dangerous driving, but there was great debate over how this should be accomplished. Speed limits were a frequent point of discussion. Automobilists claimed that "speed" and "danger" were not equivalent terms, any more than "slowness" and "safety." Horse breeders and dealers, fearing the

The Selden patent plaque[4]

NOTICE

To Dealers, Importers, Agents, and Users of our Gasoline Automobiles

WE will protect you against any prosecution for alleged infringements of patents. Regarding alleged infringement of the Selden patent, we beg to quote the well-known Patent Attorneys, Messrs. Parker & Burton: "The Selden patent is not a broad one, and if it was, it is anticipated. It does not cover a practicable machine, no practicable machine can be made from it, and never was, so far as we can ascertain. It relates to that form of carriage called a FORE CARRIAGE. None of that type have ever been in use; all have been failures." "No court in the United States has ever decided in favor of the patent on the merits of the case; all it has ever done was to record a prior agreement between the parties."

We are the pioneers of the GASOLINE AUTOMOBILE. Our Mr. Ford made the first Gasoline Automobile in Detroit, and the third in the United States. His machine, built in 1893, two years prior to the issue of the Selden patents Nov. 5, 1895, is still in use. Our Mr. Ford also built the famous "999" Gasoline Automobile, which was driven by Barney Oldfield in New York on July 25th, 1903, a mile in 55 4-5 seconds, on a circular track, which is the world's record.

Mr. Ford, driving his own machine, beat Mr. Winton at Grosse Pointe track in 1901. We have always been winners.

Ford Motor Company
688-692 Mack Ave., Detroit, Mich.
Write for Catalogue

The Ford notice[5]

competition of the new invention, put up a constant effort to limit the speed of the automobile to the same as their own animals. Motorists argued that speed limits were of no use in preventing accidents and that the use of discretion by the driver was a better guarantee of safety to the public than the mere limitation of miles per hour.[6]

British motoring enthusiast the Honorable John Scott-Montagu, a fervent advocate of eliminating speed limits, identified several stages of legislation in 1904. He branded the first stage as contemptuous indifference, wherein legislatures believed it was not likely that the automobile would become popular or numerous. The second stage was fear and jealous dislike due to the inability to understand the great power of the new machines. The third stage was panic legislation, once it was seen that there was a rapid increase in motorcars in every country. Railway companies were a good example of this. They first ignored the automobile, then feared it, then began to use it in conjunction with their own established systems.[7] Scott-Montagu said, "Future generations in all civilized countries will laugh at the cumbrous and illogical efforts their forefathers made to restrict the use of the automobile, and smile at the assumption that it was a dangerous and uncontrollable vehicle."[8] He spent a great deal of time trying to convince legislators that motorists value their own lives like other people and they did not have a desire to maim or kill their fellow man. He maintained that the mere ownership of a valuable machine such as a motorcar tended to make the owner more cautious as to what he does with it.

Scott-Montagu also suggested that a reasonable solution to automotive legislation to protect the public be fashioned on the precedent of maritime laws. The underlying principle of marine legislation is that the onus of avoiding collisions lies upon the faster and more easily controlled vessel. Thus the fast liner must give way to a sailing ship or pleasure yacht, providing the liner itself is not forced into a dangerous position. Using this logic, motor vehicles would give way to the less maneuverable horse-drawn carriages.

As clashes between the automobile and the horse-drawn carriage sharing the same roads became more common, so did the number of lawsuits. One case in Bridgeport, Connecticut, in 1901 involved a silent electric vehicle (a Riker surrey) approaching a doctor's horse-drawn carriage from behind. The horse was spooked and the doctor was thrown down and dragged about fifty feet. He sued for $50,000 for the dislocation of one finger and "general nervous shock." Part of the complaint argued that the electric vehicle was too noiseless in its running. The doctor lost the case, but its historical importance lay not in the verdict but in the judge's instructions to the jury. He articulated several important points that were becoming clear at the time: "[T]he mere fact that an accident happens does not make it the fault of someone else.... The highways are for us all; all can use them, with reasonable regard, to be sure, for others who use them. The most common motive power on the highway is a horse; but the horse has no paramount exclusive right to the road; and the mere fact that a horse takes fright at some vehicle run by new and improved methods, and smashes things, does not give to the injured party a cause of action.... You and I, in our experience, have seen a great change in the highways, not only in this town in which we live, but in the highways out of town. The great advantage is that people can exercise their right of locomotion more easily and accomplish more; that we can go to and fro ... much more swiftly.... Within limits, too, the swiftness with which persons are enabled, by modern vehicles, to go from place to place, is of great moment also."[9]

Between 1895 and 1905 many laws, rules and regulations were passed in Europe and

North America addressing speed limits, licensing and registration. In general there were parallel ideas put into law, but there were also many variations. In every case, the national government did not take control, but left the legislation to the states, counties, cantons and cities.

In the early 1800s, the stagecoach and horse-owning industries set to work to establish laws restricting steam carriages and any other road locomotive. This began in Britain with the Red Flag Act of 1836, which required all self-propelled vehicles to be preceded by a man carrying a red flag by day and a red light by night to warn fellow travelers of the locomotive's approach and to help keep any frightened horses under control. The Act also restricted speed of the vehicle to two mph in town and a maximum of four mph in the country. This regulation stifled innovation by placing limits on speed and discouraged travel in the motorized vehicle by making the adventure a group effort. By 1895 the laws were being reexamined to keep up with the new auto technologies. Great Britain passed the Locomotives on Highways Act of 1896, also called the Light Locomotives on Highways Act, which abolished the red flag rule (along with many other restrictive enactments concerning self-propelled carriages) and increased the speed limit to fourteen miles per hour. It defined light locomotives as those under two tons, not used for hauling other vehicles and emitting no smoke or other vapors. It also held the driver of such a vehicle accountable for a fine not to exceed £10 if he drove negligently or lost control of his vehicle. Motorists celebrated the occasion of the effect of the new law by holding an "Emancipation Run" from London to Brighton on November 14, 1896. After several years of public agitation by motorists about this speed limit, Parliament enacted a new law in 1903 establishing a maximum speed of twenty miles per hour. This was seen as a compromise between those who wanted a twelve mile per hour speed limit and motorists who wanted no speed limit at all. This new act also required vehicle identification by numbers, registration of the vehicle under the authority of county governments and a license for the driver.

In the United States, government officials were also facing disputes between horse and motor owners. The popularity of motor carriages was growing, and in many cities rides through the parks were becoming trendy social outings. Controversy arose when horse-drawn and motor carriages appeared in parks side by side. The New York City Park Commissioner made a serious political *faux pas* in November 1899 when he declared that no automobiles would be allowed in the city parks. One editorial to the *New York Times* objected thus: "The old ladies of both sexes and of every age who are alarmed at the effect of automobiles on their horses may be commended to imitate the example of the most eminent of living old ladies."[10] The editorial was referring to Queen Victoria, who had her carriage horses put through a course of special training to accustom them to the sights and sounds of the automobile in all its varieties and modes. "People who will not take the trouble to educate their horses should at least have the grace not to make the ignorance of their horse a matter of public complaint."[11] Uproar concerning the ban was so constant that later in the month the Park Commissioner reversed his decision and allowed the automobile the right to use all public roadways. He established rules and regulations to ensure safe driving conditions for both horses and automobiles. The conflict was settled for the time being. Baltimore, Maryland, showed another example of a community establishing a means for promoting safe driving through its parks. To drive in the Baltimore parks in 1900, drivers had to secure certificates of competence from the general superintendent.[12]

France was viewed as a country naturally receptive to new ideas in 1904 and generally had more liberal legislation than other countries. It had passed some legislation in 1899 requiring that construction of the automobile be safe enough to prevent explosive material or fuel that might cause a fire. Each automobile must be equipped with two lamps, one white and the other green, to increase its visibility to others, and to have secure steering gear and brakes. If the vehicle was to be manufactured for sale, the automobile must bear the name of the maker, the type and number of the machine and the name and address of the owner.[13] It also established a certification of capacity of owners and an examination by an official of the Mining Department. As for the question of speed limits, the law only required a special permit from the Prefects of Departments to hold races through communities at a speed of no more than eighteen miles per hour in the open country and twelve miles per hour in congested districts. Since the races were bringing a good deal of money into the districts, permission was easily obtained and the laws rarely enforced. There was no general speed limit for the touring car and the police were seen to be applying common sense in the enforcement of the regulations. They did not set speed traps between cities and would seldom interfere with the driver of a touring car, unless they spotted reckless driving near or through towns. One law that was never enforced was a requirement that the approach of the automobile must be signaled by means of a trumpet. This broadminded treatment made France a very popular touring place and French hotels benefited greatly from this liberal outlook on regulating vehicle speeds. France became a more popular country for touring than its neighboring countries or Great Britain.

At the same time in Germany, a total prohibition of automobiles was in effect in some provincial towns in order not to frighten children and horses. Other German cities established a number of minute regulations concerning what a driver should or should not do, including a speed limit of four miles per hour. Berlin laws required that each motorcar be equipped with two separate braking systems that could bring a car traveling at a speed of nine miles per hour to a stop within a distance of twenty-five feet. The speed could be increased according to the judgment of the driver on open and straight roads; however, the driver would be liable in case of any accident. Each motorcar was required to carry identification marks and drivers needed to obtain a driving certificate from a school of instruction recognized by the authorities. Foreigners traveling into Germany were required to have their driving certificates from their own country examined and passed by the German authorities.

Switzerland had a different situation. Its steep roads were not very suitable for the automobile. Many roads had a rock wall on one side and a steep precipice on the other. Each canton had its own very restrictive rules and regulations. Several were as strict as in some German towns, prohibiting automobiles altogether. The hotel owners complained bitterly about the negative economic impact on tourist business due to the restrictions, but had little power at the time to overturn the strict restraints.

A royal decree in Belgium in August 1899 required a license plate bearing the name and address of the owner to be displayed on the left side and front of the car. It also established a speed limit of 18½ mph on roads outside towns and villages. The speed limit for Brussels and large towns was set at 6 mph. The town of Antwerp was the exception. It established a speed limit equal to that of a horse-drawn vehicle. Other than these few strict laws, Belgium generally followed the more liberal regulations of the French system. The Belgian gendarme was seen as very fair-minded and would tend to render a liberal interpretation of the laws in favor of the motorist.[14]

Austrian laws were very stringent and in 1904 the Municipal Council of Vienna proposed that even more restrictive regulations than those existing at the present time be imposed. An Austrian law in 1903 required severe official inspections of all vehicles and the use of identification numbers and a speed limit of only 7½ mph. It was also the only country that passed a regulation forbidding women to drive a motorcar.

The laws in Italy during this time were very lenient, framed on those of France. The government alleged that speed limits were of no use in preventing accidents.

In the United States in 1904, each state controlled its own laws and regulations concerning the motorcar. The state laws did not differ as much from one another as they did in European countries. In towns, the speed limit ranged from 8 to 12 mph. The speed limit was generally 20 mph on open roads, and the motorist was to be held responsible for any accident occurring while passing another vehicle or any domestic animal. This became a controversial clause and the Automobilists of America club named it the "pig and chicken" clause. The sense at the time was that the western states were more lenient in their penalties and more lenient in enforcing their speed limits than states in the East. This could have been due to the fact that many roads in the West were in such poor condition that it was almost impossible to drive a car, much less exceed any imposed speed limits.

By 1906, with the help of "automobilists" squarely in favor of good roads and uniform laws concerning the use and licensing of automobiles, automobile legislation debates at a national level were beginning in earnest in the United States. The states were intent on setting their own standards for motoring laws. Senator Gorman of New York said, "I do not think the [federal] Government can ever pass a law to regulate the speed of motor vehicles or make other stipulations. It appears to me that this is more in the line of State legislative action."[15] Gorman proposed federal involvement in the "laws licensing machines, and the regulations governing tourists while passing from one state to another."[16] He was particularly interested in convincing farmers in the "western states" that improved roads would add value to their property. Many farmers at the time were opposed to automobiles, having seen some wild tourists careening through their property and would just as soon keep the bad roads as opposed to being "invaded" by automobilists. Gorman encouraged farmers to see the benefits of greater opportunities to take their goods to market and that the increased travel would bring more money to their district. He claimed railroads would also benefit as freight could be more easily handled and larger shipments could be made from longer distances.

As cars toured from one state to another, they ran into state licensing wars. In 1906 New Jersey required motorcars licensed in other states to obtain a license to operate in its state. The license fee was $3 for machines under thirty horsepower and $5 for machines of greater horsepower. New York adopted a similar stance and the fight was on. Massachusetts and Connecticut were a little more tourist and commerce friendly. They allowed vehicles from other states to visit for a few days with no additional fees. General discussion suggested that the federal government could be helpful by providing good roads and promoting consistency among state laws.

During the first decade of the 1900s, the eastern United States began campaigns to improve safety and promote revenue. New Jersey, in addition to enacting legislation requiring a speed limit of 8 mph in cities and 20 mph in open locations, also established a Commissioner of State Vehicles office, with the power to inspect vehicles and register them at a rate of seventy-five cents per horsepower. An age limit of eighteen was set for a license to drive and chauffeurs were required to pass an examination. More than 100 women drivers were licensed in the state and some were "practiced chauffeurs."[17] One prominent woman driver was Mrs. Margaret L. Johnson, daughter of Thomas Edison, who claimed she had traveled 5,000 miles in her automobile in seven years. Licensing violations included a fine of up to $500 and possible imprisonment. The money collected went to the State Road Fund. Monies from the Road Fund were to be used to improve roads and to provide street signs and possibly lights at dangerous intersections in the roads.

New York State believed it could prevent automobile accidents by providing perfect roads from one end of the state to the other. To accomplish this plan it appropriated $50 million over a ten-year period for road improvement to insure that the state would have the best roads in the country. As much as $11 million had been spent on road improvements by cities and counties from 1898 to 1905.[18] A committee of citizens in Elizabeth, New Jersey, in 1906, charged that automobiles injured the roads. The state engineer called this idea "ridiculous" as the wide tires on the vehicles prevented any damage to the roads. This attitude had changed greatly by 1909, when state engineers recognized that they had a serious problem with automobiles being the most active agent in the breaking down of macadamized roads. They believed there were only two solutions to the problem: either restrict automobile traffic or create new and improved methods of road construction. In either case, the states recognized well-kept roads as an element for the successful driving experience.

By 1906 automobile accidents were being reported regularly in the daily newspapers. New York state had twenty-five thousand automobiles with five hundred persons injured by motorcars annually. Many of these were charged to the stupidity of the street-crossing public.[19] The rest were considered to be a small percentage and were ascribed to the "road hog." London and Paris combined had fewer automobile accidents than New York. This was attributed to the perception that people in Europe were more accustomed to both driving and seeing cars. It was more likely due to the severe penalties that offending chauffeurs were dealt. One well-known American in Paris was given a jail sentence and a heavy fine payable to the family of the person he killed. The fear of being jailed was being used as a deterrent to prevent accidents. America looked to the driver to behave responsibly. An *Outlook* magazine article in 1906 outlined a series of "Don'ts" for motorists to prevent accidents. Some of these included:

Don't allow your chauffeur to drink liquor while in charge of your car and if running
   your own car avoid rum yourself.
Don't try to see how close you can run to pedestrians.
Don't put oil on your registration number and throw dust on it. An honest man isn't
   afraid of identification.
Don't toot your horn at passing horses.
Don't blow your Gabriel horn in a city street.
Don't grab at things that concern the chauffeur.
Don't run away after hitting somebody. You'll stand a better chance if you stay.
Don't ever act like anything but an intelligent gentleman.[20]

There were an estimated 75,000 cars in the United States in 1906. Reckless driving, accidents and lawsuits led many states to enact or consider legislation requiring a driver's license, as well as a speed limit and a variety of other laws. Until about 1905, any man, woman or child could drive an automobile. The electrics advertised theirs were the easiest to handle and did not require a chauffeur. They created the women's market. That market was to have some challenges, as women's competency to operate a vehicle safely was being questioned. With the rise of the suffragettes came a backlash of opinion questioning a woman's ability to handle an automobile. A 1909 editorial in *Outlook* magazine carried on extensively about the ability of women to drive a vehicle because they were unable to "think of two things at once." Men, on the other hand, were seen as being trained from the earliest youth by playing baseball to pay attention to two or three bases at once, along with home plate and "numerous other points. With few exceptions, a woman seldom reaches this particular phase of mental activity, called for time and again in automobiling." It was also observed that a woman who meets a person with whom she wishes to converse, will almost invariably stop and do so while blocking traffic. One slight exception was given if the vehicle was electric. "No license should be granted to one under eighteen, or possibly twenty one years of age, and never to a woman, unless, possibly, for a car driven by electric power."[21]

Laws governing speed had their own set of challengers, but most acknowledged the need for some regulation for safety. The 8 mph speed limit in New York City in 1906 had its share of dissenters and advocates. Some argued the speed limit had two disadvantages: (1) that the speed of an automobile can only be determined by an expert with a stopwatch while the car is passing over a measured course, and (2) the speed limit is already constantly exceeded without protest from the authorities and seems to be impossible to enforce.[22] Charles S. Adams wrote an editorial in the *Scientific American* in October 1906 in favor of speed limits. He stated his theory in a very logical scientific manner, claiming that drivers did not realize that danger increases to the square of the speed. He used an example of three identical vehicles, one traveling at five miles per hour, one at twenty miles per hour and one at forty miles per hour. The second vehicle has sixteen times as much "stored" energy than the first. It will take sixteen times the distance to stop, and if it leaves the road and strikes an obstacle such as a tree, it will strike with sixteen times as much force. The third vehicle will do the same at sixty four times the force of the first vehicle. Although enforcement was a problem, the dangers of too much speed were acknowledged.

By 1907 there was great concern about "speed mania" and how to cure it. The perception was that the automobile provided "an exhilaration in flying through the air at forty miles an hour that no other sports could give."[23] Actually, automobiles were beginning to reach speeds of a mile a minute at the time. An article in *Harper's Weekly* identified the type of man given to reckless speeding as the same type "who speculates in more stocks than he is able to carry, eats and drinks more than he can assimilate, covers himself with gaudy jewels [and] makes an objectionable exhibition of himself at every possible occasion." There was a call for more speed limit laws and for their enforcement. The state of New York speed law was general in nature, stating, "No person shall operate a motor vehicle on a public highway at a rate of speed greater than is reasonable and proper, having regard to the traffic and use of the highway, or so as to endanger the life and limb of any person or the safety of any property."[24] An editorial suggested that perhaps policemen should position themselves in wait for motorists on a downgrade, where the motorcar is apt to run faster and thus "make a case" against a greater number of motorists. At the time, some "speed maniacs" would merely laugh at a fine and then boast about it to their friends. It was also suggested that the driver's license of reckless motorists be revoked, and if he were subsequently found driving without a license, to put him in jail. The public wanted action against reckless speeding.

The automobile magazines were in agreement as countries struggled with this new technology. In 1908 *Punch* magazine recognized there was an automobile problem in Great Britain and queried, "How shall it be regulated?" Testimony before Parliament declared, "the enjoyment of English country life has been spoiled for all who do not take to motoring." The speed and dust seemed to be the major complaints. Some argued there should be no speed limits and the law should hold anyone responsible for any damage done; they were ignored and a speed limit of 12 mph was set in law. Max Pemberton of the *London Times* listed a code of rules that he said would end the complaints about automobiles. Some points included:

(1) Submission to and observance of a speed limit of 12 mph.
(2) Faithful observance of the following rules of safe driving:
    a. Never take a sharp corner at more than a walking pace.
    b. Never overtake another vehicle uphill or on a corner.
    c. Never drive the engine downhill.
    d. Slow down while passing pedestrians.
    e. Give cyclists plenty of room.
(3) Be unselfish by lessening the evils of dust.

John Burns, a cabinet minister, "officially warned the fraternity that their fate is in their own hands, and that drastic results will ensue if they do not put their house — or their motor car — in order."[25] Many laws concerning vehicles were soon to follow.

German law in 1908 required the automobile owner to be personally accountable for the least misbehavior of his car.

In June 1909 a jury in New York City convicted a chauffeur of manslaughter and sentenced him to confinement in the state prison for not less than seven nor more than twenty years. The man had approached a boy who was playing in the street with other boys at what witnesses agreed was a high rate of speed, hit him in the back and dragged him half a block, slowed for a moment, then sped on at a higher rate of speed. He left the city and was later arrested in Port Arthur, Texas. This was the first case in the United States of a chauffeur's being convicted of reckless driving and manslaughter with a motor vehicle. There was much outrage at the time over "speed-maniacs" and this case was seen to serve notice to all chauffeurs that no leniency would be given.[26]

In May 1911 the Touring Club of America and the American Automobile Association combined forces and called for a national movement to improve the highways in all states. The American Association for Highway Improvement was formed and Walter Page, Director of the United States Office of Public Roads, Department of Agriculture, was elected its president. The object of the Association was to promote public awareness and to establish a uniform system of road building.

By 1912 many states had enacted legislation requiring automobiles to be licensed, but licenses were valid only in that particular state. The concept was changing. In March 1912 Maryland recognized reciprocal licensing, with a restriction that touring to New Jersey was limited to a fifteen-day period. The statute was not as well received as expected. District of Columbia motorists feared a lack of revenue for D.C. coffers if they were allowed to travel to Maryland on a reciprocal basis. Maryland visitors had been a lucrative revenue source for D.C. Part of the Maryland bill also required the use of one bright light from one hour after sunset to one hour before sunrise. In that same year Massachusetts called for standardization of traffic regulations. New Jersey also enacted a law requiring mufflers to quiet the internal combustion engines. In April 1912 New Jersey granted reciprocity between it and New York state, allowing travel from one state to the other without fear of interference by the police. The states began to see the value of honoring each other's licenses.

In April 1917 France stopped all private motoring because of gasoline shortages. With the advance of World War I, they expected that there would be only enough gasoline available to cover military requirements.

New York state enacted several laws concerning automobiles in 1917, including requiring adequate brakes and sufficient lighting to "reveal any person, vehicle or substantial object on the road straight ahead of the motor vehicle for a distance of at least two hundred and fifty feet."[27] The same law mandated the use of low/high beam headlights because of the high number of accidents caused by uncontrolled headlight glare. That same year New Jersey decided to mail out blank applications for drivers' licenses to save owners a visit to the office and to ease the problems that arose from trying to process all the new applications.

Deaths from automobile accidents in the United States in 1922 were estimated at fourteen thousand, 1,600 more than in 1921. The number of automobiles in use had increased five-fold since 1915. The Boston *Herald* in 1923 said, "There is only one way to eliminate that class of accidents. Keep such drivers off the highways. Never relent in the search for the driver who 'speeds away in the night' ... and the public at large will support such measures." A writer for the *Baltimore Sun* suggested that the "motor car psychology" contributes to the accident rate by explaining "why a man of intelligence, experience and caution in any other environment will get into an automobile and pull a fool stunt that will probably cause his death or that of others."[28] Others put the blame on pedestrians who left the curb without looking for approaching vehicles and called for common sense and the general observance of a few plain rules of safety on the part of both drivers and pedestrians to curb the high number of deaths involving motorists.

By 1920 there was a great debate about the uniformity of state laws and whether there should be an all-encompassing federal law for automobiles. Historically, the states began legislation with the introduction of vehicle registration and a driver's license. Collection of the taxes for these fees began with the secretary of state, while the enforcement of the laws became a police matter. Eventually the automobile license bureau became a separate administrative department generally titled the Commissioner of Motor Vehicles. One argument against federal legislation stated that since the states at that time were roughly divided into manufacturing, agricultural or mining, the best interests of each state varied greatly, as did the laws to be applied. The argument for federal legislation was that the federal government could increase revenue by collecting more taxes. Concerns were raised that federal involvement would increase lawsuits through the federal courts and it seemed a new enormous clerical and judicial machine would have to be built up to accommodate the increased caseload. Officers jurisdiction would also have to be addressed. Would the traffic officer be a federal appointee or would he remain the municipal policeman who might have to appear in a federal court against offenders he might arrest? Another argument against federal overall legislation said it would be better to have a simple voluntary association among the motor vehicle administrators of several states to meet quarterly and discuss common problems and policies and work together toward common decisions. In 1921 this, in fact, was already happening. Representatives from Massachusetts, Rhode Island, Connecticut, New York, New Jersey, Pennsylvania and Maryland established a working rule (not constitutional) that all formulated policy would be arrived at unanimously. Meeting on September 23, 1921, a conference, through a variety of committees, adopted several agreements, including a uniform headlight law, licensing, registration and the right-hand, right-of-way rule. It was hoped that eventually the entire forty-eight states would be covered by six conferences.[29] This seemed to be the best solution to untangling the automotive laws in place and put an end to the controversy of a uniform federal automobile and traffic law.

By 1923 the state of New York passed a law taxing vehicles for wear and tear on the state road system. Electric trucks and some electric pleasure vehicles were penalized, i.e., taxed at a higher rate, because the assumption was made that the wear and tear on the state highways was proportionate to the additional weight of the vehicle. Heavy batteries accounted for the increased weight. The *Literary Digest* argued that the taxation on the electric trucks was unjustly rated for two reasons: (1) the rapid development of delivery trucks during the previous three years had been for the use of haulage in town and on local roads, and (2) wear and tear on the roads was not proportionate to a car's weight alone, but related also to speed and the mechanical conditions of driving. It went on to argue that tires get a longer wear life on an electric truck than on a gasoline truck of the same capacity and the smooth starting torque and the absence of shock and vibration were the mechanical reasons for this. The *Digest* called upon manufacturers and users of electric vehicles to take the initiative in reversing this type of taxation and developing some simple method of determining a license fee that would be more fair to both electric and gasoline vehicles.[30]

In 1928 the American Association of State Highway Officials created national highway concrete thickness standards of six inches, plus ten-foot lanes and eight-foot-wide shoulders. It also recommended octagonal stop signs.

By 1930, in response to public demand, laws governing automobile and driver licensing, speed limits and the means for generating revenue to keep roads passable for safe driving, were in force everywhere.

Rules and Regulations

"Politics deals with public goods— streets, parks, clean air, and so on — that are indivisible and nonexcludable, and therefore must be shared. Markets deal with private goods—food, houses, cars and so on — that are consumed by individuals and cannot be shared."[31] Government must take special care in providing assistance in the form of regulations or financial support to any industry. Changes in rules and regulations concerning an industry may have a major impact on the economy, the public's perception of the role government should play in the private sector, and the potential growth of an industry. The EV, HEV and alternate fuels industries are no exception. One example of the process can be seen in federal safety standards that require that all vehicles have adequate heating and defrosting systems. This is a disadvantage for EVs. Heating alone can reduce the vehicle's range by as much as 35 percent depending on ambient temperatures and cabin temperatures. Another example appears in California regulations. The California

Air Resources Board (CARB) policies, begun in 1990, have affected civic values and impacted market direction. Citizens, through government, create policies in the hope that the policies will shape other citizens' opinions. This would, in turn, shape the direction taken in nascent technologies. This premise proved true. Environmental groups, for example, began to promote EVs after the government, in the form of CARB, formed its policies. This prompted some in the industry to revisit EVs, HEVs and alternate fuel vehicles as a means to support a potential market of environmentally conscious buyers, and meet regulations for automotive fuel consumption.

The government's impact on the auto industry through legislation and regulation cannot be underestimated. The automobile contributes substantially to the United States Gross National Product, involving a large segment of the work force. It is a major component of the production industry. Any government rules, regulations or laws concerning EVs have a profound effect on not only the general U.S. economy, but specifically on the oil, steel, chemical and a host of service industries that are associated with the automobile industry. It was estimated in 1967 that for all road transportation to suddenly go electric, the (then) current electric generating capacity would have had to double. Even the most avid proponents of EVs agree that they must crawl in a small way before they can run on a large scale. Government must promote a balance between social and economic responsibility — between the ideal and what can reasonably be accomplished — because changes in one area of the automotive industry impacts much of our labor force and economy.

As early as 1955 Congress passed an Air Pollution Control Act, which identified air pollution as a national problem. Many state and local governments had passed legislation concerning pollution, but this was the first federal legislation on the issue. Many more would follow. The Clean Air Act of 1963 was the first to use that phrase and was passed to promote public health and welfare. Initially, it set standards for power plants and steel mills, but would later be amended to set anti-pollution standards for automobiles. It granted $95 million over a three-year period to state and local governments to conduct research on power plants' pollution and the automobile exhaust problem.

In the late 1960s, when concern over air pollution was high, at least eight branches of the U.S. government were involved in electric car research, including the Transportation Department ($10.5 million), Health, Education and Welfare ($5 million), the Post Office and the Army. There were also fifteen federal agencies funding a total of eighty-six projects in battery research (21 government laboratories, 14 universities and 51 industrial companies). Part of the government response to the concerns about air pollution was the adoption of emission control systems in California in 1966, scheduled to go national in 1968.

The eighty-ninth Congress passed three bills referred to as the Electric Vehicle Development Act of 1966. They provided funding for research and development of EVs. A fourth bill amended the Clean Air Act of 1963 to promote consideration of electric vehicles to reduce air pollution. This Clean Air Act set standards of carbon monoxide emission levels and required each state to submit a State Implementation Plan (SIP) establishing a clean-vehicle fleet program. The federal government set standards that included a certain percentage of "clean alternative fuel vehicles" to be used in state fleets. The percentage varied by areas of pollution classified as extreme, severe or serious. The government realized some of these requirements could not be met on time and continues to remain flexible in its enforcement.

As early as 1973 the Environmental Protection Agency (EPA) issued standards calling for a gradual reduction of lead emissions from gasoline. As part of its responsibility, it examines the complete economic and environmental impact of automobiles from their manufacture to their disposal. The EPA established an oxygenated fuel program and the reformulated fuel program in an effort to direct compliance. The agency has worked with the Big Three automakers since 1994 to promote electric vehicles as an alternative to the environmental impact of gasoline emissions from the internal combustion engine.

Nineteen seventy-three illustrated how difficult it is to locate a reasonable balance between government intervention and government manipulation in regulating industry. The 1973-74 oil shortages spurred the federal government to mediate in energy policy formulation, enacting price controls. This led to funding for energy alternative projects and renewed interest in the electric and hybrid vehicle. Neither the federal government nor the energy companies established much credibility in controlling the crisis. The public lacked confidence in the government's ability to provide leadership in formulating a rational energy program for the future. The public had many doubts that the oil crisis was real. This crisis shows the volatility of the public's perception when government and private industry align. A survey in Canada at the time revealed most Canadians did not perceive the energy situation as a serious issue and did not believe it to be a "real" crisis. In the United States, the Federal Energy Office was accused of creating the oil shortages. Ralph Nader, a well-known consumer advocate, contended that "the world is literally drowning in oil ... and the present apparent shortages in the U.S., and related price increases are nothing less than unarmed robbery by oil companies in collusion with governmental support."[32] Many people suspected oil companies of shuffling oil supplies to hide them and delaying delivery of truckloads of oil to take advantage of higher prices. Many also suspected the government to be in collusion with oil companies to perpetrate the hoax of an oil shortage. Public trust of the government was at an all-time low following the Watergate scandal, and seeing home heating oil plentiful in the northeast while people in Washington, D.C., were being asked to lower their thermostat settings caused many to question the validity of the crisis. The public perceived complicity. One energy administrator said, "people will say 'See, the oil companies contrived the shortage and so did President Nixon to get Watergate off the front pages.'"[33] Wall Street analysts estimated thirty oil companies would realize profits 40 to 50 percent higher in 1974 then in 1973. Oil companies' crude oil reserves were a closely held competitive secret at the time, and the public demanded that Congress get involved in forcing each company to divulge its estimates of its reserves. Mobil and Exxon were summoned before the Senate Government Operations Subcommittee to answer questions about the price fluctuations in their stocks and to what extent refined products were brought in from the Caribbean and how much was produced from Arab oil. Other oil companies did report some data to the Bureau of Mines, but the public was aware that the figures could easily be jiggled by reporting the reserves in "custody" without reporting the crude or refined products held at independent terminals. There was also a loophole called "secondary storage" which could include any tank in the distribution system other than the refiners, enabling middlemen to hoard reserves of crude oil. While the hearings proceeded, consumers voiced their distrust of government accounting and demanded an immediate solution for the shortages.

An article in *Public Utilities Fortnightly* in 1974 suggested three possible courses of action: (1) continue the present course which may lead to higher-priced service, (2) change restrictive regulations to allow prices to fluctuate, and probably increase; and (3) implement government intervention in the form of tax credits.

President Ford signed legislation in 1975 authorizing the Energy Research and Development Administration to provide $6 billion in loan guarantees to promote the synthetic fuels industry. The president also proposed to set up a new agency to be called the Energy Independence Authority, to finance $100 billion for the development of nuclear energy and synthetic fuels over the next ten years.

The fuel shortage generated growing interest in electric and hybrid vehicles. It was predicted that "Before very long, a lot of people may get their chance to ride in or even own electric vehicles."[34] The U.S. Postal Service began taking bids from several companies to contract for a fleet of electric vehicles. The two drawbacks were seen to be slow speed and limited range. The advantages were the lack of pollution and the availability of electric power. A fleet manager, Bud Tenney in Youngstown, Ohio, said, "I don't like fumes and it's getting harder and harder to get gasoline, and more expensive."[35] Electrics looked like a good alternative to ICEs.

In an attempt to address consumer concerns from the 1974 oil crisis, automakers turned to improving the average fuel mileage from about 14 mpg to about 22 mpg in 1981. The government also responded. Corporate Average Fuel Economy (CAFE) standards of 27.5 mpg were established in 1975 to recommend standard miles-per-gallon norms for the automotive industry. Because the automakers could not produce a station wagon that would meet the standards, they discontinued the model and put their efforts into manufacturing SUVs. The SUV would only have to meet the lower CAFE truck standards. In 1995 General Motors called for the government to increase gasoline prices artificially and do away with CAFE.

Congress passed the Electric and Hybrid Vehicle Act of 1976 over President Ford's veto. It established a demonstration project through the Department of Energy and assigned a budget of $160 million. The Energy Research and Development Agency (ERDA) was set up to administer the act and was committed to the view that the United States would have an all-electric economy by the year 2000. The act authorized the secretary to enter agreements or arrangements with other major government departments such as the Department of Transportation, NASA, the Department of Agriculture and the Environmental Protection Agency. Its purpose was to promote research on batteries, controls and motors, and vehicle design. It was to conduct feasibility demonstration projects to determine possible commercial use of electric and hybrid vehicles, identify potential customer markets and determine impacts on the long-range planning for roads, utilities, urban design, taxation and maintenance facilities. Much of the funding went to government national laboratories. Interest in researching alternative fueled vehicles began to decline in the late 1970s when it became evident that the EV and HEV were not practical competitors to the ICE. Automakers were improving the efficiency of the ICE and gasoline was flowing freely again. By 1978, ERDA had not received any funding and there was great congressional debate over the fiscal budget to reduce the amount and defer the demonstration project called for in the act.

The international community was also responding to environmental concerns. People wanted research into the health aspects of automobile pollution. Some international events during the mid–1990s included:

• England—"No new road-building" protestors wanted to save money and protect the trees that would be taken down to build new roads.

- France — A clean air policy was enacted that allowed city governors to close cities to car traffic in times of heavy pollution.
- Italy — The city center of Milan was closed to gasoline-powered cars.
- Japan — Protestors demanded new road designs to accommodate noise and pollution.

In 1990 the U.S. Congress approved a contract with the Department of Energy (DOE), Ford and General Electric to design commercially viable modular propulsion. This Modular Electric Vehicle Program was part of the larger Electric and Hybrid Vehicle Program.[36] Also in 1990, the Clean Air Act required the EPA to set air quality standards. The law recognized that the states must be in charge of their own pollution control problems and the means they would use to meet those standards.

The Energy Policy Act (EP Act) of 1992 was designed to reduce dependency on foreign oil and to improve air quality. The EP Act established the State and Alternative Fuel Provider Program, a Department of Energy regulatory program that required state and alternative fuel provider fleets to purchase AFVs as a portion of their annual light-duty vehicle acquisitions. Fleets earned credits for each vehicle purchased and credits earned in excess of their requirements could be banked or traded with other fleets. This gave fleets flexibility in meeting their requirements. Part of the act required federal, state and fuel provider groups to purchase increasing numbers of alternative fuel vehicles (AFVs) each year to meet a 10 percent reduction in petroleum use by 2000 and 30 percent by 2010. By 1999 only 1.6 percent of alternative fuel vehicles on the road were electric.

To promote compliance with the Energy Policy Act of 1992 and the Clean Air Act of 1990, the Department of Energy established the Clean Cities Program. The voluntary program was designed to encourage local communities to find economically sustainable markets for AFVs. The program was founded on the principle that individuals working toward a common goal can best achieve the nation's objectives through local action. Since 1993, Clean Cities International has over eighty cities in the United States, and five countries (Brazil, Mexico, Chile, Peru and India), involved in the program. Clean Cities' purpose is to bring private industry, utilities, government agencies and the public together to create a viable alternative fuels market. Some groups work on policies and government initiatives to encourage public support and market interest in electric vehicles and other AFVs, others have begun using AFVs in fleets and shuttle services, still others are instigating public awareness campaigns to promote usage. Each Clean Cities Program contributes to the goal of private industry working with community governments to promote the use of alternatives to gasoline and diesel vehicles.

Also in 1992 a study by the Southern California Edison (SCE) company showed that nearly two-thirds of Californians would buy an electric vehicle if, and again this is a big IF, it was comparable in price to the internal combustion engine (ICE). Nearly half in the study said they would accept a $1,000 annual battery replacement cost as a necessary expense. Michael R. Peavey, president of SCE, said, "If you build them, they will buy."[37] He claimed that electric vehicles could reduce air pollution in California (attributed to the ICE) by two-thirds and would reduce dependence on foreign oil. An air quality official at the New York Department of Environmental Conservation said, "There's a wealth of Yuppie environmental guilt out there to be exploited."[38] Allan D. Gilmore, vice president of Ford Motor Company, commented on some focus group studies conducted in California. "Basically, what the people told us was this: 'I think these alternative types of vehicles are marvelous. I'm in favor of protecting the environment, and I think my neighbor should get one.'"[39] Automakers insist that incentives from utility companies and federal and local governments are necessary to get the EVs on the road.

In 1993 Michigan Senator Carl Levin proposed a consortium of the utilities and the Big Three automakers in Michigan to build electric cars. The Big Three balked, responding that they all knew how to build cars, what was needed was new battery technology and infrastructure. They also noted that having customers was an important detail that would increase their efforts to produce electric vehicles and suggested that the government should put in an order for fifty thousand vans by 1998.

In 1994 a thirty-member advisory panel was charged by President Clinton to achieve a long-term Global Climate Action Plan in a three-stage strategy for the years 2005, 2015, and 2025 to reduce carbon dioxide emissions. The CAFE standard was still 27.5 mpg. The panel was portrayed as an attempt to bring together the automotive, environmental and utility industries. The thirty-member panel contained only five seats for automakers. The Sierra Club considered the effort a shield for the administration to get credit for a clean-air program and an attack on global warming and as a way to appease the auto industry by keeping regulation at bay.

In 1995 oil companies and auto manufacturers were accused of trying to kill the electric car. A spokesman for Mobil stated that they did not fear the competition of electric cars, but at the same time were opposed to the government's mandating "unproven technology" and subsidizing the competition with public tax monies. A Carnegie-Mellon University study concluded that recycling lead-acid batteries on a large scale would discharge large quantities of lead into the environment, an amount that would outweigh the benefits of the removal of lead from gasoline. The more efficient ICEs of 1995 were already emitting 95 percent less tailpipe emissions than the cars of the 1960s.[40]

A study conducted in 2001 by the American Council for an Energy Efficient Economy (ACEEE), a non-profit research group in Washington State, found that new technology improved standard ICE engines to the point of getting about forty miles per gallon. The better engines added about $1,000 to the cost of the vehicle. The same study found that a hybrid Taurus could get fifty-three miles per gallon, but the added cost to the vehicle was about $3,500.

The Canadian government is taking a key role in the development of hydrogen and fuel cell technology. The federal government of Canada allocated $30 million in 1999 to support small and medium-sized businesses in the research and development of fuel cells and the creation of a hydrogen infrastructure. The move is meant to promote high-tech industries, job creation and environmental awareness. Ford Canada introduced its TH!NK city car at the Montreal 2000–Electric Vehicle Project symposium in September 2000.

Most Western European countries have passed legislation to reduce air pollution by reducing auto emissions. In 2001 the United Kingdom passed regulations allowing buses to have remote controls to change traffic lights to green. They are also widening the bus lanes and requiring cars to stop and wait behind the buses when picking up passengers. Some areas have legislation to restrict driving motor vehicles in city centers. Switzerland provides direct subsidies for buying cars to individuals who take part in demonstration programs involving electric vehicles.[41] France is experimenting with electric vehicle fleets for utility companies and is offering recharging services and reduced parking fees for electric vehicles.

The oil market once again came to the public's attention when the Arab community voted to reduce production early in 2000. The price of gas at the pumps shot up immediately, with more cries for government involvement. The government's roles to date have been to attempt to socially engineer and spur industry through mandates (rules and regulations) and tax incentives (rebates and subsidies).

State Incentive Programs

Almost every state offers tax credits or deductions for developing and implementing alternative fuel vehicles. A few examples are:

- Alabama — Low-interest loans for Alternative Fuel Vehicle (AFV) projects.
- Arizona — State income tax deduction of 25 percent on the purchase cost of AFVs.
- Arkansas — A 50 percent tax credit for any Arkansas taxpayer who constructs a facility in the state that will manufacture EVs, fuel cells or photovoltaic cells.
- California — $5,000 rebates on the purchase cost of EVs. $1,000 tax incentive for NGVs.
- Colorado — Up to 50 percent rebate on the cost of AFVs.
- Florida — Low-cost loans of up to $5,000 for conversion or purchase of an AFV.
- Georgia — A business tax credit of up to $2,500 for vehicle rechargers used for vehicles registered in the state.
- Kansas — Up to 50 percent tax credit on the cost of converting a vehicle to an AFV.
- Louisiana — Zero-interest loans for fleet conversions to CNG or LNG vehicles.
- Maryland — A tax credit of up to $2,000 for EVs, $500 to $1,000 for hybrid electrics based on their energy efficiency, and $125 to $500 for their ability to regenerate through braking.
- Minnesota — Excludes the sale of propane or natural gas for vehicles from the motor fuel tax.
- Montana — A 50 percent tax deduction for the purchase cost of an AFV.
- Nebraska — Low cost loans (5 percent) toward the purchase or conversion of fleets to AFVs.
- New Hampshire — excludes electricity sold for vehicles from the state franchise tax.
- New York — Rebates up to 80 percent of the cost of converting vehicles to CNG.
- Ohio — A ten percent tax credit for vehicles using ethanol.
- Oklahoma — A 10 percent tax credit for the cost of AFV conversions.
- Oregon — A 35 percent tax credit for AFV projects.
- Pennsylvania — Exempts AFVs from annual vehicle registration fees and the differential cost of EVs from sales tax.
- Rhode Island — A 50 percent tax credit to businesses for constructing EV recharging stations effective January 1, 1998–January 1, 2003.
- Texas — A $2,000 rebate for CNG conversions.
- Utah — A tax credit for up to 50 percent of the cost of a new EV to a maximum of $2,000 per vehicle.
- Virginia — No local motor vehicle license fees for AFVs.
- West Virginia — Up to 50 percent matching funds for conversions or purchases of AFVs.

In December 1996 the city of Portland, Oregon, opened two electric charging stations downtown that were capable of charging two electric vehicles at once at any time of the day. The city also announced it was considering adding electric vehicles to its fleet.[42] By 2001 Portland experimented with a few alternative vehicles such as electric, propane and compressed natural gas (CNG) and has plans to buy three dozen Toyota

Prius hybrids in the near future. Portland's Department of Sustainable Resources (formerly the Energy Department) discovered a "Catch 22" during this experimentation period, one that has plagued AFVs throughout the history of the automobile. They found it easy to buy CNG vehicles, but the infrastructure was not in place to support them. On the other hand, the infrastructure is in place for electrics, but they are too expensive to buy.

In 1997 Massachusetts and New York enacted low-emission vehicle programs (LEVP) with tighter standards than the 1990 California LEVP. The LEVP set sales mandates for LEVs, ULEVs and ZEVs. In 2000 federal courts overturned the stricter northeastern state laws in favor of the lower California standards.

In 1999 Arizona enacted a program to promote alternative fuel vehicles. It allowed buyers to recoup up to half the cost of a vehicle if it was outfitted with a natural gas fuel system. The program did not require actually using the system. Many people took advantage of this law (more than 22,000) without following through with the conversion and estimated costs to the state went from $5 million to over $500 million before the state took action to reverse the program in 2000.

State-supported programs in California also fell under scrutiny. In early 2001 California experienced rolling blackouts. Due to power shortages, the electric grid was shut down at various times during the day in many populated areas. California had to buy electricity from Washington, Oregon and Texas. How does this affect EVs? CARB commissioned UC Davis and AC Propulsion to study the potential role of EVs as energy storage devices, which could conceivably feed electricity back into the power grid. The public concentrated on reasons for the problem and the wisdom of state-supported EV projects. Opinions on causes for the shortage varied from persons blaming environmentalists for not wanting power facilities in "their backyard" to citizens disavowing the concept of deregulation of the industry. Whatever the reason, those supporting electric vehicle development became a group of citizens questioning the state's endorsement for promoting electric vehicles when the electric power system could not produce enough power to keep the lights on all day. Others suggested that California not allow any imported cars, but only electric cars manufactured in the U.S., and then only sell the number that could be supported by electricity produced in California to minimize any problems with future electrical energy shortages.

Pennsylvania announced in February 2001 that it would provide funding in the amount of $7 million for projects promoting the use of alternative fuels in vehicles. The ultimate goal is to reduce air pollution and dependence on foreign oil. This money supplemented $17 million funded during the previous six years to develop alternative fuel vehicles, build refueling and recharging stations and fund research and development of the various technologies. The alternative fuels being considered included natural gas, bio fuels, methanol, ethanol and hydrogen. The Pennsylvania Department of Environmental Protection estimated that this program in the last six years has reduced the hydrocarbon and carbon monoxide emissions to a degree that would equal the removal of 200 ICE vehicles from the roads every year.

The California Air Resources Board (CARB) has shown itself to be the most influential political association affecting vehicle emissions in current history. It has passed many regulations which impact the auto industry and its suppliers, beginning with a requirement of an 80 percent reduction in new car emissions between 1992 and 2003, and a minimum of 10 percent of vehicles sold to be Zero Emission Vehicles (ZEV) by 2003.

California is not the only state to have made this type of legislation, but it has had the greatest influence in regulating the behavior of automobile manufacturers. CARB's adjustments to these regulations also depict the fluidity needed when government and the marketplace combine forces.

California initiated the low-emission vehicle (LEV) mandate on September 28, 1990. This initiative also contained the zero-emission vehicle (ZEV) mandate, which included special rules to allow manufacturers to "bank" credits as well as trade them. In 1994 CARB introduced the ideas of emission averaging, trading and banking credits, as a departure from uniform standards. The board realized it might have to change its standards because the industry could not comply in such a limited time frame given the current technology and consumer market. This led to the decision in 1996 in which CARB changed the relative importance of some technical criteria evaluations and changed the factors it was using to assess consumers' willingness to purchase EVs. The free market's lack of enthusiasm for the products had become evident. CARB's research on consumer acceptance had proved to be flawed. A survey submitted to CARB in 1994 showed that the consumers' lack of enthusiasm was primarily due to their lack of information. From this CARB falsely concluded that once consumers were properly informed, they would convert to wanting and buying EVs. This did not prove to be the case. Buyers were not willing to purchase the more expensive environmentally friendly vehicles if the cost was substantially higher and the owner was inconvenienced by the fuel supply. The primary objections to these vehicles, as it had been throughout the century, were still lack of range and high price. People were not influenced by civic benefits or citizenship for the public good if the product offered less performance than their current choices. By 1996 CARB realized that their survey tool was unreliable and that they could not create or convert consumer behavior by trying to sway them through data and environmental impact information. CARB returned to adjusting incentives for the manufacturers to encourage compliance to their mandates. CARB provided an incentive for smaller manufacturers with its ZEV credits program. In 1995 a coalition called Californians Against Utility Company Abuse (CAUCA) was formed by 2,700 companies and groups, including some oil companies, to actively attack attempts by utilities to increase rates to finance EV promotion and develop infrastructure. The coalition stated that Southern California Edison should finance its EV involvement by company profits and not by customers. The California Manufacturers Association (CMA) was also working in 1995 to prevent the CARB mandates from going into effect in 1998. CMA claimed the EV mandate was a "well intentioned, but misguided attempt by government to force technology into the marketplace prematurely."[43] "We absolutely oppose any government mandate that forces manufacturers to make a product that isn't ready for the marketplace," stated CMA president William Campbell, citing a U.S. Government Accounting Office warning "that automotive batteries are not well developed, fueling and repair infrastructure is lacking, safety and environmental effects are not known, production costs are high and the market potential is uncertain."[44] He further added that the government should be mandating clean air and not the technology to achieve it. It was also felt at the time that technological improvements in the ICE would bring emissions down close to zero. These factors led in part to CARB's backing away from and revising some of the mandates in 1996.

Since sales were not meeting expectations, banking and trading emission credits provided flexibility among the manufacturers to balance their inventories and still meet the letter of the regulations. For each vehicle sold, CARB gives the company a ZEV credit, which can be sold to any of the Big Seven manufacturers for $5,000. In 1996 CARB voted unanimously to do away with the requirement that 2 percent of automotive sales for 1998 be ZEV and 5 percent for 2001. In 1998 automakers convinced CARB to relax the standards by postponing the 10 percent quota until 2003 and allowing 6 percent of the 10 percent quota to be made up of partial zero emission vehicles (PZEVs). In 1998 CARB allowed partial credits for vehicles that achieved near-zero emissions, such as hybrids, and those meeting a new standard for super ultra low emission vehicles (SU-LEVs). In 2000 CARB announced it would allow carmakers to substitute up to 2 percent of the 4 percent ZEV quota with Advanced Technology Partial Zero Emission Vehicles (AT-PZEV). This would allow the acceptance of cleaner engines due to reformulated gasoline and hybrid and fuel cell vehicles to be counted as part of the solution. To qualify for PZEV status, the vehicles must meet three criteria: (1) meet the SU-LEV standards, (2) have zero evaporative emissions, and (3) ensure 150,000-mile warranty on emission control equipment. These decisions slightly favored the manufacturing industry, while recognizing that the current "state of the art" battery technology is not yet marketable. CARB offset the possible reluctance by the manufacturers to produce more ZEVs by offering to provide funds to consumers who purchase or lease ZEVs prior to 2003. The initial cost of the vehicles being manufactured required subsidies from California as high as from $10,000 to $20,000 per vehicle sold.

In 1999 the Federal Environmental Protection Agency proposed new regulations that were effectively a de facto adoption of CARB's requirements as a national standard.[45] Little progress was made, and in 2000 the House and Senate cut the $1.25 billion subsidy for alternative fuels in half. "Representative John Sununu (R-N.H.), who led the charge to slash the project, says the success of the Insight and Prius demonstrates why subsidies won't work. 'It may well be precisely because the federal government has been subsidizing certain areas of innovation that we're behind the Japanese.'"[46]

In late 2000 CARB advanced the target date of ZEVs to 2007 with the hope of seeing 14,000 annual sales by year 2012. They put all their efforts toward a battery solution. They did not promote the sales of alternative hybrid vehicles to help accomplish their goal. New battery technology, such as NiMH and lithium ion batteries, costs more and will not be purchased by manufacturers until the cost comes down. The cost won't decrease until suppliers launch volume production. The technology has not yet been able to produce an efficient low-cost battery to use for EV mass production. CARB's short-sightedness in supporting one energy alternative to achieve their ZEV goals resulted initially in less research being devoted to other power sources that could do more to reduce pollution in the long run. They temporarily lost their objectivity and global view for finding viable solutions. This resulted in their having to adjust target dates to give the industry more time to comply. Their view reversed by 2003 when they began backing fuel cell research. This adjustment makes it more probable that they may come close to their goal in 2012.

GM filed a lawsuit in 2000 claiming that CARB, as a state regulatory agency, has no authority to require a zero emission vehicle. A General Motors spokesman noted that the mandate would require the government to provide subsidies amounting to between $500 million and $1 billion annually. Dealers note that consumer demand is not present because of the high price and short range and feel they will suffer, as the mandate only states the cars must "be available" without knowing how many will actually be sold and eventually wind up on the road. In 2002 GM contracted another manufacturer to build

NEVs that may help to meet California's ZEV mandate when the decision is made on what the mandate will specify. The concerns about the reality of the economics of ZEVs illustrate the repercussions that government regulations can have on industry.

In January 2001 CARB revised its requirements from its original idea of 10 percent ZEVs to 2 percent ZEV, 2 percent hybrids and 6 percent natural gas or other clean burning cars. The January 15, 2001, meeting of CARB readdressed the issue of selling EVs, not just making them available. The chairman of the board emphasized the word "sell" and not just "offer" vehicles to earn the ZEV credits. By 2002 many automakers had accumulated enough banked credits, many from NEVs (Neighborhood Electric Vehicles—like golf carts) (four credits each), to prolong any serious production of EVs through 2005 and beyond.

A short news article in *AutoWeek* (February 15, 2001) noted that CARB reduced the number of required ZEV sales in 2003 from 22,000 per year to 4,670. This was due to automakers' claims that no one is buying electric cars and the battery technology is not yet capable of satisfying consumers' needs. CARB claims it does not want to eliminate gasoline-powered cars, but to replace two out of every one hundred. CARB maintains that mandates and subsidies should be used to correct consumers' and automobile makers' bias against the more expensive EV. Support for state standards for that effort grew on the east coast as well. By January 2002 thirteen northeastern states have adopted the California standards with only New York sticking to the 2 percent goal and thereby imposing stricter limits than California.

A number of CARB staff "strawman" proposals were submitted in December 2002 to a workshop open to the public for discussion. The public had until the February 2003 board meeting to respond. The proposals included:

- Move the start of the mandate from 2003 to 2005. This could also allow manufacturers to extend the banking of credits to 2005.
- Lower the 2 percent ZEV requirement to 1 percent until 2012. During the interim 2005 to 2011, automakers could split the 2 percent ZEV requirement into a 1 percent pure ZEV and 1 percent transitional EV section. This would allow hybrids to earn credit in the transitional portion.
- Split the "gold" section from 4 percent to 2 percent. This would allow advanced technology partial zero emission vehicles (ATPZEVs), like the Honda Insight and the Toyota Prius hybrids, to get credits under the 2 percent status.
- Change the requirements for ZEVs to get credits. This would create a four-tier system of categorizing vehicles into NEV, City EV, Full Function EV and fuel cell vehicles. Each would be required to meet a specific mileage range. The NEV would remain the same, the City EV would need to get a 50-mile range, the Full Function EV would have a minimum of 120-mile range and the fuel cell vehicles would need a 100 mile range.[47]

This flexibility on the part of CARB shows its willingness to cooperate with manufacturers during a period of new technology development and that it realizes merely instituting a mandate does not change the market. The move to putting more EVs on the road will be a slow and incremental process involving government standards, the manufacturers and consumers.

Government and Private Partnerships

In a 1980 study, the U.S. Department of Energy identified eighty-one attempts in which one or two hybrid electric vehicles were made to yield extra range.[48] The problem of increasing range is being approached today using hybrid engines, fuel cells and improving batteries. The Partnership for a New Generation of Vehicles (PNGV) was formed in 1993. It was intended to be a high-profile $250 million effort, funded by the Department of Energy, NASA, the EPA and the Departments of Defense, Transportation and Commerce to promote Hybrid Electric Vehicle (HEV) technology. The goal was to produce an 80 mpg family sedan. PNGV also includes the "Big Three" automakers who contribute about $500 million per year. The preferred HEV design is an electric car with a small internal combustion engine and an electric generator on board to charge the batteries. In addition to hybrid development, PNGV put efforts toward developing new batteries, focusing on replacing the lead-acid battery with NiMH batteries and encouraging manufacturers to develop enabling technologies to make the HEVs more efficient. These include lighter-weight bodywork, more efficient gasoline and electric motors and better batteries and generators.[49] They propose to have test vehicles in 2004. The automotive industry supports voluntary programs such as the Partnership for a New Generation of Vehicles that promote collaboration between industry and government. The Sierra Club claims this collaboration on battery and fuel cell development between industry and government is merely a "scam to keep regulation at bay."[50] Automakers like this type of program for its flexibility. It is not binding and they do not have to commit to mass production. The arrangement allows greater freedom to concentrate on improving product lines.

The U.S. Advanced Battery Consortium (USABC) was established in 1991 to improve the performance and range offered in electric vehicle batteries. It included three U.S. automobile manufacturers (Daimler/Chrysler, Ford and General Motors), the Electric Power Research Institute, battery manufacturers and the U.S. Department of Energy (DOE). The consortium is investigating NiMH, lithium polymer and LiION battery systems. Its goal is to accelerate EV acceptance and sales by supporting R&D in advanced battery systems and to help develop electric energy systems to be competitive with the ICE. USABC is now under the umbrella of USCAR (United States Council for Automotive Research) formed in 1992 by Daimler/Chrysler, Ford and General Motors. Among their goals are cooperative efforts to share results of research projects, coordinate with PNGV and seek out funding for joint R&D from public and private resources.

In 1992 California started CALSTART, a state-funded non-profit consortium, calling itself a "business incubator" for the alternative fuel automobile. Some members include the City of Camarillo; HaveBlue, LLC; and the California Electric Transportation Coalition. They are concentrating on hybrid vehicles at the beginning, with an eye on developing the emission-free fuel cell in the not-too-distant future. CALSTART did run into opposition initially from some in the automotive industry who emphatically stated that battery technology for electric vehicles was not in place and it was impossible to comply with the California zero emissions mandates. The manufacturers lobbying turned public opinion in their direction, resulting in the 1996 modification of the requirements for 1998. Melanie Savage of CALSTART expressed concern about the amount of money being spent by automobile manufacturers on this anti–EV campaign, stating, "For every dime we [CALSTART] spent, they spent a dollar."[51]

The Southern Coalition for Advanced Transportation (SCAT) is a non-profit technology consortium of more than sixty-five public and private institutions. SCAT provides mechanisms for business and government to bring together resources in electric and hybrid electric transportation technology research and to demonstrate direct market viability. It was formed to promote development and public acceptance of AFVs. Its members include such diverse companies as GM, Delta Air Lines, Advanced Vehicle Systems and various battery companies.

The Surface Transportation Efficiency Act of 1991 authorized $12 million for the Advanced Transportation and Electric Vehicles Program. Four consortia were selected to receive funds to promote the development of electric vehicles. These consortia were to be an example of public/private partnerships. They would receive 50 percent of their funds from non-federal sources.

- Cheasapeake Consortium — Consisting of Westinghouse, Daimler/Chrysler, Baltimore Gas & Electric and the state of Maryland, it received an initial $4 million from the Federal Transit Administration (FTA), $2 million from the state of Maryland and $4 million from other sources. They have concentrated on developing electric transit buses and school buses.
- New York State Consortium — Members include the New York Metropolitan Transportation Authority, GE and various utility companies. They received an initial $2.3 million from the FTA and a matching $2.3 million from non-federal sources. FTA supplied an additional $750,000 in 1995 with matching non-federal funds of $750,000. The N.Y. State Consortium has developed a hybrid transit bus.
- CALSTART — Formed in 1992, it consists of forty public and private companies representing utilities, state, local and federal agencies. CALSTART initially received $4 million from the Federal Transit Administration and $2 million from the state of California. By 2001 they had received $11 million in federal funds and $22 million in state and local funds. They have completed over 140 public recharging stations in California, developed several electric buses and been instrumental in establishing EV components such as energy management systems, batteries and safety systems.
- Advanced Lead Acid Battery Consortium (ALABC)— Consisting of battery manufacturers and suppliers, it received an initial $2 million from the FTA with matching $2 million from local funds. ALABC is evaluating rapid recharge systems for electric buses.

One of the major partnerships among government agencies and private industry occurred just before the turn of the 21st century with the forming of the California Fuel Cell Partnership (CaFCP). In April 1999, twenty-eight members, including auto manufacturers, fuel distributors, fuel cell manufacturers, and government and transit agencies, came together to work on fuel cell solutions in a real-world test ground to explore the viability of this technology for commercial use. Its purpose is to explore the viability of infrastructure technology and to increase public awareness by making fuel cell technology more visible. GM and Toyota joined the CaFCP in October 2000 stating their belief that the activities of the partnership would ensure that consumers and the environment would benefit from advanced technologies. In early 2001 GM and Ford announced they would produce cleaner-burning hybrid gasoline engines for SUVs by 2004, improving fuel economy by 25 percent. CaFCP partners are actively looking for ways to make alternate fuel vehicles a market alternative.

Some agencies that provide funding for alternative vehicle research and development include:

- DOT's Advanced Vehicle Program.
- CALSTART.
- Alternative Fuels Infrastructure Development.
- International Energy Technology Assistance Program.
- Renewables Subject Area.
- Energy Innovations Small Grant Program.
- Public Interest Energy Research (PIER) Program.
- Alternative Fuel Infrastructure Program.
- Pennsylvania Department of Environmental Protection.

Federal Incentive Programs

"Government should be creating mechanisms such as taxes, tax credits, fees and marketable credits that marry technology and regulatory initiatives. This would lead to a more flexible, incentive-based public policy...."[52] The Federal Transportation Efficiency Act of 1998, managed through the Department of Transportation, set aside $9.1 billion for addressing environmental problems and created the Advanced Vehicle Technology Program (AVP) to encourage the development of AFVs. The AVP is designed to work in conjunction with PNGV to advance technologies that will reduce vehicle emissions beyond the 2004 standards, provide a 50 percent improvement in fuel efficiency, promote a globally competitive U.S. industry in AFVs and increase public awareness and acceptance.

Federal transportation programs have been in effect for many years. The most recent are the Transportation Equity Act for the 21st Century (TEA-21) and the Federal Transit Act (FTA). TEA-21 was initiated in June 1998 as the successor to the Intermodal Surface Transportation Efficiency Act (ISTEA) to provide federal money for AFV projects. Three parts of the act, under the Federal Highway Administration's purview, are:

- The Congestion Mitigation and Air Quality Program (CMAQ) that funds projects that reduce carbon monoxide and small particle emissions. CMAQ will pay up to 80 percent of a project's cost with the other 20 percent coming from non-federal sources.
- The Clean Fuel Formula Grant Program that provides funding of $100 million per year to assist fleet operators in purchasing low-emission buses.
- The Access Jobs and Reverse Commute Program which provides grants to local governments to offer transportation services for welfare recipients for employment and support services. The idea is to provide a public transportation link for people transitioning from welfare to work. Funding for this program began in 1999 at $50 million with increases to $150 million by 2003.

The "Securing America Energy Act of 2001" was passed in August 2001. Its goal is to reduce dependence on foreign energy sources from 56 percent to 45 percent by 2012. Some of the highlights of the tax incentives include:

Battery Electric Vehicles (BEV)
- A 10 percent tax credit for low-speed BEVs (up to $4,000).

- A $4,000 tax credit for passenger vehicles and light-duty trucks with a driving range of at least seventy miles on one charge.

Fuel Cell Electric Vehicles (FCEV)
- A $4,000 tax credit for light-duty FCEVs.
- An additional tax credit of $1,000–$4,000 for vehicles that show a 150–300 percent increase in fuel mileage over FY 2000.

Hybrid Electric Vehicles (HEVs)
- A $250–$1,000 tax credit for HEVs less than 8,500 lbs. gvw.
- An additional tax credit of $1,000–$3,500 for HEVs that show a 125–250 percent increase in fuel economy over FY 2000.

Hydrogen R&D — Authorizes $250 million for hydrogen research for FY 2002–2006.

Fuel cell research — Authorizes $84 million for a three year research program.

Fleets — Requires the federal fleet program to increase acquisitions of alternative fuel vehicles by five percent by FY 2005.

Utility Incentive Programs

A variety of utility companies incentive programs are available in almost every state. Some examples are:

- Colorado — Financial assistance for CNG fueling stations.
- Connecticut — Financial assistance for NGV purchases.
- Florida — $300 free CNG for private fleets.
- Illinois — Tax rebate of $1,500 on the purchase cost of a NGV.
- Maryland — $1,500 tax credit for hybrids.
- Montana — Ten percent tax credit on the purchase of an EV.
- North Carolina — Discounted charging rates for EVs.
- Oregon — A 35 percent tax buy-back credit on the purchase of an EV.
- Wyoming — Ten percent tax credit on the purchase cost of an NGV.

Southern California Edison operates one of the nation's largest electric car fleets. In 2000 Southern California Edison started an eighteen-month-long project to test a hybrid utility line truck. SCE, with additional funding from the Department of Transportation's Advanced Vehicle Program, began conversions of existing line trucks to hybrid vehicles using a battery pack and an internal combustion engine. Edison Electric is also investigating fuel cells for fleet use.

Manufacturer Fleet Incentive Programs

- Ford has offered a $1,500 rebate on its Ranger EV pickup and $2,000 on all of its natural gas vehicles.
  - GM has a variety of incentives for its EV1 and S-10 pickup.
  - Honda offers comprehensive collision and roadside assistance.
  - Toyota offers a home connecting device for its RAV4-EV.

City and State Fleet Funding

Idaho operates a Central Facilities Area (CFA) as a home base for its fleet of EVs. It includes more than 1,100 buses and other vehicles ranging from carts to large trucks. Research is also being conducted on other vehicles, including passenger buses, using liquefied natural gas (LNG).

Idaho's INEEL (Idaho National Engineering and Environmental Laboratory) has been testing hybrid electric vehicles (HEVs) since 1984 and results show a constant improvement in the trend toward improved energy consumption per kilogram of vehicle weight. It also participates in the Field Operations Program designed to test vehicles over several years of traditional real-world fleet-use operations. Infrastructure continues to be a key factor in the success of AFVs. INEEL established a compressed natural gas (CNG) fueling station in Idaho Falls in July 2001. The station will be used to fuel the state's fleet of CNG light-duty vehicles and will be available to regional businesses and the public.

The Electric Transportation Applications (ETA) program is a private corporation in Phoenix, Arizona. It has offered fleet services to private and government fleet managers since 1996 to support electric vehicle fleets. It has coordinated the development of electric fire and rescue emergency vehicles, promoted infrastructure, and is supported by the Advanced Lead Acid Battery Consortium.

Arizona Public Service (APS), in Phoenix, Arizona, began using electric vehicles in 1979 and in 2002 has over forty-one vehicles in its fleet. The vehicles have logged over 750,000 miles. Its fleet consists of GM's EV1, Solectria E-10, Chevrolet Electric S-10s and Ford Electric Rangers and is used on a daily basis by executive staff, meter readers and R&D departments. The object of the program is to test and evaluate electric vehicles in fleet use by collecting battery data and operation and maintenance data. In 1996 APS started a Charger Test Project to explore the use of fast charging to extend battery life.

The Salt River Project (SRP) in Tempe, Arizona, started an electric vehicle fleet in 1991 with four G-Vans and currently runs Ford Rangers and EV1s. By 1998 it had established eight recharging stations in convenient locations such as the Biltmore Fashion Square, Arizona Mills, Scottsdale Fashion Square and Fiesta Mall.

Southern California Edison (SCE) created an Electric Transportation (ET) division in 1991. In 2001 it operated about seventy EVs and planned an aggressive expansion of its fleet in the near future. The fleet includes the EV1, Chevrolet S-10, Chrysler EPIC, Honda EV-Plus and Toyota RAV4-EV. Meter readers, field representatives, service managers, mail handlers and security patrols use the vehicles on a daily basis. Primary testing and serving areas include battery and charger technology testing and SCE's "Pomona Loop," which is a twenty-mile urban driving test run.

Potomac Electric Power Company (PEPCO), an investor-owned electric utility of Washington, D.C., and the state of Maryland, began its electric vehicle leasing program in 1997. It leased ten Chevrolet S-10s to the federal government (GSA) and later supplied thirty S-10s to the Naval Public Works Center in Anacostia, D.C. PEPCO also purchased five S-10s in 1997, two of which are being tested by the DOE in Arizona. PEPCO has committed to encouraging the development of the necessary infrastructure for EVs. It is working closely with the federal DOE, EV America and the electric utility industry to promote fleet applications.

The Electricity Council of England promoted the practicality of electric cars by purchasing seventy Enfield 8000 vehicles in the 1960s to be used by the electric utility companies. During the same time, the Batronic Truck Company of England delivered electric trucks to the Potomac Edison Company in Maryland for fleet use. General Electric worked with Batronic from 1973 to 1983 developing passenger buses and fleet vans for the utility industry.

Federal Fleet Funding

The Energy Policy Act of 1992 provided federal funds for alternative fuel vehicles for fleets. Some incentives for fleet operators included:

- A 10 percent tax credit on the cost of an EV until 2004.
- A $100,000 tax deduction for alternative fuel refueling stations.
- A $2,000 tax deduction for converting vehicles to alternative fuels.
- Low-interest loans by the DOE where a state could provide 20 percent of the cost to implement alternative fuel vehicles for fleet use.

As of 1995 electric car buyers qualified for a 10 percent federal tax credit, up to a maximum of $4,000. Also in 1995 Vice President Al Gore, with the Big Three auto executives, announced a program to develop clean-fuel-burning cars that would get eighty mpg. This was in conjunction with an update of the Energy Policy Act of 1992. Part of the act required a 10 percent reduction in fuel use in the U.S. by year 2000 and a 30 percent reduction by 2010. The DOE failed to promulgate regulations by mid–1995 and manufacturers were given extra time to comply with the requirements for the model year 1996. The act also required the government to involve itself in providing a nationwide alternative fuels infrastructure. Title IV of the act provides for a financial incentives program for the states. Title V allows for credits for alternative fuel vehicles acquired beyond what is legally required. These credits could be sold or traded by fleet owners.

In 1998 Executive Order 13031 mandated that the U.S. Department of Energy (DOE) provide incremental funding to federal fleets of EVs under the "Federal Alternative Fueled Leadership" group. Under the Incremental Funding Program, the United States Postal Service (USPS) ordered sixty-one EPICs used in three fleets, the DOE ordered fifty-nine vehicles used in eight fleets and the DOD ordered forty-one vehicles for six fleets. After delivery of 209 EPICS and Rangers, 59 percent experienced a variety of mechanical problems, primarily concerned with battery packs, coolant pumps and wiring harnesses. Most of these problems were considered a minor inconvenience and were replaced readily. A survey of thirty-seven fleet managers taken in 2000 showed a positive response of 2 to 1. General positive comments included "very happy with vehicle," "ideal vehicle for mission," "very nice ride," "responsive," "perfect for our site" and "no complaints." General negative comments were "winter drains batteries quicker," "mileage not as good in mountainous areas," "distance a limitation," "looking at hybrids" and "lack of range."[53] DOE estimates there are more than 1,350 commercial and government fleets in the Washington, D.C., area using about 150,000 AFV vehicles.

Executive Order 13031 was replaced on April 21, 2000, by Executive Order 13149, "Greening the Government through Federal Fleet and Transportation Efficiency." This new order removed the incremental funding, and:

- Requires each agency to reduce its fleet's annual petroleum consumption by 20 percent by the end of FY 2005, compared with FY 1999 levels.

- Requires agencies to increase the average EPA fuel economy rating of passenger cars and light trucks acquired by 1 mpg by the end of FY 2002 and 3 mpg by the end of FY 2005 compared to FY 1999.
- Stresses the alternative fuel vehicle (AFV) acquisition requirements of the Energy Policy Act of 1992 (EPACT section 303) which states that 75 percent of the vehicles acquired by each agency should be AFVs.
- Requires agencies to use alternative fuels to meet a majority of the fuel requirements of AFVs, rather than only using alternative fuels "to the extent practicable," as stated in Executive Order 13031.
- Encourages agencies to team with state, local, and private entities to expand use of fueling at commercial facilities that offer alternative fuels for sale to the public.
- Increases the credit values for dedicated AFVs and Zero Emission Vehicles towards fulfilling the AFV acquisition requirements of EPACT.[54]

In July 2002 California's Governor Gray Davis signed bill AB 1493 into law. The new law seeks to reduce greenhouse gas emissions from automobiles sold in California starting with the model year 2009. This law is unique in that it spells out a direct connection between "global warming" and exhaust emissions from automobiles. As the Conference Board "pointed out recently, whether you believe global warming exists or that man-made CO_2 has a role in it, the perception of its existence is now a reality and businesses need to starting living with it and planning accordingly. AB 1493 may be the sire of many similar, perhaps even more draconian measures to come, if we fail to act in a prudent and timely fashion."[55]

Cooperation, coercion and partnerships between government and industry provide incentives for change. Their impact is seen in technological development of fuel cells, batteries and alternate fuel sources and in government, utility and manufacturer fleet projects. The interest is in supporting change to promote marketable alternatives to the traditional ICE and provide a kinder impact on the environment.

3 Environment

"Civilized is the word for the electric car, not only because it is environmentally clean, but also because it conveys the impression of friendliness and serenity. They offer efficient transportation, yet still they proceed with civility and show compassion for lovers, joggers, bicyclists and walkers."[1]

Families love their personal transportation vehicles. Whether the vehicles are powered by gasoline, natural gas, hydrogen or electricity, they have become part of our culture and our public environmental concern. They symbolize our independence and freedom to move where we want, when we want. Discussions about the use and type of automobiles reflect our society's wants and fears as we try to meld the independence and freedom we strive to protect with the perceived needs of public interest in sustaining a healthy environment. Ride sharing and carpooling programs over the years have failed because people want independence and individual automobility.

The number of persons owning cars has grown exponentially with growing economies. In 1911 there were 578,000 automobiles in use in the United States, with 70,000 in New York and 40,000 each in Pennsylvania and California. Today, there are between 150 and 200 million vehicles in the United States, 18 million vehicles in Canada and about 100 million vehicles in Europe. In 1950 the world's population was 2.6 billion people with 50 million cars. Fifty years later, there were six billion people and 800 million cars. The population doubled while car ownership rose over tenfold. The world's car manufacturers are producing about 50 million vehicles per year, and, as economies in developing countries grow, more people want more cars. Economists estimate that when the average annual family income in a country reaches $6,000, car sales rise dramatically.[2] Governments in these developing countries want to attract manufacturers and it is likely that the automobile industry will expand rapidly as these local economies grow around the world.

How will this automobile expansion affect the global environment? Cars are the biggest producers of carbon emissions, emissions which environmentalists point to as causing global warming. Today's urban areas are growing at a 66 percent property use rate and an 89 percent population rate, but suburbs are still a popular place to live and people in America are not giving up their cars, nor are our world neighbors. Other options need to be examined. Using technology is one viable alternative, developing cleaner-burning ICE engines and introducing hybrids and EVs should help reduce the amount of harmful emissions. But just expanding the options available for auto buyers is not the only change needed. If electrics are to be an option, where is that power going to originate? There are still questions about how to produce the electricity needed to power the electric vehicles without adding more pollution, and how to dispose of batteries, tires, etc. in an environmentally friendly way. Partnerships among manufacturers and government agencies are forming to find solutions to lessen the environmental impact caused by increased demand and auto ownership.

Pursuing both new and return buyers to consider non-polluting vehicles is a key factor to those wanting to protect the environment. In the early years, electric automobiles were seen as the answer to horse pollution, and the noise and fumes of their ICE counterparts. The environmental problems that accompany our favorite form of transportation have changed only in degree. It is obvious that cars have had and will continue to have an adverse affect on air quality. John Barber of the *Globe and Mail*, Toronto, in a 1999 article, adds:

> But, we would never dream of giving them up, let alone using them less. The current fascination with new gizmos actually disguises the incredible advances in conventional technology that have occurred over the past 20-odd years. Unfortunately, the explosion in car use over that same period of time has virtually cancelled out all environmental benefits we might otherwise have gained.[3]

Emission patterns in the United States provide a guidepost for air quality concerns for the new world markets, but current economic plateaus must be reached before concern about environmental impact becomes a public issue in those countries. It is clear that at some point, if we want to protect the environment, we must change attitudes about car use, including increasing fuel efficiency and reducing the use of the ICE automobile in its current design.

The U.S. transportation industry is about twenty years ahead of other industrialized countries in emissions volume. Carbon emissions from U.S. motor vehicles contribute to about 5 percent of the world's total carbon emissions, more than any other industry sector, including the airline industry.[4] As nations grow into economic viability, the people in them tend to use public transportation less and buy individual vehicles more. Environmental concerns evolve after a level of economic prosperity has been reached. It is predicted that by 2015, 90 percent of the oil in the Middle East will go to the Far East. Most of Asia and China will be growing economically and, as they become more affluent, will use more oil and gas for energy for personal transportation. Europe, with over a century of automotive experience, is a leader in recognizing the damage done to our environment by engine emissions and is promoting a number of environmentally friendly transportation policies to discourage the use of private automobiles. The European Union is cooperating with automakers to reduce carbon emissions in new cars.[5] Germany, in particular, has committed to supplying 10–30 percent of its energy from renewable energy resources, such as wind farms. It already has three times the number of wind farms as the United States.[6] But these positive efforts are balanced by the growing use of more traditional energy sources in the emerging economies. As nations improve economically, more people move to individual automobiles instead of relying on public transportation. Despite efforts among more-established industrial nations to promote the need for adherence to strict environmental quality standards for the burgeoning markets, we can assume, based on existing buying patterns for ICEs over alternate fuel vehicles, that the buying trend will duplicate the U.S. pattern initially. This trend will lead to more carbon emissions globally and the need to address its impact on the world's air quality.

Advocates of the global warming theory are bringing renewed interest in alternative fuel vehicles. In 1998 supporters stated that, given the current patterns of fossil fuel use worldwide, by 2050, we will see dramatic climatic changes causing drought in the Amazon, Mediterranean and eastern U.S. The weather changes experienced in 1998 due to Hurricane Mitch and excessive flooding in China and India were just the beginning, according to this environmental faction. These extreme weather patterns reflected the effects of the excess in carbon dioxide (CO_2) emissions from ICEs and utility plants from thirty years earlier. The global warming theorists see a pattern of increased CO_2 from ICEs and the corresponding cycle of rising temperatures caused by the greenhouse effect, leading to decreased rainfall and a shortage after 2050 in the number of plants (which absorb CO_2) needed to deplete the extra CO_2. They predict this will magnify the greenhouse effect for the second half of the 21st century, resulting in droughts, killer storms and widespread disease.[7] Many adhering to this theory see the agreements made by the scientists of the Intergovernmental Panel on Climate Change in 1990, the Rio conference in 1992 and the Kyoto Agreement in 1997 to be very slow-moving and effective only in their efforts to create a groundwork, in their view, for much-needed worldwide regulation on the use of fossil fuels. The global warming theory has renewed interest in the alternative fuels possible for the automotive and transportation industries.

Pollution Problems

Environmental issues have been a part of the story of the automobile from its inception. In New York and Chicago in 1890, horse-drawn carriages were as major a traffic problem as cars are today. They were "bumper to bumper" or nose to carriage. Crossing the street in front of mammoth draft horses and avoiding the pollution of manure was a daunting effort. There were ordinances concerning where horses could be stabled to protect the citizenry against possible disease. Although these restrictions were necessary, they were inconvenient. Persons wanting to use public carriages had to wait for livery to arrive from these set-apart areas. Street cleaning in the 1890s was a major industry in New York City, employing 1,600 men engaged in removing 1,035 cubic yards of sweepings per day and carting them to the dump. The average cost for this service was eighteen cents per cubic yard. The advent of the horseless carriage was expected to reduce this expense considerably. The horseless carriage was looked upon as an environmental godsend. Not only could it be conveniently housed, but there was no need for street cleanup after it passed, and it decreased the need to find places to dispose of the stables' by-product — manure from thousands of draft and carriage horses. A *New York Times* editorial in 1899 suggested "automobilitors" have the right to freedom of the road, and moreover not they, but users of horses, should be paying fees to use the roads: "...horses [owners should] be charged a license to travel upon the parks and boulevards, inasmuch as they are a source of considerable expense to the public in wearing out the surface of the streets, and causing a considerable additional expense in maintaining forces of men to keep the roadways clean over which they pass."[8] An analysis by the *Scientific American* in 1899 discovered that two-thirds of the dust and mud in city streets was caused by horses. The writer concluded that if automobiles could replace the horses, two-thirds of the dirt in cities would disappear. It was also estimated at the time that a horse would eat 12,000 pounds of food a year, or about five acres, while being only 2 percent efficient. The article stated that the ten million horses in the United States employed thousands of stable and street cleaners, and that the iron hammered out for horseshoes by blacksmiths in one year could be turned into 40,000 farm tractors or 60,000 motor vehicles.

Converting from horse to automobile would clear mud and dust pollution in the local environments, but other pollutants also brought distress to the public. Probably the first recorded complaint about automobile air pollution came in 1900 from Burton Peck. Peck had made two gasoline-powered vehicles, then stopped, saying, "There is one great obstacle that must be overcome and that is the offensive odor from gasoline that has been burned and that is discharged into the air. It is a sickening odor and I can readily see that should there be any number of them running on the street, there would be an ordinance passed forbidding them."[9]

Noise pollution was also becoming a problem. In 1899, the "noise and clatter" of horse-drawn carriages "which makes conversation difficult on many streets of New York at the present time will be done away with" by the nearly noiseless electric vehicle.[10] In a lawsuit in 1901 involving an electric vehicle, the judge advised the jury, "Much has been said about the swiftness of the vehicle and its relative freedom from noise. Within limits, freedom from noise is of very great moment to the whole community, not merely to the persons who use the vehicles, but persons living by the roadside and the persons who use the road."[11] Electric vehicles seemed to solve some of these problems. Ladies especially liked the quiet-running electrics. The New York Fifth Avenue line service added electric vehicles to its trolley lines in 1904. "It is not probable that tracks can ever be laid in any part of Fifth Avenue, as public opinion as well as property holders are extremely opposed to it. There are no objections, however, to the noiseless and clean horseless [electric] omnibus, which will leave the street in good sanitary condition."[12] "Electricity continues to assert itself as the most suitable power for city and suburban traffic. In the former, it is supreme and for suburban travel, it is growing in favor."[13] Kevin A. Wilson, in an editorial in *AutoWeek* in 2002, illustrates that noise pollution is as much a part of the current environment as it was in the early 1900s. On a vacation in the Maine woods, Wilson discovered he could find no silence. ATVs, powerboats, jet skis, etc., all contribute to the noise pollution near and within campgrounds to the point where silent campers can be disturbed even at night. He suggests this is a wonderful marketing opportunity for silent-running fuel cell electric-drive machines to provide "quiet transport through the wilderness."[14]

Roads that were in a constant state of disrepair were another early environmental issue. If roads were left to dirt, motoring autos would create clouds of dust; if stone covered, the small rocks would be kicked by tires to the neighboring fields, yards and walkways. Road repair became a public priority. In the West in the early 1900s, the Iowa State Highway Commission opened a course in road building at the State College in Ames, Iowa. Across the country, motor vehicles were penalized through taxation for wearing out the roads faster than horse-drawn carriages. Electric vehicles were taxed at a higher rate because they generally weighed more due to the batteries, and it was assumed that the extra weight caused more wear and tear to the road surface. New York State appropriated $50,000,000 to be spent on roads in 1906.[15] There were 74,000 miles of roads and highways in the state; 38,000 miles were repaired and maintained under the "day work program," under which a person could work out taxes owed at $1.50 a day instead of paying the taxes in cash. From 1898 to 1906 the amount of money spent by towns, counties and the state amounted to about $11,508,000. These monies accounted for an estimated 16,000 miles of "good" roads in the state. It was predicted that the appropriated $50,000,000 to be spent over a ten-year period would result in "perfect" roads from one end of the state to the other. Much time and expense went into keeping the roads maintained to promote a safer, cleaner environment.

By 1909 road resurfacing was a serious problem throughout the country. Many of the highways were being surfaced using John L. MacAdam's process of layering small stones on the roadbed and binding them with tar or asphalt. The auto caused the greatest damage to the macadamized road surfaces. The initial breakdown of the surface, when it was first noticed, was called "suction." This would occur when the rubber tires picked up the finely crushed binding material of the surface, and threw it to the rear, exposing the broken edges of the top layer of macadam. These loosened "marbles" would in turn be broken down and again picked up by passing vehicles and thrown by the wind into adjacent fields, lawns or other property. Chains and other non-skidding devices on tires intensified the breaking down and pulverizing of the road surface. The damage was accelerated by the road's popularity. So many automobilists were attracted to the new macadamized roads that, when a new stretch of highway opened up to the public, they would travel a considerable detour just to drive on it instead of using inferior roads. This caused greater traffic volume and faster breakdown of the surface. With a high level of traffic, the underlying foundation of macadam was exposed much sooner than road builders projected and the roadway had to be rebuilt on an accelerated schedule. Legislation was considered to limit the traffic or impose fines for speeding and using chains. Regulation was not pursued because it was recognized that this solution might slow the problem, but would not stop it completely. The only workable solution was to build more durable highways that could stand up to the increased traffic demands by the public. Engineers looked for a material that would shed water in the winter and prevent the surface from being ground up into dust in the summer. They began experimenting with tar, but found it almost more objectionable than the original problem. Eventually, it was decided to use tar with a surface layer of sand to give a sufficient crown to the surface to drain water. Even with this new approach, the roads needed day-by-day attention by a repair gang who continuously patched the surface and prevented the polluting of the adjacent roadsides.[16]

Hard surfacing all roadways was not economically feasible, so auto enthusiasts looked for other possible solutions to reduce the dust churned up by the automobiles. It was noted that some cars running at high speeds were not accompanied by as much dust as others at lower speeds. *Motor World* magazine in 1909 suggested manufacturers should make designs tending toward the abatement of the public nuisance, dust. This would include devices on the front and rear of cars to accommodate the direction of air currents, and building highways with cohesive surfaces.

By 1917 the dangers of carbon monoxide from the internal combustion engine surfaced as a topic of discussion. Deaths in garages were being reported as men worked on their cars' engines without proper ventilation. The running engines would consume oxygen and expel more and more of the harmful gas. "Many persons have succumbed to its poisonous fumes, and scientists have given the cause of death from the gas the name of petromortis."[17] Media of the day encouraged that auto maintenance be done in a well-ventilated area to prevent such poisonous carbon monoxide tragedies from happening.

During the World Wars and the time immediately following, concerns for sustaining a viable economy outweighed concerns about pollution-producing vehicles, but in the early 1950s industrial areas of the country were beginning to see haze in the air. Air quality became recognized as an important aspect for community health. Rachel Carson's *Silent Spring* (1962) reawakened awareness of the damaging effects our culture was having on the earth. In the late 1960s air pollution was the topic of the day. Advocates of electric vehicles at the time admitted that if it were not for air pollution, the interest in EVs would be nil. They also realized that some of the reduction in air pollution gained by driving EVs might be offset by the increased exhaust pollution from the generating plants needed to supply the energy for those vehicles. The federal government responded to the public's increased concern for air quality by passing first the Air Pollution Control Act of 1955 which ear-marked air pollution as a national problem, and then the Clean Air Act of 1963 which set standards for power plant and later for automobile emissions. Congress identified the issue, but did little to answer the post–World War II dilemma of how electricity to support battery-operated EVs on a large scale could be safely generated by power plants without having detrimental effects on the air, water or earth. In 1970, in an effort to address environmental quality, Congress and the executive branch of the government formed the Environmental Protection Agency. Its primary purpose was to develop standards for air, water and land quality. Environmental interests were surfacing to temper the needs of the economy.

Providing a persistent alternative, renewable energy source for vehicles continues to impede acceptance of environmentally friendly personal transport. Fossil fuels have brought their own share of problems for consumers, but not enough to dissuade the masses from the ICEs. At the time of the 1973–74 oil energy crisis, 6 percent of the world's population (the United States) consumed 40 percent of the world's oil. After the Watergate scandal, the public's trust in the federal government was waning. Environmentalists noted that the United States began decreasing imported oil in April 1973 and requiring that Congress enact legislation demanding full disclosure of all oil industry data, suspecting that the crisis was being artificially induced to raise consumer prices. They also lobbied to require auto manufacturers to produce cars with 20 percent more efficient fuel usage. The Federal Energy Administration did not ask Congress for gasoline efficiency standards or a horsepower tax, but suggested the auto industry should aim to increase gasoline efficiency by 1985. During the same time period, the Environmental Protection Agency issued standards for automobile emissions to comply with its mandate to improve air quality. The standards, along with another oil crisis, emphasized the government's interest in the potential for alternate fuels. Tax dollars were spent on researching the feasibility of electric and hybrid vehicles for commercial and consumer use. Research showed little support for the alternate fuel vehicles and by the late 1970s, attention turned from EVs to encouraging more efficient ICEs. The efficient ICE continues to be a preferred economic choice for consumers. Air quality auto emission standards require higher fuel-efficient engines in the vehicle consumers prefer. The distinction between the environmental impact of the ICE or HEV versus electrics continues to narrow. For electrics to be the better option, clean power generators must be available. Environmentalists are in strong disagreement about how that alternate power source might be established and maintained. A constant reliable energy source is key to the electric's feasibility and survival as the preferred "green machine."

In order to have power available to energize EVs as an environmentally friendly alternative to ICEs, a balance must be reached in generating the power needed to operate them. Sometimes laws and court rulings, intended to improve the environment, become far more influential than originally intended, and have a negative impact on the EV industry. Environmentalists, while being advocates for EVs, have thwarted the efforts to promote electrics by decreasing the expansion of the power stations needed to support the high volume of energy needed to keep electrics in service. The number of cars tapping into the energy resources cannot be supported until enough power can be generated to meet recharging needs.

There is much disagreement among the environmental factions on how power might be generated, and whether private automobile ownership is in the public's best interest. The objections are varied. Hydroelectric power plants cover over Indian ruins in Arizona, deplete salmon runs in the Pacific Northwest and generally disrupt the flow of wild rivers. Wind power is bad because the whirling blades kill birds, including protected species. Solar energy takes up too much land space. Geothermal sites are mostly in protected areas like Yellowstone and have a limited non-renewable capacity. Coal-fired and natural gas plants are air polluters. Nuclear plants have the problem of waste product storage.[18] Their successful lobbying was considered a major contributor to blocking the construction of new energy facilities during the 1990s while energy needs continued to increase. The 2001 brownouts in California are one example of negative impact.

In the summer of 2003, Cape Cod has become another controversial ground for a renewable energy source. Residents of the area are voicing opposition to Cape Wind Associates' being allowed to build 130 wind turbines approximately six miles offshore. Cables from the generating source would be routed to shore to the regional power facility. According to Cape Wind, the facility would offset one million tons of carbon dioxide and supply 74 percent of the energy needed for the area. Residents voice concerns along a wide spectrum, from the politicians remonstrating that local jurisdiction has authority over regulating wind turbines off their shores to the aesthetics of wind turbines on the horizon of a popular tourist spot to environmental and commercial concerns about possible disruption of local oyster beds, estuaries and fishing areas. Mark Rogers of Cape Wind Associates believes this protesting to be a NIMBY (Not in My Backyard) objection.[19] Although opinions differ on the amount and source of energy needed by our communities and the reluctance of some to agree to support new energy sources, it is a generally accepted belief that it is easier to control emissions from a utility plant that supports EVs, than try to control people's use of their cars. Compromises must be reached if consumers are going to support non-polluting alternatives to the ICE.

Developing a stable, cost-effective energy source has been and continues to be the main roadblock to electrics' joining the mainstream market. Current research has branched in many directions, using theories and concepts formulated in the early years. Each has its positives and negatives. Some continue to be cost-prohibitive, others are plagued by the historic problem of lack of infrastructure to provide wide area service. Batteries, fuel cells, alternate fuels, each struggle to find environmentally friendly solutions the market will accept.

Energy Sources — Batteries

The environmental impact of the battery, with its limited range and high cost, continues to be an obstacle to the EV's development. There are many unanswered questions about pollution generated from old batteries and traditional power plants, the possible toxicity and recycling of current lead acid batteries and the advanced (NiMH, LiION) forms being developed, and the cost of generating electricity to recharge these batteries both at home and using commercial recharging stations. In 1996 discussions heated up over the effectiveness of reducing pollution at the tailpipe level, but creating more pollution at the lead mining/disposal and power plant levels. Researchers estimated that the mining, smelting and recycling of more than 500 Kg of lead batteries per vehicle would cause a far greater environmental problem than the air quality problem it might solve. They estimated that the battery lead hazard to the environment would increase by 20 percent if emphasis were placed on using battery-powered electric vehicles to combat the ICE air pollution.[20] In 1998, an estimated three billion batteries were sold in the U.S. with a projected increase of about 6 percent per year. The disposal of the volume of batteries needed to power EVs is a major problem.

Although the battery disposal problem continues to be an issue, it is being partially addressed through recycling. Most parts of the batteries can be recycled. The electrolyte can be neutralized and the lead can be recovered by a controlled-temperature process and refined for resale. This process looks promising in reducing the environmental impact of pollution from the EV batteries as long as the industry finds a market for the battery's recycled by-products. The disposal problem becomes solvable when addressed as an environmental recycling issue. By 2001 environmentalists generally agreed that pollution from tailpipes expose more people to noxious fumes than pollution from power plants, as the plants are more likely to be located in remote areas and have tall stacks that allow the pollution to disperse before reaching populated areas.[21] Power plants also have stricter regulations to adhere to concerning pollutants. Interest in alternative electricity-producing sources such as fuel cells, solar, wave, nuclear and wind are also being revisited. The problems of EVs' batteries and utility plants emissions as they affect air and ground pollution are obstacles, but accommodations are being found in regulation and recycling.

Fuel Cells

Using fuel cells to generate electricity for the EV has caught the environmentalists' attention. In a perfect world the only by-products of fuel cells powered by hydrogen are water and heat. People could actually drink water from the tailpipe of fuel-cell-equipped buses in a Chicago test program. Realistically, the emissions vary depending on the type of fuel used, and developers face obstacles in packaging, marketing and supplying the product to potential consumers. Hydrogen produced by the electrolysis of water would be the ideal solution, but it is not economically feasible at this time. If hydrogen is produced using gasoline, methanol or natural gas, there are trace amounts of pollutants, such as nitrogen oxide and carbon monoxide. The emissions are still far less than the current ICEs but air quality is still negatively affected no matter which alternate fuel is used. As with the shortage of charging stations that electrics have faced historically, a convenient fuel supply also continues to be a problem with these alternates. The infrastructure is not in place for the hydrogen or methane fuel sources and natural gas carries its own drawbacks in the volume it consumes, even when compressed or liquefied. Developers are looking for solutions for these roadblocks. One possible solution to this is to extract the hydrogen from the natural gas in large reformers located at filling stations and then storing it in a solid metal hydride form. This would provide about the same amount of energy as a same-sized tank of gasoline.[22] The benefits appear slowly as the market sorts out which infrastructure to support, but innovations like these for using the low- to zero-polluting fuel cells are raising expectations for people interested in a cleaner environment.

The Pembina Institute of Alberta, Canada, an environmental "think tank," estimated the impact of using hydrogen derived from fossil fuels against a benchmark traditional ICE to illustrate that just changing to fuel cells would not provide the greatest opportunity for cleaning the air. The choice of fuels used to generate the hydrogen makes a difference in the percentage of CO_2 pollution reduced by this method.

- The ICE creates 248 kilograms of CO_2 per 1000 kilometers driven.
- A car using electricity from a fossil fuel plant would create 237.
- Hydrogen extracted from an onboard gasoline reformer, 193.
- An onboard methanol reformer from natural gas, 162.
- Hydrogen fuel cell reformer from natural gas at urban outlets, 80.
- Hydrogen supplied from large refineries, 70.

The Canadian Institute's research found that hydrogen pulled from fossil-fuel generating plants (comparisons of hydrogen gained from hydro, solar, wind power or methane escaping from landfills were not addressed in the study) would have minimal impact on changing levels of greenhouse gases and increase smog and heavy metal pollutants such as arsenic and mercury. Pollution would be reduced by 35 percent using hydrogen refined from methanol; hydrogen from natural gas would reduce it 70 percent [23] The good news here is that this method produces only half as many pollutants as an ICE.[24]

Again, the existing infrastructure, not ideals, is key to what will and will not survive in the marketplace. Gasoline has the existing infrastructure and is familiar to car owners. It is customary and readily available, but is the least efficient hydrogen source. Natural gas has a small infrastructure built in and may be expanded, but is less likely to be the major resource for the fuel cell's hydrogen supply. For some urban areas, natural gas may provide the cleaner alternative, but its limited availability makes it a distant second option for most consumers. In April 2002 the Bush administration put its support behind the development of hydrogen powered fuel cell vehicles, acknowledging that the technology for getting the autos on the road may be a decade away. Even with the limitations, fuel cells show promise for decreasing pollution from autos and a high possibility for gaining market share.

Fuel cells powered by hydrogen, even in their current emerging state of development, are already proving to be "green" conscious. They eliminate the immediate problem of piles of dead lead acid batteries accumulating in landfills and show future potential to further reduce landfill expansion as new designs in fuel cells are being developed as reusable resources. The components of the Ballard fuel cell, for example, are completely recyclable. After thousands of hours of use, the parts can be disassembled, cleaned and reassembled into new fuel cells. The drawback with hydrogen is that currently energy generated through it is more expensive than coal, oil or natural gas. It also has the added disadvantage of being associated with the *Hindenburg* disaster in 1937 in which the airship burned at its mooring in Lakehurst, New Jersey. Hydrogen is non-polluting and safe, but is still perceived by many to be an unsafe gas that could explode in disaster, not a comfortable feeling for use in the family car. Even with this stigma, environmentalists and those in the industry see the fuel cell's potential for success, if care is given to the source fuel used.

Major industries are experimenting with ways to supply the automobile industry with fuel cell technology. The automakers are branching out and partnering with fuel cell manufacturers. Each wants its market share and is pushing to have its version of the product become the industry standard in the manufacturing of the new auto lines. Research and development expenses are still a reality, and the competition has not had the needed effect of reducing cost for these products. No main industry idea for the most effective product has yet surfaced to standardize production for cost savings.

"Researchers are helping to develop technologies to tap into this natural resource and generate hydrogen in mass quantities and cheaper prices in order to compete with the traditional energy sources. There are three main methods that scientists are researching for inexpensive hydrogen generation. All three separate the hydrogen from a 'feedstock,' such as fossil fuel or water — but by very different means."[25]

- Reformers — Reforming is the name of the process used to extract hydrogen from a variety of materials including natural gas, methanol, ethanol, propane and even gasoline. One type of reforming is endothermic steam which combines the fuels with steam and then separates hydrogen using membranes. A problem here is that the process uses energy. Another type of reformer is a partial oxidation process. It has a drawback of having CO_2 as a by-product.
- Enzymes — Cyanobacteria are single-celled organisms that can produce hydrogen when growing in water. The organisms use enzymes to split the molecules to produce hydrogen. This process is especially attractive because the by-product is water, which can be used for the next process cycle.
- Solar and wind power — Photovoltaics, solar cells or wind turbines can also generate hydrogen by using power to electrolyze water into hydrogen and oxygen. Hydrogen becomes an energy carrier and can be transported from the generation site to another location for use in a fuel cell.

Each of these methods shows that fuel cell technology is developing into a viable option for providing an environmentally friendly energy source for powering electric vehicles. Both industry and those looking for clean ways to generate power are following progress in its development.

Catalytic Converters

After the energy crisis of 1973–74, many regulations were enacted to conserve fuels and reduce tailpipe emissions to improve air quality. Tailpipe exhaust emissions consist of carbon monoxide (CO), unburned hydrocarbons (HC) and nitrogen oxides (NOX). One of the solutions to reduce these emissions was the catalytic converter. Evaporative emissions are the fuel vapors that seep out of the fuel tank and carburetor. These vapors are prevented from escaping into the atmosphere by sealing the fuel system and storing the vapors in a canister for later reburning. The catalytic converter captures the pollutants that make it into the exhaust and sends them back to be reburned before they can exit the tailpipe. High sulfur levels in gasoline tend to clog up the catalytic converters. This sulfur content problem was addressed by the Clinton administration in April 1999, when it announced new standards, known as Tier 2, to clean up heavily polluting light trucks. The new plan lowered the acceptable levels from 330 parts per million to 30 ppm, with 15 ppm being the goal for 2005. The idea was to lower the amount of soot released in the air. The proposal is expected to have little effect due to several loopholes. First, it will not take effect until 2004 for cars and not until 2009 for light trucks. Second, it does not apply to trucks weighing over 8,500 pounds, and third it does not apply to diesel engines, which produce far more soot than gasoline engines. The Tier 2 program is still in a position of being amended and the EPA is producing reports annually. The rulings involve certain provisions for small refiners to average, bank and trade gasoline sulfur baselines for credit with foreign refiners.

Success using this catalytic converter technology dramatically decreases ICE pollutants. This may have an impact on the allure that electrics have as a "green machine" by lessening the gap between tailpipe and no-tailpipe emissions.

CNG and LNG

Demand increased in the late 1990s for clean-burning compressed natural gas (CNG) and liquid natural gas (LNG) engines. By 1998 there were about 50,000 CNG and LNG vehicles in the United States. Most were in fleet use with about 5 percent being transit buses; a few were consumer vehicles. The transit bus segment is growing; about 22 percent of all new bus orders are for natural gas vehicles. Infrastructure is also growing, with about 1,300 fueling stations from Vermont to California.[26] One-third of these are privately owned and the rest are run by utility companies.

This clean-air alternative is in direct competition to the electric fleet and mass transit markets. It also shows promise for providing an infrastructure for hydrogen fuel-cell vehicles.

Bio-diesel

Bio-diesel fuel is a clear liquid similar to diesel oil, but obtained from plants. Bio-diesel oil may be made from any type of oily vegetation, including seeds from peanut, castor, sunflower, etc. A plant called rape is being used extensively in the United Kingdom to produce this fuel. The crop grown will produce about three tons of seed per hectare, and 30 percent of this will produce oil. Its one possible drawback is the potential for having a harmful effect on natural rubber seals in an engine. This product burns cleanly. It does not produce carbon dioxide or sulfur oxide emissions when burned.

Reformulated Gasoline

Reformulated gasoline (RFG) is a specially processed and blended product, using methanol, ethanol or MTBE. It is intended to reduce the emission of pollutants such as hydrocarbons, carbon monoxide and nitrogen oxides. RFG is estimated to reduce hydrocarbon emissions by 15 percent. There are side effects. The mileage is reduced by 2 to 3 percent, and it may also shorten the life of rubber hoses and seals in the engine. In June 2000 the Environmental Protection Agency (EPA) proposed to make it easier for refiners to use ethanol in cleaner-burning gasoline. The use of ethanol reduces the amount of carbon monoxide from the tailpipe. The adjustment would allow refiners to slightly increase the evaporative property of gasoline in exchange for reducing the carbon monoxide level from the tailpipe. The EPA called on Congress to decrease or eliminate the use of MTBE in gasoline, citing that it can render ground water supplies undrinkable if leaked into the soil. Although this solution looked like a promising competitor to the EVs, its impact on the environment is taking it out of the running.

Foreign Oil

At the turn of the 21st century Russia is becoming a major producer and exporter of oil. Oil production is expected to increase and then peak around 2010. Russia also has vast quantities of natural gas in the Arctic region, perhaps as much as one-third of the world's supply. The Caspian Sea is one of the oldest oil production areas in the world, and after the breakup of the Soviet Union, capitalism emerged in Azerbaijan, Kazakhstan and Russia and they began exporting large amounts of oil to the West. This prompted hope in the United States that the West could be less reliant on Middle East oil supplies. This has not happened.

Alternate Energy Sources

In 2002 a Sierra Club press release called for senators to promote the development of solar and wind power, claiming that 20 percent of our energy could come from these sources as early as 2020. They began a radio advertising campaign calling for a forward-looking vision in developing an energy plan that would provide for a cleaner environment using diversified technologies. "We don't have to dig, drill and destroy to meet our energy needs. We need leadership from senators to ensure that our energy policy is clean, safe, and secure."[27]

If electric vehicles become popular, utility companies will be faced with a demand for more electricity to recharge batteries. This concerns environmentalists who monitor emissions from generating plants that use fossil fuels. Currently about 50 percent of the electrical energy generated in the United States is from coal. The problems with coal are varied, on both an environmental and personal health level. The generation process is only about 30 percent efficient. There are also problems with coal miners dying from black lung disease. The federal government has paid out about $35 billion in benefits to miners and their survivors since 1973. Coal-fired plants also cause acid rain, found primarily in the northeastern United States, but also seen in Europe and Asia. Alternatives are being sought to meet increased power demands around the world. Having a clean power source for battery recharging must be in place for the EVs to be a success as an environmentally friendly alternative.

Wind Power

It is predicted that wind-powered turbines placed in the Midwest could provide up to 30 percent of the energy currently produced by coal, without the disease and pollution problems. Currently there are about 12,000 turbines operating in the United States. This could double with a federal investment of $70 billion.[28]

Using wind power to generate electricity is not a new idea. In 1923 A. J. Root, the dean of the American bee industry, constructed two windmills in his backyard to generate electricity for his electric car. He proposed this as a solution for "free" energy for electric vehicles; however, the initial cost was about $1,500. The windmills kept his car fully charged for its regular duty of five or six miles a day, and in addition lit his house.[30] The idea never caught on with the public.

Currently, the largest number of wind turbines in the United States is located in California. The wind farmers lease land from ranchers and sell the electricity to power marketers, electric utilities and government agencies. There are another fifteen states, located primarily in the Midwest, that have wind energy potential higher than California, yet to be developed.

In May 2002, the British Parliament approved the building of Britain's largest wind farm in the Cambrian Mountains to generate electricity for 40,000 homes. The project cost £35 million ($51 million) and has a total of thirty-nine wind-powered turbines. The government had previously pledged to produce 10 percent of Britain's electricity supply from renewable resources by the year 2010. Work on the wind turbines began in the summer of 2002 and the finished product is expected to have a working life of thirty years.

British Petroleum (BP) has invested millions of dollars in "green" technology and declared a profit in its wind business operation in 2001. It

Wind fever — Wasco, Oregon[29]

predicted its solar business would be profitable by 2003. BP's Connect service stations, for electric-vehicle recharging, are partially powered by solar power. BP is also researching fuel cells for cars. To advance its new image in alternate power technologies, British Petroleum is shying away from that name and using BP in advertising to promote itself as "beyond petroleum." Royal Dutch Shell has designated half a billion dollars over the next five years for research and development of wind and solar power. They will also be looking at geothermal, biofuels and hydrogen fuel cells.

Ocean Power

Tidal and wave power are being tested as a positive approach to generating energy without pollution. In the 1970s Japan and England began research on generating electricity using the power of ocean waves. More experimental programs began in the 1980s in Australia and Norway. The two basic designs for wave-powered generating devices are fixed and floating. The fixed device is mounted to the seabed or the shore (cliffs). Some consider the best way of capturing wave power to be the oscillating water column (OWC). It consists of a fixed column filled with air that is compressed when the waves come up to it. The compressed air, as well as the air sucked back by the retreating waves, is forced through turbines that produce electricity. Only a few of these devices have been built. The most successful plant, in Tofteshallen, Norway, was unfortunately blown out to sea in a heavy storm in 1998. Another fixed device, called TAPCHAN, consists of a tapered channel. The channel forces the waves into a narrowing channel, increasing the amplitude of the wave (kinetic energy) and forcing the water up to a reservoir (potential energy). As the water falls by gravity back to the ocean, it is run through a turbine to generate the energy. There are only a limited number of sites for fixed generators. Floating devices that rise and fall with the motion of the waves and generate electricity through the motion are another type of wave power. Cockerell's Raft, one type of floating device, consists of a line of rafts connected to hydraulic pumps that drive turbines to produce energy. Salter Ducks are floating devices connected in a series that bob up and down in the water. The name comes from its creator Steven Salter and the fact that the devices look similar to floating ducks. The ducks are connected by a stiff shaft. The shaft contains hydraulic fluid that drives a pump to produce electricity. These fixed and floating devices have been experimented with since the 1970s.

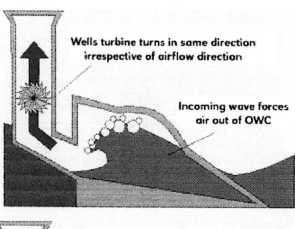

Wells turbine turns in same direction irrespective of airflow direction

Incoming wave forces air out of OWC

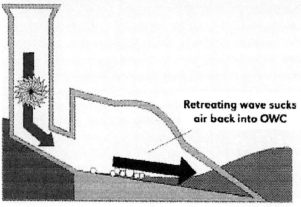

Retreating wave sucks air back into OWC

Wave Power[31]

Tidal power operates by building a barrier across a river estuary, an area where the tide meets the current, to allow the tide to drive turbines to produce electricity. One tidal power station, at Rance in northern France, has operated successfully since 1966. As of 2001, North America's only tidal power plant is located on the Bay of Fundy near Annapolis Royal, Nova Scotia. Powered by 20-foot tides, the plant's turbine produces 30 million kilowatt-hours per year, enough to power 4,500 homes.

Even with the setbacks, tidal and wave power continue to be researched for their clean energy source potential.

Thermal water-based power also holds promise, although it is less cost-effective than the tide and wave models. Ocean Thermal Energy Conversion (OTEC) power plants make use of the difference in water temperature between warm surface waters heated by the sun and colder waters found at ocean depths (about 1,000 meters). A temperature difference of 20°C or more between the warm and cold water is required. A great deal of the electricity generated must be re-used to pump the cold water from the depths to the surface, making the process less efficient.

Tidal and wave power does come with drawbacks. Plants may be damaged by powerful waves and storms. Some tidal power devices that are placed in estuaries may affect the habitat of fish and seabirds. And, generally, due to the tidal currents, many of these devices will produce electricity only about ten hours a day, leaving a fourteen hour gap in which power must be provided by other means.

Although the technology is currently available to build these power plants, the construction costs are high enough to make the electricity produced from them more expensive than traditional energy plants, but, even with the setbacks, research continues. Many environmentalists view wave power as a clean acceptable alternative to land bound sources.

Solar Power

Solar power plants have very little negative impact on the environment, but the drawback is they can only operate efficiently when the sun is shining. At night or during overcast days, backup power generators must be in place. Natural gas is used for the power source during these gaps to maintain consistent service. Solar thermal plants use the heat from the sun to boil water to create steam that is passed through a turbine. The collectors are expensive and the solar industry is working on new technologies to become more efficient.

Nuclear Power

Nuclear energy has perhaps the lowest initial impact on the environment of any energy source because it does not emit harmful gases and requires less area to produce the same amount of electricity as other sources. The nuclear fuel is used to heat water to create steam that is used to turn a turbine to create electricity. The emission-free energy generated by nuclear power plants meets the standards of the 1970 Clean Air Act. The problems with nuclear energy generation are the safety concerns of reactor failure and how to dispose of the nuclear waste by-product. The Nuclear Waste Policy Act of 1982 and its 1987 amendments authorize the Department of Energy to build deep, mined geological sites for the storage of high-level nuclear waste. Although it is a solution, nuclear energy is less favored because it generates extreme potential public safety concerns.

Partnerships

The California Fuel Cell Partnership (CaFCP) is a consortium of automakers, fuel cell makers, energy companies, government agencies and associated partners. Currently, a gas/electric hybrid vehicle will use about $600 worth of gas per 20,000 miles. An SUV will use $2,600 per 20,000 miles and produce four times the amount of pollutants. CaFCP is committed to promoting fuel cell vehicles by advancing new technology, developing alternative fuel infrastructure and educating the public about Alternative Fuel Vehicles (AFVs). One of its near-term goals is to put 40,000 fuel cell vehicles (FCVs) on the road in California by about 2008, as a mark for a viable market entry. Most auto manufacturers are targeting 2003–4 for their FCVs, primarily to be tested in fleet use. They are conducting studies to determine which type of fuel will dominate the new market. Four current alternatives are hydrogen, methanol, ethanol and gasoline. Infrastructure is still the key problem, part of the chicken/egg riddle, with (a) when will the cars be ready and/or (b) when will the fuel be broadly available? Fuel cells powered by gasoline do not require a new infrastructure, but are less friendly to the environment than hydrogen-powered cars. High cost is also a key problem in the present, and this must be offset for FCV marketability. Some of this expense is being absorbed by government agencies to assist the consortium in their program.

The Partnership for New Generation Vehicles (PNGV) has added SUVs to the list of vehicles targeted for improvement. It wants to triple the gas mileage of SUVs and help diminish the impression that SUVs are gas-guzzlers. The PNGV is a longstanding joint research effort between the U.S. government and Ford, General Motors and Daimler/Chrysler. Its research helps increase automobile efficiency through the development of new materials, fuels and propulsion systems. The Daimler/Chrysler merger may also open the program up to participation by other foreign manufacturers.

The Vehicle Recycling Development Center (VRDC) is a joint research project to improve recycling of car parts. It was established in 1996 by Ford, Chrysler and General Motors. Currently, of the ten million vehicles scrapped each year, about 75 percent of the material by weight is being recycled. The VRDC is focusing on the remaining 25 percent of the vehicle not being recycled, consisting primarily of fluids and plastics. Removing fluids can be profitable only if it can be done rapidly. VRDC is promoting an industry standard of design guidelines for fluid caps on all vehicles to aid the fluid removal equipment. Plastics recycling presents a bigger problem, as there may be as many as fourteen different types of plastics used to make just the instrument panel, in addition to a number of different bonding materials. A new method of removing, cleaning and reusing seat foam was developed in 1996. The goal of the project is to take the American automobile, not from cradle to grave, but from cradle to cradle.[32]

In 1998 Toyota announced an alliance with British Petroleum, Enron, United Technologies and Lockheed Martin to address the global warming issue. It was the first automaker to take this step.[33]

Hybrids

Hybrid engines deliver better fuel efficiency and emit fewer pollutants than their ICE counterparts. Vehicles using a hybrid concept generate the power they need from more than one source. How the power is integrated depends on the inventor's and designer's ideas of what makes the most sense. Some use small gasoline motors to generate electricity needed to run the auto and its accessories, while others use a combination of electric and alternate fuel motors or fuel cells to move the vehicle. To provide fast acceleration, for example, both might be used, while in stop-and-go traffic only the electric is needed. Each manufacturer has its concept of what will catch the imagination of consumers and put them in line to buy the product. Regardless of design, this mode of power is a cleaner option both for fuel consumption and air quality.

Two fairly successful hybrid (gasoline-electric) vehicles entered the U.S. market in 2000, the Toyota Prius and the Honda Insight. Toyota has taken an environmental approach, not only to the use of hybrid energy, but also to the product materials themselves. Ninety percent of their Prius is advertised as being built from recyclable materials. The Toyota Prius has been in production and sold in Japan since 1997. Toyota also produces the Estima minivan and Crown luxury sedans that are known as "mild hybrids" in that they use a cheaper and less efficient system. The Estima, introduced in June 2001 in Japan, is a seven-passenger van using a hybrid engine to drive the front wheels. The van's "E-Four" system regulates the drive to the rear wheels and coordinates distribution of electric power to all wheels. Toyota is promoting this vehicle as the world's first electric four-wheel drive system that represents an achievable environmental solution for a cleaner planet. Both Honda and Toyota products rallied enough consumer interest to have competitors consider expanding their offerings, and Toyota and Honda continue developing hybrids as part of the companies' product lines.

Prototype hybrids of limited production among major auto manufacturers show a willingness for the industry to test the market, but none are expecting to have a competitive mass-produced product until late in the first decade of the 21st century. Toyota is also producing the FCHV-5, a fuel cell hybrid vehicle that generates electricity from hydrogen derived from CHF (Clean Hydrogen Fuel), using a reformer. Seen as the next generation liquid fuel, CHF can be produced from crude oil, natural gas or coal and it has low sulfur content. CHF is also used as a fuel for gasoline engine vehicles and can be supplied by current gasoline pumps. The FCHV-5 could be useful where hydrogen supply infrastructure is not available.[34] Honda began producing its natural gas Civic GX in 1998. It was certified as a SULEV, and fleet testing proved the engine reduced the CO_2 emissions by 25 percent compared to an ICE. They rolled out the Civic Hybrid in 2001. Volkswagen tested a new concept vehicle in August 2000 by driving it around the world in eighty days. The Lupo 3L TDI uses a system of Turbo Direct Injection to combine a variable blade turbocharger with electronically controlled pump injector units to deliver a precise amount of a mist of fuel to the three cylinders. The engine shuts off automatically when the car stops and restarts when the accelerator is pressed, and the clutch disengages when coasting. These factors contributed to an average of about 80 mpg. Ford, GM and Daimler/Chrysler announced in January 2001 they would expand their offering of hybrid gasoline-electric powertrains. They showed prototypes of cars with mileage of 70–80 mpg at a Detroit auto show that year. As in the past, having a competitive product seems to always be five to ten years in the future.

The Sierra Club launched a three-year campaign in June 2002 calling for the Big Three automakers to improve the fuel efficiency of their cars. The club maintains that existing technologies could be made more widely available to increase gas mileage in order to cut dependence on foreign oil, save money at the pump and provide a cleaner environment. "The biggest single step we can take to save oil is to make our cars go farther on a gallon of gas. The technology exists to boost fuel economy in our cars and SUVs, saving 42 million gallons of oil a day."[35] The Sierra Club welcomed Honda's newest fuel-saving car, the Civic Hybrid, in December 2001, stating, "As the nation debates national energy security and the need to reduce dependence on oil, Honda's second hybrid vehicle shows how technology can help cut oil consumption, save consumers at the pump, and curb global warming. Honda's new Civic Hybrid, like the Honda Insight, combines attributes of electric and gasoline motors. The Civic Hybrid's highly efficient gas-powered engine, refillable at any gas station, powers the vehicle and also generates electricity for the electric motor, which helps provide power. The Civic additionally captures the energy typically lost in braking, directing it to recharge the batteries. Unlike pure electric vehicles, a hybrid does not need to be plugged in. Because the Civic runs on both gasoline and clean electricity, it achieves fuel economy of 50 mpg and therefore emits much less pollution than other vehicles."[36]

Environmental clubs and organizations are promoting the hybrid vehicles over the battery-only EVs. There is a Web-based car club in Japan (Priusmania) dedicated to the development of the gasoline-electric hybrid car. They are promoting environmentally conscious vehicles and automakers who support these designs, touting the belief that the gasoline-electric vehicles are "the next big thing" because their major advantage is not having to be plugged in to be charged. Many groups in the United States are concentrating on raising fuel economy and making the CAFE standards higher. They want light trucks and SUVs to conform to the same standards as cars. Currently, and for the last twenty-five years, CAFE standards for cars are 27.5 mpg while SUVs and light trucks need to meet only a 20.7 mpg requirement. The Sierra Club estimates that raising this requirement to that of cars would save consumers over $27 billion at the gas pump and reduce the consumption of oil by over one million barrels a day. The Club restates in many of its press releases that the biggest single step to take in saving oil (and gasoline) is to make cars that will go farther on a gallon of gas. They also feel that making a car go farther on a gallon of gasoline will prevent global warming. They claim the SUV is a monument to environmental destruction, mainly due to the fact that they only achieve about twelve miles per gallon. As part of their fuel efficiency campaign for the "Big Three" car manufacturers, the Sierra Club also called for more stringent CAFE standards that would require automakers to produce cleaner cars.

The *New Environmentalist* magazine is promoting hybrid cars in 2002, stating "the gas-electric vehicles offer 1.5 to twice the fuel efficiency of gasoline cars of the same size, cutting carbon dioxide emissions."[37] When the internal combustion engine is running in a hybrid electric vehicle, it emits slightly more pollutants than an electric car, but is far cleaner than a conventional car. "When pollution from the generating sources that charge its batteries is taken into account, an electric vehicle is about one tenth as 'dirty' as a conventional car with a well-tuned engine. An HEV, in comparison, can be about one eighth as polluting."[38]

In 1990 the transportation industry ranked third in energy usage. It is predicted that by 2010 it will be the dominant source of CO_2 emissions in the United States. Citizens with an interest in environmental quality have the power to influence the course manufacturers of our personal transports will take in the marketplace. Hybrids are capturing the market's attention by their practicality in using existing infrastructure while successfully reducing the noxious fumes and pollutants.

EVs have been looked to at various times in history as solutions to noise and air pollution and as a means to decrease dependence on foreign oil supplies, but the electrics have not been able to capture more than a niche in the marketplace. For the environmentalist or conservationist, the electric car is one option that must be viewed in its entirety: Not only "how does the vehicle affect the environment," but also, "how does the generation of electricity impact the earth?" Acceptance by the consumer must also be weighed. Fuel development and power generation are finding inventive alternatives to the traditional EV, but the market continues to be "just around the corner."

4 Technology

"We are at the very beginning of a new era of technology [fuel cells], comparable to the days when Gottlieb Daimler and Karl Benz were constructing the first vehicles powered by internal combustion engines."[1]

"The mechanism of an electric car is so simple that there are really only two things upon which there can be any extensive improvement, i.e., the battery and the motor."[2]

Today, technological innovation is needed for the electric vehicle. The public must have a comparable product in price and performance to move from their treasured internal combustion engine (ICE) automobiles. The excitement of competition is clear. Recent developments in battery recharging are aimed at reducing the time needed to recharge the battery from several hours or overnight to 15–20 minutes. This would still take considerably longer time at a recharging station than filling a tank with gasoline, an inconvenience the consumer might not be willing to accept. The choices are battery-powered, fuel cells or hybrids. The most promising long-term solution for a fully electric vehicle is the use of fuel cell technology. The technology itself is not a motor and not a fuel. It is an efficient, environmentally friendly, cost-effective means for creating the electricity needed to run a motor or series of motors for an electric automobile. Its fuel can be as cheap a product as methanol. Hydrogen fuel cells fit today's focus on clean green energy since the only by-products are heat and water. The ultimate goal is to have zero emission vehicles on the road, but until the technology is perfected, hybrids, using electric motors enhanced by small clean burning gasoline engines will probably be the best interim answer to pollution problems and the most marketable to the auto-buying public.

The deregulation of the energy market in the United States and Europe is another major factor in the technology development. As with the expansion of the oil industry in the early 1900s, deregulation of the energy industry has the potential for providing incentives to advance a next generation in the electric automotive industry. As of June 2000, twenty-four states have deregulation laws on the books, and the rest are considering legislation. This will increase the competitive focus for residential fuel cells making it possible to use them commercially by 2003–5. This deregulation will substantially increase the potential for competitive development of new technologies to provide low emission energy at a low cost for both the automotive and residential sectors. Observe the choices now available in the telecommunications industry after deregulation and envision the same happening in the energy industry. The energy industry is in its infancy learning about being competitive, but it is learning rapidly how to survive and thrive in a deregulated environment.

The evolution in technology to provide energy to a non-conventional vehicle is moving ahead. Inventions in batteries, fuel cells and hybrid vehicles are all options being considered and researched to create the energy needed to run an efficient, convenient automobile. The necessary advancements in these technologies will determine whether mass production is feasible and whether a vehicle with comparable performance can be produced at a competitive price. If it can, will the public accept it as a replacement for the internal combustion engine (ICE)? In May 2002 an article in *AutoWeek* stated that "automakers are in agreement in one thing: electric vehicles powered by hydrogen fuel cells represent the best hope for the long-term survival of the automobile."[3] The present argument concerns the source of the hydrogen to use to power the fuel cells. It could come from natural gas, gasoline or a solid state. Once again the problem is that a convenient infrastructure does not exist to get the fuel on board. Building a hydrogen infrastructure, it is estimated, could take ten years or more at the cost in excess of $100 billion. Alternatives are being explored. Some manufacturers are working on a hydrogen supply from on-board reformers that would convert methanol into hydrogen. Currently, these are very complex and heavy. John Wallace, executive director of Ford's alternative fuel vehicle Th!nk division, says, "It's just another layer of difficulty that no one needs."[4] The Ztec Corporation in Woburn, Massachusetts, is developing another option. It is an electric-powered hydrogen generator that could be installed in a filling station's service bay. The generator would vaporize gasoline, mix it with steam, and then pass the mixture over a catalyst stripping hydrogen from the blend. The by-products of carbon dioxide and carbon monoxide would be collected for later disposal.[5] The Big Three manufacturers see market potential and are putting resources into research and development of fuel cells. They have vowed to have cars powered by that technology on the road by 2004.

The automotive industry is at the beginning of a generational shift, a sea change that will eliminate the reliance on the standard internal combustion engine. Through this technology-driven change we may soon see an analogy to Moore's law (that computer chips will double in speed every year) in the battery and fuel cell industry. "There is an enormous backlog of innovative ideas in the technology development area."[6] There is a budding development of interest in new possibilities for generating power in the energy industry that has been lagging until now. The technology that is being created today points to solutions that will allow automobile manufacturers to produce an environmentally friendly electric vehicle that is better than the conventional technology currently used in the internal combustion engine, and at a competitive price.

Early Developments

France and England were the first to develop electric vehicles in the late 1800s. The United States joined in 1895, and in 1897 the first commercial fleet of electric vehicles appeared as taxis in New York City. Electric vehicles outsold all other types in 1899 and 1900. This would be the peak of their popularity to this point in history. Part of the reason for this popularity was that the only good roads at the time were in towns. Since the range of the electric vehicle was limited, it was a perfect choice for local commuting in cities on both sides of the Atlantic.

From 1894 to about 1900, battery technology made great strides and looked like it had a promising future with the electric cars. Total electricity production increased and battery production flourished. Technological improvements increased battery life and the durability needed to withstand the rough roads.[7] Early battery technology blossomed in about 1895 when storage batteries became more efficient and consistent. By that time, the Electric Storage Battery Company had "obtained all battery-related rights, patents, and licenses formerly controlled by Consolidated Electric Storage, General Electric, Brush Electric and Electric Launch and Navigation."[8] Electrics had the promise of a reliable power source.

As the steam, internal combustion gasoline-powered, and electric cars vied for dominance, each moved forward its their own technological advances, trying to gain market share. In 1895 one-third of all vehicles registered in Michigan were steam-powered, one-third were electric and one-third were gasoline-powered. While the electric and steam-powered vehicles were superior from a maintenance standpoint with fewer parts to repair, they suffered from short range and inconvenient refueling/recharging stations. Although strides had been made in battery technology, the technology development was not sufficient to place the electric automobile in the marketplace lead. Electric automobiles were more expensive to buy and maintain than steam, or gasoline-powered cars. The initial prices for the electric car ranged from $1,250 to $3,500, while gasoline-powered automobiles were $1,000 to $2,000 and steam cars sold for $650 to $1,500. Operating expenses for the electrics averaged $0.02/mile compared with $0.01/mile for the steam or gasoline vehicles. The range of the electrics was only twenty miles and charging stations were not readily available.[9] Increasing range would require improvement in the batteries used to provide energy, a challenge to the inventors of the 1900s, and one that would increase the chances of the electric vehicle competing against the ICE.

The electric utility industry was also expanding at this time. Chicago Edison was busy acquiring every small, local generating station it could afford. By 1898 it had a monopoly. Unfortunately for the EV, most of the Chicago utility company's efforts were spent on advertising the spread of modern electric service (light bulbs and signs) and had little impact on the advancement of sales of the electric vehicle.[10]

The power system of an electric vehicle consists of two components: the motor that provides the power and the controller that provides the application of that power. The motor converts electrical energy into mechanical energy while the controller regulates the energy flow from the battery. The motor may produce alternating current (AC) or direct current (DC). If DC, the controller converts it to AC. If the motor is reversed, the controller converts this action into a generator to recharge the battery. The controller

Automatic recharging electric vehicle, circa 1900[11]

can also be used to regulate regenerative braking to recharge the battery. This discovery came in 1900 when manufacturers began looking at ways for recharging batteries while the automobile was in motion. The concept was successful in the 1900 Waverley, for example, which used a braking system based on this bi-directional controller concept. The battery actually charged as the driver was applying the brakes. The motor used was the invention of J. C. Lincoln of Cleveland, Ohio, and was manufactured by the Lincoln Electric Company. It allowed the driver descending a hill to replace the current used in ascending it.

By 1912 there were many improvements in electric vehicles that prompted people to once again believe the electric would find far greater favor as the advantages became more well known and appreciated. The technology had made the electric car the easiest to control with no shifting of gears and no clutch. Starting the car was no more effort than turning a key. There was no noise or vibration, which led to longer life of the machinery and tires. Once again it was realized that

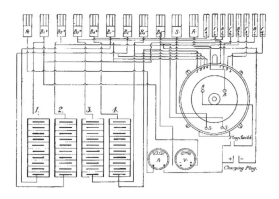

Diagram of controller circuits of recharging motor[12]

Knife-blade controller, 1911

Interior, 1911

the mechanism of the electric car was so simple that there were only two things upon which improvement could be made, the battery and the motor. The *Scientific American* touted Thomas A. Edison as a genius in bringing out the nickel-iron storage battery. The new battery was just half the weight of the lead battery and was said to increase the range from sixty-five up to one hundred miles.[13] One more improvement of note was the conversion of the transmission of power to the wheels from a chain drive to a shaft drive system.

Chassis, 1911[14]

It was silent and could be enclosed, giving a more finished appearance. One failed invention added two more wheels, with motors attached to all six wheels for greater motive power.

By 1913 there were several forms of the lead-acid battery available that could deliver a daily range of about eighty miles, or sufficient charge to travel about the town or suburbs for three days of ordinary travel. A standard thick plate lead battery was common with a medium or thinner-plate type available for lighter body styles, such as the roadster. The thinner-plate battery allowed a larger number of batteries to be installed in about the same space and for about the same weight as the standard battery. The thin-plate battery gave longer total mileage per charge, and the total life of the battery was about two to three times that of the thick-plate battery. The improved construction of this battery included a positive plate in the shape of a pencil. Installation of this new battery added about $120 to the overall cost of the vehicle. The additional expense could be justified, since the plates shed very little active material and internal cleaning was seldom required, making it more economical to operate. The nickel-iron type battery was another choice. This battery increased the cost of a car by about $600. The added initial price could be offset by reduced maintenance. There was no plate renewal needed and internal cleaning of the battery was unnecessary. The only maintenance required was adding distilled water to keep the electrolyte fluid level above the top of the plate.[15]

Ways for providing interchangeable battery systems for electric cars were being explored again around 1914. The Klingelsmith Electric Truck Company of Chicago, Illinois, devised a system of quickly replacing discharged batteries with charged storage batteries. The batteries were carried to the vehicles on small transfer rail cars. The company proposed that all service stations should own the batteries, relieving the owner of the car of that investment. They estimated that the cost to the driver for fresh batteries and some service offerings would be about half as much as maintaining the batteries themselves. A Chicago agent of the Milburn Electric Car Company developed a battery and rental exchange program in 1917. Harry Salvat, owner of the Fashion Automobile Stations, offered to sell a Milburn car for $1,485 minus the battery. The battery would be rented for $15 a month with a one dollar fee for a change. The exchange could be made at any of five stations located in the Chicago area and would take only two minutes, less time than it took to fill a gasoline tank. The company promoted its idea as relieving the car owners of the time and investment in batteries.

Battery History

Alessandro Volta invented the first battery in 1800 when he generated an electrical current from chemical reactions between dissimilar metals. "The original voltaic pile used zinc and silver disks and a separator consisting of a porous nonconducting material saturated with sea water."[16]

Milburn notice, 1917 (ad)

Raymond Gaston Plante invented the lead-acid battery in 1860 when he rolled up a combination of thin lead and rubber sheets and immersed it in a dilute sulfuric acid solution. In the 1880s, the efficiency was improved by creating a paste of lead oxides for the positive plate active materials. In the 1960s, German researchers developed a gelled-electrolyte lead-acid battery to help eliminate electrolyte leakage. The two batteries most frequently used in the electric automobiles were a lead pasted battery that contained elements of lead, peroxide of lead, and sulphuric acid, and the Edison battery, containing iron, nickel and an alkaline solution.

Battery weight challenged the industry. The problem was being approached as early as 1899. A *Scientific American* article stated, "The factor of weight is one of the features in an electric vehicle that practical men are working to overcome, and it is said that whenever a storage

Edison 4-plate
battery cell[17]

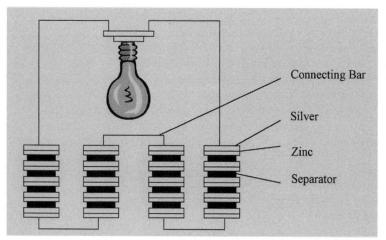

Connecting Bar

Silver

Zinc

Separator

Voltaic pile

battery or a system of storing the electric current is invented by which the weight of the battery is greatly reduced, there is certain to be an impetus given to the electric motor vehicle industry such as has never been thought of."[18] The Willard storage cell was one common system of the day consisting of forty-four batteries measuring $3 \times 5 \times 9$ inches and weighing 950 pounds. Recharging took about two hours. Other designers continued to experiment with new configurations to counteract the battery weight.

A major design obstacle in using batteries is finding the balance between the weight of the battery and the need for a large number of batteries on board to provide performance and range. The problem of large and heavy batteries was partly solved in battery-powered automobiles by redistributing weight. In 1901, to combat the weight of the battery, M. Krieger designed an electric automobile using the two-place "electrolette machine."[19] This system consisted of a gasoline motor, an electric generator and two electric motors. The energy developed by the gasoline motor was delivered to the driving wheels electrically, not mechanically. The front wheels turn at the end of a spur gear, each being independently driven by a separate electric motor. The motors represented only 220 pounds of the total weight of 1,700 pounds for the vehicle. The batteries were Fulmen type having a total weight of only 800 pounds and a range of sixty-five miles on a single charge. The Fulmen battery design was a variation on the original grid type lead-battery plate and used friction to hold the active material in place on the grid. This prevented the lead coating on the plate from "falling off" to the bottom of the battery and causing a short. This design improved battery life, especially against the physical jolts suffered in on-road use. The concept is still in use today. The speed of the Krieger on an average level grade was about 21 mph. Braking was accomplished by short-circuiting the motors.

The 1900 Waverley incorporated a recharging motor for its electric car. By continuing to run the motor downhill instead of immediately applying the brakes, the motor continues to increase in speed "until the counter electromotive force of the armature equals that of the battery, which would be 80 volts with the controller on the third position or notch. At this point the motor will take no current and ... if the speed increases ... will generate a current in the

Krieger electric, 1901[20]

opposite direction."[21] The inventor claimed this process would provide from 20 to 40 percent greater distance of travel than the conventional wound motor.

Current Battery Technology

Dramatic improvement in battery technology is still needed if the industry is to develop a marketable electric car. The consumers' acceptance of the electric vehicle depends upon the manufacturer's ability to provide the range, durability, performance and convenient recharging that consumers expect from conventional automobiles. The battery is the single biggest obstacle to the development of an efficient electric car. The battery is the most critical component of fulfilling the dream of an electric vehicle revolution. Unless this technology improves, we are stuck with the same roadblocks as in the early 1900s, cost and convenience.

The Department of Energy (DOE) spent $7 million on advanced battery research in 1976 and increased that to $12.5 million in 1977. The U.S. Postal Service had 350 EVs in operation in 1976 and was slated to purchase 750 more in 1978. In 1978 the Lead Industries Association claimed the lead-acid battery to be the "only viable power source for electric vehicles for the present and near-term future."[22] Partially because of this attitude, almost all research concentrated on boosting the lead-acid battery's performance. The DOE, in a joint project with Argonne National Laboratory, called for the purchase of several hundred electric vehicles with improved batteries by 1979 and for a further 5,000 additional electric vehicles with more improved batteries by 1984. The DOE estimated

	Specific Energy (Wh/kg)	Energy Density (Wh/kg)	Specific Power (W/kg)	Cycle Life	Range (Miles)	Recharge Time (Hours)	Energy Efficiency (%)	Recyclability of Materials (%)
Present Lead-Acid	33	30	130	400	60	8 to 17 hours	65	97
Horizon Lead-Acid	42	93 Wh/L	240	800	100	< 5 hours	na	100
Nickel-Cadmium	57	56	200	2000	120	8 hours	65	99
Nickel-Iron	55	50	100	2000	110	4 to 8 hours	60	99
Nickel-Metal Hydride	70	80	250	600	250	< 6 hours	90	90
Lithium-Ion	100	100	300	1200	195	< 3 hours	na	50

Energy storage devices[23]

that people would buy an electric car if it had a range of eighty-eight miles. The lead-acid battery of the day was getting a range of only about forty miles. Zinc-nickel batteries were smaller and lighter, but cost-prohibitive.

In 1991 Arizona Public Service and Southern California Edison sponsored a new type of battery, a bipolar zinc-air unit. This battery was shown to produce eight times the energy of a lead-acid battery. The system uses oxygen from the atmosphere to combine with a zinc paste and a catalyst to produce electricity. The manufacturer, DEMI, claims a twelve-minute "flash" charge will produce a range of forty miles at thirty miles per hour, while a one-hour charge will give a range of one hundred miles. Honda used the bipolar zinc-air battery in its CRX EV to win the first electric vehicle race in Phoenix with an average speed of sixty-two miles per hour for 108 miles.

In 1996 the United States Advanced Battery Consortium (USABC) awarded seven contracts to research companies to develop mid-term and long-term solutions for the electric vehicle. Looking to physics for an answer, lithium is the lightest metal on the periodic table. Research began to explore the possibilities of a lithium polymer battery (LPB) with a five-layer design consisting of an insulator, lithium fuel (anode), solid electrolyte, cathode and a metal-foil current collector. The current focus of the USABC and the Department of Energy (DOE) is on nickel metal hydride (NiMH) and lithium-ion (Li-Ion) batteries. NiMH batteries have the immediate advantage, offering increased range, but the Li-Ion may take the long-term command in the marketplace. Li-Ion batteries are a solid-state technology that uses carbon as the anode and shuttles lithium back and forth in ion form between the carbon and a metal oxide. Lithium is also recyclable. Each design holds promise as an electric car power source.

NiMH batteries use a metal-hydride electrode that has a theoretical capacity approximately 20–40 percent higher than the equivalent cadmium electrode in a nickel-cadmium battery. From 1991 to 1996, the NiMH battery evolved from small cells used in consumer electronics to larger units capable of powering an EV. It is projected that the next stage of nickel metal hydride batteries will be more cost effective and last the life of the car.

Lithium-Ion (Li-Ion) batteries are currently popular for portable electronics like video cameras and laptop computers, but are being ramped up for electric vehicles. The cost is very high, but they offer longer range and have a long life cycle. The advantage of the Li-Ion battery is light weight and small size. The current technology allows cells to be constructed with thin films 100 micrometers thick. The resulting battery is still too large for commercial use in an automobile, but may be a strong contender if the evolution of its technology mirrors the size reduction seen in the evolution of the computer microprocessor.

Fuel Cell History

In 1802 an English chemist, Sir Humphrey Davy, built a fuel cell that used carbon electrodes and nitric-acid electrolyte.[24] This was the first fuel cell. In 1839, British scientist Sir William Grove discovered that when combining hydrogen and oxygen electronically to form water, you get by-products of heat and electricity. In 1894 Wilhelm Ostwald, a German chemist, foresaw the dangers of pollution caused by internal combustion engines and stressed the importance of using an electro-chemical process to provide energy. The process was not fully understood at the time and his strategy was not pursued. Fuel cell research surfaced again in the 1930s and '40s, but results produced too little power to be practical for vehicles or utilities. It was not until research completed by NASA for the Apollo space missions that fuel cell technology resurfaced as viable for automotive applications. The phosphoric-acid fuel cells showed excellent prospects for better efficiency at lower cost. In the 1960s Karl Kordesch, of Union Carbide, combined a six kilowatt (kw) alkaline fuel cell with storage batteries to provide greater power and a longer range for electric vehicles. This hybrid concept would be revisited at the Los Alamos laboratory in the late 1970s using a phosphoric-acid electrolyte fuel cell and battery. The hybrid produced a vehicle where the fuel cell provided a steady speed of 55 mph and the battery provided brisk acceleration.[25] The problem since the turn of the century has been that although fuel cell generators are less expensive and more efficient than battery operated units, the fuel cells created to do this are large and expensive.

The current focus by companies such as Ballard, Plug Power, Fuel Cell Energy, Inc., and International Fuel Cells (IFC) is to make these fuel cells small and inexpensive. Ballard Power Systems is the leader in developing the proton exchange membrane (PEM) fuel cell technology, making alliances to develop fuel cell stacks that cost less, are smaller and weigh less. They are developing an oxygen enrichment system and a hydrogen purification system to increase high performance and contribute to cost effectiveness. The Ballard concept consists of a membrane electrode assembly placed between two flow-field plates. The membrane electrode assembly has two electrodes, an anode and a cathode separated by a solid polymer membrane electrolyte. Hydrogen is broken into free electrons and protons. The electrons are used to create electrical current and the protons combine with oxygen to create water and heat. The last decade has shown a great reduction in cost and could make household use a possibility soon. The advantage of a fuel cell over a battery is that while batteries eventually lose potency, fuel cells keep producing power as long as the fuel and oxidant supplies are maintained. The industry as a whole is progressing from creating these new technologies first for industrial buildings, then for residential homes and next to automobiles and computers.

Fuel Cell Technology

Like the battery, a fuel cell is an electrochemical engine. The fuel is fed in, but not burned, as in an internal combustion engine. Instead, it fuel and air reacts electrochemically in a clean environment. Fuels that can be used in this process include hydrogen, methanol, ethanol, natural gas and liquefied petroleum gas. It could also include energy from biomass, wind and solar sources. Biochemists are developing a method of harvesting hydrogen from algae. The algae is first grown in a standard medium, then sulfur is removed from the mix and hydrogen is produced. Currently this method is operating only on a small scale. Wind and solar power are also providing only small amounts of hydrogen until demand becomes higher or the costs go down. The market and developing technology is so diverse that none of these hydrogen-producing methods have emerged as a single winner. Availability is not a problem with other hydrogen sources, but each has its drawbacks. Methanol reformation plants produced a world glut of the product in 2001.[26] Petroleum reformers are not as efficient because the gasoline molecule carbon bonds take a lot more energy to break apart. Petrol reformers therefore need to run at high temperatures, while methanol reformers can operate at about one-third of that temperature. Fuel cells powered by methanol use a chemical reactor, a reformer, to release the hydrogen. The process has a small amount of carbon dioxide as a by-product. As the inventors scale down from large facilities to auto-size fuel cells, they also face another problem — the smaller the reformer, the more carbon dioxide it releases. An argument for gasoline, of course, is that it is already in place and no new infrastructure is needed. Probably the best advantage fuel cells have is that they are about twice as efficient as the internal combustion engine, converting about 30 percent of their fuel into useful energy.

The industry is concentrating on three types of fuel cell technology today — molten carbonate, PEM and solid oxide.

- Molten carbonate is a high temperature fuel cell technology available in the 1990s and has a market of large buildings, like hospitals, malls or universities. The fuel cells use nickel-based electrodes to convert (or reform) fuel into electricity inside (internal reformer) the fuel stacks. They are called a Direct Fuel Cell (DFC). DFCs are more efficient than external fuel cell systems. The cells produce electricity with heat as a by-product. The heat can provide for the heating needs of large buildings. One example of this application is a 200 kw fuel cell plant in Hamburg, Germany, that was a result of a partnership between the German electric and natural gas industries. Since the by-products are water and carbon dioxide, it is clean enough to exist next to residential areas and supply additional heat to a nearby apartment building. This shows the potential for fuel cell technology to be cost effective and environmentally sound.

- PEM is a proton exchange membrane fuel cell that operates at low temperature and is a good model for uses under one megawatt, such as automobiles and possibly cell phones and small stationary power plants or portable generators. The PEM fuel cell consists of the membrane electrode assembly and two flow-field plates. Hydrogen flows through a flow-field plate, while oxygen from the air flows through the other plate, attracting the hydrogen protons through the PEM. This electrochemical process produces electricity, with water and heat as by-products. Fuel cells are similar to batteries. They produce electricity from an electro-chemical reaction and use the electricity to power an electric motor. Unlike the battery that uses up the chemical reactants during the reaction and must be recharged or discarded, a fuel cell stores the reactants externally, so it will keep producing electricity as long as fuel (hydrogen) is delivered to the fuel cell. This allows a fuel cell vehicle to be refueled instead of recharged. The main drawback of the PEM fuel cell is that it requires an external hydrogen reformer and therefore a new hydrogen infrastructure. One possibility in PEM technology might see the consumer buying a tank of hydrogen (like we now buy propane) instead of gasoline at the pump. While hydrogen or methanol would require a new infrastructure, extracting hydrogen from natural gas could build on an existing service. Natural gas, because of its availability, is the best choice for a hydrogen source, as it is mostly methane and has four hydrogen atoms for every carbon atom. The initial disadvantage of natural gas is that it takes up a lot of space, even when compressed or liquefied, but a product made by the Energy Conversion Devices Co. in Detroit in 2000 is providing the technology breakthrough needed here. It is a solid form of natural gas known as metal hydride. It can provide a tank of energy about the same size as an average tank of gasoline. Hydride powder can be produced and sold as a replaceable sealed canister to be inserted at the bottom of the fuel cell stack. Just add water to the top of the stack to activate. Though natural gas is currently only available at some gas stations, it is widely on sale and could be made conveniently available. Will the consumer see this alternate fuel as acceptable?

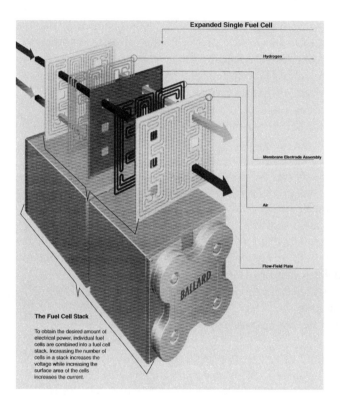

The Ballard Mark 900 Series fuel cell[27]

In another advance in PEM technology, QuestAir, in a joint venture with Ballard, is currently developing a proprietary revolutionary pressure swing adsorption technology that separates and enriches selected hydrogen/oxygen gas streams making the process more effective. This will have uses in many applications beyond fuel cells, such as industrial gas applications, diesel emissions reduction, and medical oxygen devices.

In 2000, solid hydrogen storage was being considered by some companies as the key to commercializing fuel cell electric vehicles (FCEVs). It is stored in a safe, solid compound container at low pressure. The technology has increased the limit of two grams of hydrogen per one hundred grams of hydride to seven grams of hydrogen per one hundred grams of hydride. A typical fill up would require only three to four minutes. Hydrogen gas inserted into the container absorbs into the interface regions of the metallic powder and the molecules dissociate into individual hydrogen atoms forming a metal hydride. Adding heat releases the hydrogen atoms to reform into molecules. The resulting pure hydrogen gas can then be fed into a fuel cell to produce the energy to power the vehicle. In September 2000, GM, in collaboration with ExxonMobil, announced they had developed a unit that would generate hydrogen from gasoline. GM claimed an efficiency of 80 percent and predicted a gasoline processor fuel cell car could be delivered to the consumer within ten years.

• Solid Oxide is the next generation to be developed, within five to ten years, and uses heat to produce hydrogen for the fuel cell. This fuel cell uses a coated zirconia ceramic electrolyte as an internal reformer. The electrochemical conversion process produces electricity, with a large amount of heat as a by-product. Mass production of this type of fuel cell is faced with a number of basic manufacturing challenges that are being studied. An advantage to this technology is that it will not require a separate hydrogen infrastructure. A faction of the environmental community is emphatically promoting the development of this last type of fuel cell technology.[28]

In an ideal green environment, the hydrogen for the PEM fuel cell would be produced directly by the electrolysis of water, using electricity generated from a renewable source. This is not presently economical. The alternative is to extract the hydrogen from fossil fuels using the reformer, realizing that some carbon dioxide will reach the environment.

The by-products of fuel cells are water and large amounts of heat. The Modine Manufacturing Co., Racine, Wisconsin, specializes in heat transfer. They have created a fuel cell products group to develop heat exchangers for the PEM technology to assist in production of heat cell engines. GM began developing a catalytic converter in 2000 that generates hydrogen directly from gasoline. It still creates carbon dioxide as a by-product but is 50 percent cleaner than the conventional ICE. The positive aspect is that no new infrastructure is needed as gas stations are already in place. GM wants to have a car ready and using this concept by 2004. Fuel cells follow the tradition of a "green" machine.

People want home energy to be cheap and reliable. The same goes for cars, but powering an automobile by fuel cells is much more complicated than producing a home generator. Fuel analysts' opinions vary in their predictions for the use of PEM fuel cells in automobiles. Some analysts claim it may be ten years before a reliable fuel cell automobile will be available. (General Electric owns 12 percent of Plug Power and Ford and Daimler/Chrysler own 32 percent of Ballard.) Other analysts predict PEM fuel cells will dominate the automotive market with an 80 percent share by 2010. Skeptics imply GM is not really interested in developing an EV because of its links to "Big Oil" companies. Enron, before its demise, invested in Fuel Cell Energy, Inc., to accelerate the commercialization of fuel cell products.

In March 2000 Purdue University started experimenting with another possible power source. It is a fuel cell that runs on chemical reactions between hydrogen peroxide and aluminum. The hydrogen peroxide works as a "catholyte" with the properties of both an electrolyte (a liquid that conducts electricity) and a cathode (the part of a battery that attracts electrons). The current disadvantage is the time it takes to provide a steady current flow.

> Fuel cell vehicles have many advantages, including zero emissions, quiet operation, long range and unparalleled energy efficiency. Perhaps most compelling of all, though, is that they might realize the elusive dream of solar hydrogen. Fuel cells that run on methanol, natural gas or petroleum would dramatically reduce pollution and cut green house gas emissions and energy consumption at least by half. But, solar hydrogen would push the fuel cell one giant step further — to a future that would come close to being environmentally benign. No other transportation technology or fuel holds the same promise.[29]

The California Fuel Cell Partnership, founded in April 1999, is an alliance of automakers, fuel cell distributors and manufacturers, government and transit agencies and fueling companies dedicated to developing environmentally friendly vehicles. Its automotive partners include Honda, Daimler/Chrysler, Volkswagen (joined in October 1999), Ford, Nissan and Hyundai. Daimler/Chrysler introduced its Necar 4 vehicle in March 2000, using liquid hydrogen to power a PEM fuel cell. It can go 90 mph for 280 miles. Toyota introduced its Prius (hybrid) in the U.S. in June 2000. In December 1999, Ford ordered $4.5 million worth of fuel cells from Ballard Power Systems to integrate into its engines. In May 2002 Nissan confirmed a $2 million order of the Mark 902 series fuel cell from Ballard. Daimler/Chrysler is also directing its efforts toward public transportation. It is building a fleet of buses powered by fuel cells and predicts them to be available in 2004. Volkswagen demonstrated its Jetta (called the Bora HyMotion in Europe) ZEM sedan during the California Fuel Cell Partnership meeting in November 2001. The car's fuel cell engine is most efficient when operating at mid-throttle, the range used during most normal driving. It has a range of about 350 kilometers and accelerates from 0 to 100 km/h in 12.6 seconds. [30]

The hydrogen-powered fuel cell is a true zero emission vehicle product. There are no air pollutants and the only by-product is water. Electric vehicles with a range and speed comparable to current internal combustion engines, driven by a hydrogen-powered fuel cell, would be a true competitor.

Hybrid Vehicles

One of the first hybrid vehicles was the 1902 French Lohner-Porsche Electric automobile, which combined electric and gasoline motors. It eliminated the inconvenience of battery recharging. Similar to the Krieger automobile, the electric motors were mounted on the wheels and the armature was part of the hub. It provided 12 hp and had a range of seventy-five miles.

Two other examples of early hybrid vehicles are the 1904 Krieger and the 1902 Columbia.

Hybrid vehicles are coming to market a little sooner than the fuel cell vehicle. Most automakers believe the immediate practical answer to the demand for a car that is environmentally sensible is the hybrid gasoline-electric vehicle, with the fuel cell vehicles soon to follow. However, future hybrids could also include a combination of fuel cells and batteries. Ballard predicted a fuel cell bus line in 2002 and fuel cell cars by 2003–5. Hybrid drive system technology is likely to take a significant market share sooner than electric vehicles because the technology is already on the road in the form of the Toyota Prius and Honda Insight and Civic, and the infrastructure is already in place. Toyota's hybrid

Lohner-Porsche coupe, 1902[31]

vehicle Prius was introduced in Japan in November 1997 and was being marketed in the United States by mid–2000. The Toyota Prius was the world's first mass-produced gasoline-electric hybrid car. The electric motor starts acceleration and the gasoline-run engine kicks in at higher speeds. Performance is comparable to conventional vehicles and it gets up to 70 mpg. The key to the Toyota system is a power-split transmission that constantly varies the amount of power supplied by the engine to either the wheels or the generator. Emissions are halved, with toxic gases cut by 90 percent. In addition, like the cars of the early 1900s, when going uphill, the battery and electric motor join the gasoline engine to provide more power. When going downhill, the wheels are turning the motor, which is charging the battery. The problem is its price. Toyota is losing over $20,000 per vehicle; selling it for $20,000 while it costs $41,000 to build. The Honda Insight, another gasoline-electric hybrid, began selling in the United States in early 2000. The Insight

Columbia hybrid automobile, 1902[33]

Krieger tonneau, 1904[32]

gets up to 73 mpg, and like its predecessors does not require external charging. The electric motor assists when more power is needed. It uses nickel metal hydride (NiMH) batteries, which are recharged by regenerative braking. When you take your foot off the accelerator, the motor becomes a generator, similar to the 1901 concept used by the Waverley and the Krieger. Another similar concept is that the energy spent climbing uphill

Toyota hybrid dash information display panel[34]

is recovered going downhill. Demand was so high for the Insight that the average dealer in year 2000 was getting only one car every two months.

Hybrid vehicles' primary attractions are that they solve the problem of extending range and don't require special fuels or a need to plug into an electric source. This is an important factor for a transition vehicle from the internal combustion engine to the ZEV. They offer a solution of less pollution and less usage of natural resources, right now, today, registering 70 mpg. However, there is a marketing issue: most Americans still think the battery in hybrid vehicles must be plugged in to be recharged.

The disadvantage of the hybrid vehicle is that two systems are more complex, requiring a higher degree of technical expertise to repair if problems arise, but technology in many areas of manufacturing has become more complex. As the 21st century begins, complex computers and mechanical operations are prevalent in our homes, our appliances and our manufacturing processes. The reappearance of the hybrid fits with this more intricate technological trend.

Toyota's Prius is a good example of a smooth transition from one energy source to another, with test drivers reporting that the switch between the electric and gasoline power is a non-event for the driver. This is important because acceptance in the marketplace relies on performance as well as cost and convenience.

Toyota also introduced a hydrogen-fuel-cell-powered Highlander car called FCHV-4 in mid–2000. The fuel cell stack replaces the batteries and is based on the same drive train as the Prius. It hopes to be competitive in the fleet market.

The Honda Insight uses an Ultra Low Emission Vehicle (ULEV) gasoline engine with an ultra-compact electric motor. The gasoline engine is the primary source of propulsion. The electric motor assists when additional power is needed. Regenerative braking recharges the NiMH batteries. *AutoWeek*'s year-long road test of the Insight found it to be very drivable and practical. They reported sufficient power. The only complaint was that the heater struggled to maintain a comfortable temperature. Overall, they found it to be a "dependable, fun little car."[37] Honda introduced its Honda Civic hybrid in 2002, hoping to rely on crossover sales. The Honda Civic is the best-selling compact car in America. The hybrid version also uses regenerative braking to charge the batteries and the battery pack itself is guaranteed for eight years or 80,000 miles. The Civic Hybrid has four doors, seats five passengers and has a functioning air conditioner.

Toyota Prius — hybrid technology[35] (David Dewhurst, photographer)

Honda Insight — hybrid technology[36]

In January 2001 GM announced plans for researching specific fuels for its fuel cells. It will concentrate on using hydrogen in the long term and a clean hydrocarbon fuel in the short to medium term for development. GM is working with Toyota and collaborating with Exxon Mobil in this venture.

GM's Precept uses a dual-axle set-up with a 35 kw three-phase electric motor driving the front wheels and a lean-burn compression-ignition gasoline engine driving the rear wheels. GM's Triax is a unique concept car. It has three propulsion options: all-wheel-drive electric, all-wheel-drive hybrid electric or two-wheel-drive internal combustion.

Electric-Only Vehicles Around the Turn of the 21st Century

The world's major automakers are not the only ones to experiment with new technology. Corbin Motors, located in California, is an example of a small company entering the electric car market.[38] Founded by Mike and Tom Corbin in 1999, the company produced the Corbin Sparrow, an electric three wheeled zero emission vehicle.

It is rechargeable in two hours at a 220-volt outlet or six hours at a 110 volt outlet and will travel at 50 mph for a range of fifty miles on one charge. The Sparrow uses lead-acid batteries that are rechargeable for 800 cycles, or about 25,000 miles. Replacement cost of the thirteen-pack battery system is about $1,500. The advantage of electric cars is that they have 100 percent of torque available at 0 rpm for rapid acceleration. The Sparrow does the quarter mile in fifteen seconds at 95 mph.

GM's Saturn division is developing the EV1, an all-electric zero-emission vehicle. It is being advertised for what it doesn't have. No engine, valves, pistons, spark plugs,

Corbin Sparrow

GM EV1 (Gen II)[39]

crankshaft, transmission, starter, clutch, muffler, exhaust or oil changes. It is being called a two-passenger sports car that can accelerate from 0 to 50 mph in less than seven seconds. It has a top speed of 80 mph and its range is 80 miles. The car can be recharged in about three hours using a 220-volt/6.6 kilowatt charger. GM's EV1 operates with high capacity lead-acid batteries and has a range of 55–95 miles; nickel-metal hydride batteries increase the range to 75–130 miles. Honda's EV+ uses nickel-metal hydride batteries and provides a range of 90–100 miles. It takes about six to seven hours to charge. The GM and Honda vehicles are available for lease only as the manufacturers want to maintain control over the emerging technology. The lease includes coverage of all maintenance, though there is little to maintain as they do not require a tune-up or oil change and there is no transmission, clutch or water pump. They do, however, have a negative factor — both of these cars require a special recharging station. GM maintains about sixty-five stations in northern California and far more in southern California, while Honda has about thirty. Both will provide free towing, if needed.

Ford's Th!nk City car is a sub-compact battery-powered vehicle designed for urban transportation. It provides acceleration of 0–30 in seven seconds and has a range of fifty-three miles. It was introduced in Norway with a positive response and became available in the United States in 2002. The car was available by lease only, in Southern California, at rate of $212 per month, including taxes. The body is constructed of biodegradable thermoplastic that can be recycled. Southern California Edison provides the lessee with a special meter to attach to the normal house meter to identify power used for recharging the EV. SC Edison charges a much cheaper kilowatt-hour rate for charging the vehicle.

In September 2002 Ford decided to discontinue promotion and production of its Th!nk City car and Th!nk Neighbor car in the United States. About fifty people currently

Ford's Th!nk City Car — battery powered technology[40]

leasing the Th!nk City car organized a protest in San Francisco, probably the first of its kind planned to save an automobile from becoming extinct. Protestors claimed there were many people on waiting lists for the vehicle and that thousands could be sold if some marketing efforts were applied. One spokesman said that every person who owns one has three or four friends who want one. While many of these people may own an SUV, they have disposable incomes high enough to afford an environmentally friendly vehicle for trips around town. Ford said it would continue to support the infrastructure and agreements for the cars already on lease.

Reformulated Gasoline for ICEs

The attraction of electric vehicles' technology has been that they are environmentally friendly clean transportation. Technological changes in fuels for internal combustion engines may have an impact on that current advantage.

Gasolines are being reformulated (RFG). The U.S. Clean Air Act of 1990 required RFG in areas with severe ozone non-attainment status. The actual program began in 1995. The act required that oil companies add oxygenates to gasoline. Oxygenates are additives such as ethanol or ethers such as MTBE. This is an added expense for operating internal combustion engines. A 1999 report from the Wisconsin Department of Natural Resources estimates a loss of about three miles per gallon and an average cost of two cents per gallon more than conventional gasoline. The initial introduction of RFG was met with some negative reports of having a bad smell, giving poor mileage and concern about health problems and possible leaks of MTBE into the ground water. These problems were addressed during the next five years and the public has generally accepted RFG. Phase two began in the summer of 2000. Compared to conventional gasoline, this phase of RFG is reported to reduce toxic emissions by 22 percent, volatile organic compound emissions by 27 percent and nitrogen oxide emissions by 7 percent. The process added approximately an extra two cents per gallon over the phase one RFG. The product has been extensively tested and shows no changes in performance or mileage when compared to the phase one RFG. "The new gasoline cars, for all practical purposes, are zero emitting. It's extraordinary what auto makers have done."[41] This simple adaptation for the internal combustion engine may again prove to give the electric vehicles ominous competition. The Nissan Sentra CA exemplifies the clean-burning ICE competitor.[42] It qualified and received CARB credits for meeting the standards for a super ultra low emission vehicle (SULEV). ICEs are closing the environmental gap.

New Charging Systems

There are two basic types of electric-vehicle chargers: conductive and inductive. The conductive has a metal-on-metal contact with direct flow of electric current between the two contact points. The inductive has two metal connectors separated by a small gap filled by a magnetic field. The electricity used to recharge the battery flows through a magnetic field.

Fast-charging stations can recharge an EV in fifteen minutes or less, doubling or sometimes tripling the daily mileage for the vehicle. This could become a major factor in establishing a charging station infrastructure in the United States. As early as 1995 some charging stations were offering a "short" charge of one hour, using a paddle system that transferred electricity through a magnetic field rather than a metal plug. In November 1997 the Ford Motor Company purchased a fast-charge system produced by AeroVironment called PosiCharge. This would be used to test its fleets of Ford Ranger EVs. The time required for a charge by this device was between six and fifteen minutes.[43] The fast-charge system will recharge a lead-acid battery to 80 percent in less than twenty minutes. The range using this system is about 150 miles. In February 1998 GM announced a new high-speed version of its Magne Charge system. The unit could recharge a lead-acid battery in 7.5 minutes and a nickel-hydride battery in about 10 minutes, and would provide a range of sixty to one hundred miles. The fast charging can allow EV owners to charge their vehicles while having lunch or while on a short shopping trip and increase their range with little inconvenience.

The search for improvements in ways to generate the energy to power our vehicles continues to evolve. Designs for smaller, more efficient motors and engines spark the industry's imagination. The problems in developing new battery technology seem to be the same as those encountered one hundred years ago. If this does not change, new technology will continue to be directed toward developing cleaner-burning ICEs and a variety of hybrid vehicles. This seems to be the most logical next step away from our heavy dependence on foreign oil supplies and toward a cleaner environment.

5 Marketing

"[Of] all the electric runabouts I ever saw, while they were very nice cars, [they] didn't seem to go very fast or very far."[1]

Marketing in general is a matter of knowing when to form alliances, when to believe in yourself, when to go your own way and when to follow advice. Automobiles provide more than a means to go from one place to another. They reflect our ingenuity, give a sense of freedom and express our personalities. The automobile has an emotional aspect tied to our lifestyles that is not associated with other machines, not even our computers. For more than a century the automobile has given a stimulus to our economy and shaped and mirrored our social values.

In the early 1900s many people thought that the electric, steam and gasoline-powered vehicles would share the market equally, each finding its own market space. The ICE won the market early and has retained its popularity through a variety of reasons, including technology, infrastructure and catering to the prospective customer's wants. The EV reflects our social changes. It symbolized women's independence along with the suffrage movement, patriotism during the world wars, and environmental solutions for air and ground pollution. Its market shifts with the social and political climates.

Marketing EVs has posed many challenges. At their inception they fared well in urban areas, but have had difficulty capturing the consumer's attention during an expanding economy. When roads between towns were limited and in poor condition with ruts and mud, travel for the majority of the population was confined to cities. Electric cars provided convenient, reliable transport not requiring a chauffeur. Their performance was adequate. They took less space than a horse and buggy, were quiet and left no tell-tale reminder on the road for the street sweepers, as horse-drawn vehicles did. The short range of the electrics was acceptable for city trips. As roads between cities improved, spurred by a blossoming economy, interest in the electrics declined. The availability of the internal combustion engine cars grew to meet consumer demand. The electrics could not compete with the greater range and speed of the ICEs. The electrics' usefulness returns during times of fuel shortages and increased interest in limiting the environmental impact of ICE emissions. Their potential effectiveness as fleet vehicles for corporate utilities and government operations continues to be examined and tested. Electrics are a possible alternative to what is viewed as a major air pollutant — the carbon monoxide by-product of the ICE. Through their ebb and flow in popularity, electric cars continue to be quiet, clean and easy to operate, but are not convenient or inexpensive enough to capture more than a fraction of the auto market's need for extended mileage and speed. Their reliability, easy maintenance and low environmental impact are major selling points, but their short range and the high cost of batteries are still drawbacks. It seems the pathways to developing an effective electric vehicle are blocked by fundamental limitations of chemistry or physics, and by the limits of our technological capabilities in the development of batteries and fuel cells.[2]

Very few consumers will pay a significant premium just to know they are driving a "clean, green" car that does not pollute the environment. Battery-only electrics must have a competitive price to effectively gain market share. The ICE and hybrids are making great strides in creating an environmentally friendly auto, attacking the EV's major selling point by designing more efficient engines. Marketing the electric vehicle requires greater incentives if it is to compete with the power and range offered by its major competitor, the internal combustion engine.

How did Henry Ford turn the "inferior" internal combustion engine into a viable force?[3] Not with technology, but by using a better business practice. He understood the nature of the market. He knew that bad roads were a problem to be addressed, and incorporated a design that would ride high, over mud and ruts. He felt the machine should be easy to buy and repair by the common man. He perfected the moving assembly line to produce large quantities of vehicles with interchangeable parts. Ford was mass-producing 650 cars per day when Stanley was producing 650 steam cars per year. He sensed the market wanted to settle on one quantity and go with it. As people saw more Fords on the road, they wanted to buy Fords too. The low cost and availability produced a "snowball" effect. Then, discovery of oil in Texas in 1901 made people think they almost had "free" energy and the infrastructure was established. His Ford had won the field.

Finding an effective approach for catching the consumer's eye hasn't been easy for the EV manufacturers. At the turn of the 20th century automobiles fell into two basic categories, "city" cars and "touring" cars. Most automobile owners preferred the romance of the touring car over the practicality of the city car. The city car (electric) became the province of women, doctors and business delivery vehicles. The speedier, more dangerous, complicated and more "masculine" gasoline-powered car took over the market and never looked back. Is the electric car a "real" car? Hans Fogelberg argues that

> The first two decades of the century were ... characterized by converging technology and converging views on what a car was, what it should be able to do, and where and when it should be driven. Thus the range of interpretations (i.e. the degree of interpretative flexibility) of the technology and the use of that technology decreased drastically during a short time period. Simultaneously, the opinions about the "losers," the failed alternatives of steam and electric propulsion, were also cemented, and have since then been fairly consistent. We "know" that lead-acid battery cars do not fulfil [sic] the requirements of a "car." since the notion of the car was integrated and constructed along with gasoline car technology.[4]

He points this out as a consistency since the very early days of marketing to establish the electric as a women's car. This tactic did create some interest, but it was for a limited audience.

Electric vehicles, with the exception of some campaigns in the early 1900s, have struggled to identify and sell to their potential market. There is a perceived difference between men and women in their attitude toward what they want from a vehicle. Men are generally felt to want power, racing, travel and luxury, while women are thought to want reliability, comfort, safety and cleanliness.[5] In 1908 Clara Ford preferred an electric vehicle to Henry's loud, lumbering, backfiring gasoline-powered Model T. "Toys for Big Boys— That's what automobiles still are for many men, and that's why electric cars can't cut the mustard."[6] The earliest automobiles weren't sold on functionality; they were sold on the romance of the open road. People took mass transit to go to work. Since the middle class of that day could afford only one car, the male in that culturally patriarchal structure invariably opted for the touring car, not the car that may have made the most economic sense.[7]

In the early 1900s automobiles for family use were looked at romantically for the freedom and elegance they could provide. It was an era of inventions that freed the homeowner and homemaker. Families were emerging from the Victorian model household to a more egalitarian family life. A strengthening middle class was finding income for luxury items already afforded to the society classes. Women's groups were ardently campaigning for more independence for women, and for women to take advantage of that freedom. Mrs. M. R. W. Harper of New York, interviewed in 1971 at age 104, recalled her early advocacy for women drivers. She credits Henry Ford with "emancipating women."[8]

Advertisers understood these symbols and began to focus on the automobile's image of freedom, romance, refinement and fun rather than its reliability. Advertisers recognized women and physicians as major potential markets for electric vehicles and slanted the ads in their direction. "Milady can seek a shady spot with children or friends until the cool of the evening, then glide swiftly back to the city before the dinner hour, rested by the perfect relaxation that an electric makes possible."[9] "There is no question but that an electric automobile is an advantage to a physician. Capable to the last degree of well-rounded usefulness, an electric meets the social, as well as the professional requirements of the professional man, whose wife and daughter are certain to find it most desirable."[10] Advertisers appealed to the fashion conscious by depicting elegance in their coaches, and the owners' sophistication as they took their car to the theater or park in style.

There was some controversy in

Detroit ad, July 1912[12]

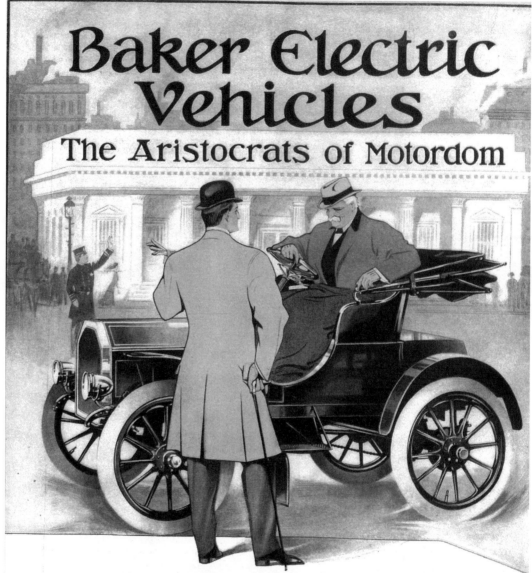

The Baker Electric Runabout has unusual speed and a mileage capacity of one hundred miles. It is swift, noiseless, and easy of control in congested streets.

Baker ad, March 1909[11] (color)

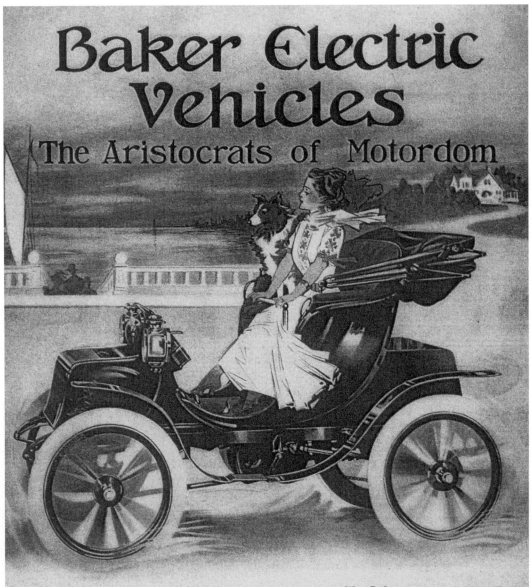

Baker Electric ad, 1909[14]

1906 about automobiles' encouraging the spread of socialism. Automobile ownership, although it began with the upper classes, provided a commonality among the economic classes as more types of automobiles became available and prices became more afford-able. President Woodrow Wilson of Princeton University stated, "Nothing has spread socialistic feelings in this country more than the use of automobiles. To the countryman they are a picture of arrogance of wealth with all its independence and carelessness." The American Automobile Association disagreed and explained that many farmers of the day were buying automobiles for "hard usage."

> Automobiling more than any other sport tends to bridge the poor man with his small runabout into close sympathy and fellowship with the rich man who owns a high powered and expensive machine. If a runabout meets with a mishap on the road the touring car owner does not hesitate to stop and offer such assistance as he can ... In short, a touch of automobiousness makes the whole world kin, and the sport tends more and more to draw the divergent classes together.[14]

Early magazines explored the adventure of electric auto touring. An article in the 1907 *Scientific American Supplement* described a long-distance touring trip with an electric automobile. The travelers started from Cleveland, Ohio, on September 21, 1906, and covered a total of 314 miles to New York. They averaged 13.2 miles per hour. Charging stations along the way were sometimes as close as eleven miles apart. They charged up at a street railway plant, a power and heating company, and regular charging stations. The only real troubles encountered were a flat tire and rain. It began to rain just as they were approaching a hill outside of Erie, Pennsylvania. They waited until the rain was over, but could not climb the hill. The wheels just skidded in the mud. It took them four hours and twenty minutes to cover a forty-four mile stretch. They estimated the car had a range of sixty-two to seventy miles on country roads and were quite satisfied with their experiment.

Touring became very popular by 1907 and many peripheral products were being developed to help the motoring camper. Leather waterproof bags or a steamer trunk could be attached to the deck of the vehicle to carry the necessities of touring, such as a tent, ponchos for rain, and blankets, food and cooking utensils. A speedometer and odometer were recommended equipment, the latter for calculating distances listed in route books, such as "After passing a large red farm house on the left continue straight ahead a mile and a half and keep to right at fork in road."[15] The speedometer was to prevent getting a ticket or being brought before the country justice of the peace at a time when speed limit laws were becoming more common and more severe each year. Many tips about touring could be gained from the publications of the day.

By 1909 electric vehicles were advertised as economical, simple, handsome and free from the complications "which often bewilder the owner of a gasoline car who is not of a mechanical turn of mind."[16] "For park, city and suburban use, the electric is the ideal carriage and will ... remain so, for it is essentially a woman's car."[17] The ads stressed simplicity.

By 1913, manufacturers were expanding their product lines and widening their appeal. EVs came in a wider choice of models. A limousine was the highest-priced model, costing from $3,000 to $5,000. It was claimed to be a direct rival to the gasoline-powered cars and its "debut proves unmistakably that the maker of electrics is going to demonstrate that the electric is not simply a vehicle for women, but a general utility machine."[18]

A brougham model was available in a price range of $2,500 to $3,000 and a roadster model was priced from $2,250 to $2,500. The roadster copied the curved hood of the gasoline car. The feeling at the time was that the electric Roadster could hold its own in competition with the gasoline vehicle for general utility purposes.

Another new concept also appeared on the scene that year to further the sales of electric cars. One of the largest department stores in New York decided to switch from selling gasoline cars to electrics exclusively. Part of the business plan included selling the vehicles on the installment plan. A customer could buy the car on an easy payment plan, including a year's worth of service on the car. It also offered, for a proper price, arrangements to house and care for the car in the garage nearest the purchaser's residence. The company would pay all the garage bills and see that it is "kept in perfect condition, washed, oiled, charged and so on, and to attend to repair work."[19] The agreement included everything but driving the car, and this could also be arranged if the buyer required the services of a chauffeur. The sales floor consisted of a huge area for the "indoor demonstration of the silent-running machines, with little clumps of foliage here and there, like oases in a desert, sheltering dainty tea tables, where the ladies— and their husbands, if they care to come along — will be taken care of while they are being told about the polished cars flitting about on the floor."[20] They were obviously trying to offer and create a pleasant buying experience for the "fair sex" with a plan that would fit most household budgets.

In 1914 Dr. Charles P. Steinmetz gave a glowing report to the Electric Vehicle Association of America. He stated that the "electric vehicle will surely drive the gasoline car from the limited area of service required in town or suburban life. High speed will not be a requirement of the future small electric car, nor will long mileage per charge be necessary. The distances to be covered are too short for the saving in time effected by high speed to be worthwhile. Even the busy physician rarely exceeds 10 miles to 20 miles per day in his rounds. The electric car is superior to the gasoline car in control and is intrinsically more reliable."[21] He strongly advised the central station owners to perceive and take advantage of the electric vehicles. He concluded with a prediction that "within ten years the electric truck is likely to produce a revenue equal to that of the light business and pleasure car."[22] George S. Walker, chief mechanic of the Philadelphia Fire Department, presented a paper to the Electric Vehicle Association titled "Electric Fire Apparatus." He pointed out that numerous tests conducted to compare the horse-driven, gasoline-driven and electric equipment demonstrated the electric to be superior in every fashion. The electric trucks were so reliable they never failed to respond to a call, which was not true of the horse or gasoline equipment. The electric eliminated the offensive odor of horses and gasoline and also reduced the element of fire characteristic of gasoline tractors. Flammability was a major concern for a fire department. The electrics could also be started up and driven off in less time than it would take to crank an engine. This EVA member demonstrated that the electrics had a great deal to offer to the service industries.

In January 1915 there were 25,000 electric passenger cars in use in the United States and over 12,000 commercial vehicles. New York state led the field with 7,455 passenger cars and 2,461 commercial vehicles. Pennsylvania followed with 5,000 passenger cars and 1,000 trucks. When the figures provided by the Electrical Vehicle Association were divided up by cities, they showed that greater New York had 2,850 passenger cars and Chicago had over 2,000, Cleveland 1,800, and Denver nearly 1,000.[23]

Why did the electric car become popular in some cities and not others? Peoria, Illinois, a hilly city with a population of 100,000, had a fairly high number of electric cars in 1917 for several reasons. The successful electric auto dealerships dealt with electric cars only and did not sell gasoline cars; and the Central Illinois Light Company provided cheaper rates for central stations. The local roads were also a factor. Peoria was not a favorable location for touring. Once a car left the smooth paved streets in town, it would encounter roads nearly impassable, turning the joy of touring into anxiety and distress. The town also made storage and maintenance convenient. Three public electric garages were also available for maintaining and housing the EVs, and individual families were building private garages attached to their homes for their pleasure cars. Many prominent families were also buying electric cars, which helped to make them fashionable. The auto dealers and the garages were producing income in the community. The city had 179 private garages that produced an annual income of about $11,000 while the public garages were generating about $3,000 per year. Many families at the time were able to afford two vehicles and bought both an electric and a gasoline car.[24]

World War I created a boom for electric vehicles in Europe. It was estimated in 1914 that the whole of Europe had approximately 3,200 electric vehicles. About 25 percent of the passenger cars in England and about 10 percent of those in France were manufactured in the United States. Commercial electric vehicles were made primarily in Europe. The commercial electric vehicles were developing along highly specialized lines such as taxi cabs, fire trucks and postal vehicles. England had about 150 electric trucks in 1915. Great Britain's Board of Trade removed the embargo tax on American electric vehicles in 1916, allowing for increased sales, especially for commercial vehicles. By 1918 there were about one thousand electric trucks in operation in England with many more on order. The electric vehicle was drafted in the United States to "make the world safe for democracy." Norway and Sweden had a large electric commercial vehicle market, which looked like it would expand after the war. Italy was generating electric power using waterfalls. Australia, Japan, Mexico and France were exporting electric vehicles in large numbers and the future looked very bright. Demand was high.

Motor travel and touring broke all records in the United States in 1917, due partially to the war in Europe. Many motorists, who had spent years touring in Europe, were forced to do their motoring in the United States. "See America First" became the slogan of the day, and many foreigners were pleasantly surprised by the picturesque beauty of the Northeast and the fine hotel services offered. New England, in particular, spent many advertising dollars to promote the good condition of its roads and its beautiful scenery. The result seemed to be a steadily increasing army of motorists each year. New York state had the most extensive highway system at the time, but was somewhat hampered by repair work being completed on many of its important highways. Tourists could also travel at no charge into Canada for a period of three or four days.[25]

In an interview with Thomas A. Edison for *Electrical World* in 1917 the lack of charging facilities was brought to the reader's attention. Mr. Edison said he would think that central stations should realize that there is a waiting market for selling current to charge electric cars. "The public is in the curious position of wanting to buy something for which there is no place to go."[26] He proposed that the central station should go into the garage business and should not sell current for charging, but for mileage. The garages should also provide for the washing and repairing of the vehicles at a fixed and reasonable price. "There is an opportunity for big sales of current on a profitable service basis. Business needs imagination. The electrical business is no exception. Sometimes I think the men who ought to see ten years ahead see only next week."[27]

By 1923 car ownership had become common for the ordinary citizen. Some questioned whether there would be a saturation point, and whether people could afford to pay for all these vehicles. One economist predicted a saturation point that would be hit like a brick wall, while another foresaw the doubling of car ownership in the near future. Production was estimated at a half million more cars than the anticipated consumption. One pessimist said, "Fords are likely to sell at cost, and others to retire from the field."[28] Another economist thought people were buying too many cars and not enough washing machines. It was estimated that an income of $2,000 a year was necessary to support car ownership, but statistics from 1922 showed that over a million people with an income of $1,600 owned cars. Prices for new cars were coming down and were about 40 percent lower than pre–World War I. The average price of a new car dropped in November 1922 from $350 to $300, making it statistically possible for millions more people to buy cars. As production and profits went up, the cost of making a car went down. Some in the industry were seriously predicting a $150 car in the near future. According to the census, the theoretical number of purchasers of cars was about twenty million, the same as the number of American families and of white, native-born men above the age of twenty-one. It was also about the same as the number of persons with an adequate income whose occupations indicated they might become car owners. The prosperity of the day and the new developments in the reliability, longevity and performance of the automobile made it a popular household purchase.

Fashions for Motoring

Early automobiles, whether gasoline or electric, exposed their passengers to all types of weather. Books and magazines of the time reflected a plucky attitude. The earliest cars had no tops— and sometimes no windshields— to protect the occupants from rain, wind or snow. To compensate, drivers and fellow passengers looked to the fashions of the day to provide protection. Greatcoats, ponchos, dusters, goggles, gloves, hats and veils to match the season became the fashion for these early driving enthusiasts. Advertisements touted products to protect the skin and hair from the elements. *Life* magazine, in 1909, carried an ad for the Scandinavia Fur & Leather Co. of New York, offering "Smart Auto Apparel for Up-to-Date Motorists. The Best Modistes and Tailors of Paris and London are drawn upon for our Selections of Imported Auto-Apparel…. Whatever is 'going' where style prevails can be furnished from our wardrobes at a moment's notice. Man, Woman, Child and Chauffeur can be instantly equipped with everything from a Complete Outfit to a pair of Gloves or Goggles."[29] Issues in 1916 carried ads for Hansen Gloves featuring "Automobile Gauntlets and Mittens— Exclusive styles covering the widest range in motoring demands."[30]

Women in 1912 were offered "dresses and hats you can launder"[33] and insulated vacuum bottles for picnicking. In 1913 the fashion-conscious were presented with a choice of apparel for the cold winter weather and the new spring offerings. Should one invest in a coat, skirt and hat, all knit and drab in color, but very warm, the very thing for a frosty day with the wind whipping around you while touring? Or, should one anticipate the summer's heat and dust and buy the light-weight, brightly colored silk coats suitable for the opera or a fancy ball? Prices of coats ranged from six dollars to twenty-five dollars. Wet-weather garments, for those in open runabouts, were primarily a poncho style that slipped over the head. A combination warm-weather garment that also had the styling to suggest an evening wrap in cut and richness could cost as much as seventy-five dollars. Straw hats, turbans and bonnets in bright colors, such as cerise, old blues, other blues, and greens of all degrees of brilliance were advertised. The straw hats came with brightly colored veils tied under the chin. Prices averaged about fifteen dollars. A parasol was considered to be for show only and was not a very real protection against the sun, wind or dust. The invention of the vacuum bottle allowed tourists to carry hot drinks that would remain hot and cold drinks that would remain cold to a picnic. A picnic was just the answer for those weary of roadhouse fare and prices. With a vacuum bottle and a traveling kitchen chest, the motoring tourist could enjoy a "denatured" picnic meal in the "rude state of nature."[34]

There was a discussion in *Outing* magazine in 1904 as to "Why Women are, or are not Good Chauffeuses."[35] It claimed that motoring was a natural task for a man,

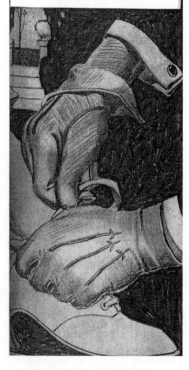
Clothing ad, 1909[32]   Clothing ad, April 1916[31]

DUST!
A CAUSE OF BAD COMPLEXIONS

The Relie...

POMPEIAN MASSAGE CREAM & SKIN FOOD

POMPEIAN MFG CO.

The vogue of the machine has meant the vogue of bad complexions. Not alone are wind and sun enemies to good, clear, soft skins. Dust is an enemy, and often the chief one. Dust gets into the pores and can't be dislodged by ordinary cleansers. A **complete** cleanser like Pompeian Massage Cream is absolut...necessary for good skin health of automobilists.

You gather the dust of the machine ahead. Your face is also continually receiving dust kicked up by your own car. This often insensibly gathered over the back by means of the vacuum created by your speed, however slight it may be. This dust g... into the pores to an astonishing degree and works havoc with the skin. Hence the necessity of a **complete** cleanser l...

POMPEIAN MASSAGE CREAM

"It Cleans Completely"

Don't compare Pompeian with cold creams. Pompeian is a massage cream. Cold creams get off a little surface dirt, and also *rub in* m... dust. This dust stays in the pores. Pompeian Massage Cream is rubbed into the pores—*and then out again*, bringing with it all the po... clogging impurities—dust, soot, soap particles, etc. It is this foreign matter in the pores that causes many face disfigurements.

You'll be astonished at the difference between Pompeian and ordinary cold creams. "When I first used Pompeian," wrote a wom... "I was as astonished as at my first Turkish bath. The dirt literally rolled out of my face pores." Wrote another: "I had no i... so much dirt could get into the pores and stay there, despite soap and water."

Pompeian enjoys the most extensive sale of all face creams, 10,000 jars being made and sold daily. Your druggist should... one of the 40,000 that sell it. But don't accept an inferior substitute on which the dealer makes a larger profit—at your exper...

Sample Jar and Book
☞ **Cut off Coupon NOW Before "Life" is Lost** ☜

You have been reading and hearing about Pompeian for years. You know it is the most popular face cream made. You have meant to try it, but have not done so. This is your chance to discover what a vast difference there is between an ordinary "cold" cream and a scientifically made Massage Cream like Pompeian. Fill out the coupon to-day and prepare for a delightful surprise when you receive our quarter ounce sample jar. A 16-page booklet on the care of the face sent with each jar. When writing enclose 6 cents in silver or stamps (United States only) to cover cost of postage and packing.

THE POMPEIAN MFG. COMPANY
25 Prospect St., Cleveland, Ohio

Pompeian Mfg. Co.
25 Prospect St.
Cleveland, Ohio

Gentlemen: Enclosed find 6c., to cover cost of postage and packing. Please send me one copy of your illustrated massage book and a special sample jar of Pompeian Massage Cream.

NAME..........................

ADDRESS..........................

CUT OUT ALONG THIS LINE, FILL IN AND MAIL TO-DAY

542

Pompeian Massage Cream ad, 1909[38]

while a woman had to adapt to it. Important factors raised were the judgment needed to control impulse and quick thought and the ability to concentrate on everyday things. "The weakness that causes a woman to read the same page of a book twice to get its meaning ... is the same weakness which, in motoring, keeps her looking too long at an attractive bit of scenery ... or for a single instant lifting her hand from the brake."[36] "The only thing about a car which a woman does not have to teach herself with patience and skill is how to dress for it." The writer might have been surprised by statistics gathered two decades later. In 1925 during a six-month period in New York state one thousand drivers licenses were revoked. Only twelve of them were owned by women.

Sun, wind and dust took their toll on the faces of early motorists. Cosmetic companies were quick to see the new market and began promoting products to protect and to soothe that chafed skin. "But the papers do say that automobiling is very harmful to the complexion and the face should be protected by layers of cold cream and powder, and a veil on top of that."[37] Besides the bad effects of wind and sun, "Dust kicked up by your own car [or] from the machine ahead" became another nasty suspect as a cause of bad complexion. Relief from this health nuisance was to be obtained by applying creams and powders.

Advertising also reflected the independence being gained by women of the time. The suffragettes were campaigning for a woman's right to vote. More women were looking for their own income, some of necessity and some for the independence it gave and the chance to afford more luxury. A popular column in the *Ladies' Home Journal* in 1912 asked "What Can I Do? How Can I Make Money Outside the Home?" and gave suggestions such as working in department stores, typing at home and becoming involved in social service. The column recommended that if a woman must teach, she should specialize. Salary ranges for these positions were listed to fall between $600 and $1,800 a year. Home products such as electric washing machines and electric irons were also aimed at freeing the family from household chores. Even paper disposable diapers, advertised in 1912, offered more independence for a woman traveling with an infant. Women who had relied on men for transportation and protection were being lured to the EV, with its promises of easy operation, need for less repairs or for knowing mechanics, and so easy to drive "a child can do it." They saw the added mobility offered by the automobile as part of this new independence. It allowed a woman to move about the city without need of a chauffeur or driver, and gave the convenience of travel whenever the fancy took her. She and her friends or children were free to travel where they pleased. Their men, in the meantime, were reading ads that pictured lovely stylish women operating electric cars on their own. When torn between the pressures of being modern in their thinking and their concern for their wife's or daughter's welfare if left alone driving a vehicle, the gentleman could gather comfort from ads that stressed the ease of operating electric vehicles, even for the delicate woman. Baker, in particular, picked up on this theme and showed their electrics driven by women in many happy scenes: women and children on a picnic, women chatting off on a drive, women being helped out of the car for an elegant evening out.

This theme was still used by Grandma Duck of Walt Disney fame in the 1950s.

Being fashionably and properly dressed for social occasions is part of our western culture. Young American women of the early 1900s were interested in being properly attired when going motoring. The *Automobile Girls* series of books was advertised with a number of other young adult series as "The Best and Least Expensive Books for Real Boys and Girls. These fascinating volumes will interest boys and girls of every age under

The Family Car
That Needs No Chauffeur

The utmost in room makes the Silent Waverley Electric Limousine
the town car ideal for the family. Ample seating space is afforded for five in this big richly upholstered car. The driver
occupies a front seat—and so always has a full view of the
thoroughfare ahead. Unusual expanse of plate glass panels,
front, sides and rear, gives all the occupants the widest view.

Silent Waverley Electric Limousine-Five

"Full View Ahead"

Design and Construction Patents Applied For

Needs no chauffeur, because the
Waverley No-Arc Controller is so
simple and so safe that a child may
operate it. It is the Town Car that
requires no cranking—presents no
mechanical difficulties—yet goes
wherever a town car can be used, winter or summer. The coldest weather
does not put it out of commission.

High Efficiency Shaft Drive, Full
Elliptic Springs front and rear. Solid
or pneumatic Tires.

Send for the beautiful Waverley Art
Book on Town Cars. It shows ten
models. Prices $3500 down to $1225.

Also the Waverley Catalog of Commercial Vehicles. Exide Battery.

THE WAVERLEY COMPANY
Factory and Home Office, 194 South East Street, Indianapolis, Indiana

New York, 2010 Broadway
Philadelphia
2043 Market Street

Boston, 25 Irvington Place
Chicago Branch
2005 Michigan Boulevard

Waverley ad, March 1912[39]

Baker ad, March 1916 (color)[40]

Grandma Duck driving an electric car[41] © Disney Enterprises, Inc.

sixty."[42] The price was fifty cents per volume. This series followed the adventures of four young women and an aunt as they motored through the countryside beyond New York City. They met gypsies, repelled robbers and kidnappers, and stayed in beautiful country homes as they toured. Although they were motoring in an automobile they had to start by cranking, the clothing and sentiments for driving reflect those of both electric and gasoline motorists of the era.

> They had got into their fresh linen suits and broad-brimmed straw hats, and were waiting on the porch with suitcases and small satchels.... "And don't forget our automobile coats," exclaimed Mollie proudly, as she shook out her long pongee duster, last year's Christmas gift from Ruth. "This is the first time we've had a chance to wear them. I feel so grand in mine!" she continued, as she slipped it on. "With all this veil and hat, I can almost imagine I am a millionaire."[43]

On women driving automobiles:

> "My dear Major," replied Miss Sallie, "you have been away from America for so long that you are old-fashioned. Do you think these athletic young women need a man to protect them? I assure you that the world has been changing while you have been burying yourself in Russia and Japan. Ruth, here, is as good a chauffeur as could be found, and Barbara Thurston can protect herself and us into the bargain."[44]

By 1917 clothing for motoring became high fashion as well as functional, providing warmth in the winter. Raccoon coats were in high demand for men. Women shopped for fur coats made of beaver, wombat, and nutria. The latter provided warmth without the extra weight. "The best styled coats of fur are noted at once by the comfortable fullness of their cut. The designers have treated the collars of the coats meant for use in a car. Most of them are cut deep and full, which allows them not only to be warm but permits them to be turned up high in the back to protect the neck and ears."[45] Prices ranged from $55 to $95 with exclusive designs upward to $250. By 1917 motoring fashions stressed comfort, especially in the winter styles. Nearly all coats had pockets trimmed with a contrasting fur. "As for the fabrics that clothe the lady of the car when furs become superfluous, they are many.... Burilla and velour top the list along with 'Anzac Bolivia.'"[46] The well-dressed motorist stayed abreast of the fashion for each season.

The electric vehicle's dependability, and its simple design and operation, made it drivable by even inexperienced men. During World War I, England was using many electric cars and trucks for delivery of goods. As men of all ages became more and more scarce, women drivers were tried as an experiment and were found to be competent. One of the largest stores in London employed women almost exclusively to drive its seventy-five electric delivery trucks.[47] Harrods department store had a fleet of sixty electric trucks and the Midland Railway Company had a fleet of seventy-three electric trucks in use.

Early Advertising

During the early years of the electric vehicle, there were no qualifications for driving, and no training was required. Any child or adult who could manage the vehicle was permitted to drive without any license or proof of skill. A 1902 advertisement claimed the electric car was so simple to drive that even a child could be taught to understand it. A 1902 National Electric ad claimed their vehicles were for "those who take no pleasure in mechanical labor. Easily controlled by man, woman or child."

A 1906 Babcock ad targeted women with the slogan: "A contented woman is she who operates a Babcock Electric. She knows there is nothing to fear." Another Babcock slogan was "When you build it right, IT IS right and works right." The EVs were promoted

National Electric Vehicles

are for those who take no pleasure in mechanical labor. Started and kept in motion without worry or tinkering. Simple, noiseless, graceful. The most practical automobile for business or pleasure. Easily controlled by man, woman or child. Write for catalog.

NATIONAL VEHICLE CO., 900 E. 22nd St., Indianapolis, Ind.

National Electric ad, December 1902[48]

as town cars for shopping and going to the theater and to dinner. A 1908 Baker advertisement proclaimed the car's simplicity and reliability, to promote the Baker as the "standard" of the industry. It also promoted luxury and elegance by referring to their vehicles as "The Aristocrats of Motordom." The company claimed to produce the simplest vehi-

cle with the fewest parts and fewer adjustments than others. One advertisement pronounced it to be an "automobile without a repair bill." A 1910 Baker ad claimed, "It outsells all other Electrics because it outclasses them. More than three times as many Baker Electrics are sold each year than any other make."

Early advertising rarely addressed the range of the electric, but a 1900 Riker ad took the problem head on. The ad features a "standard" Riker phaeton with a map showing the route the car took on its "run" from New York to Philadelphia, a distance of 110 miles, on one charge. Another characteristic rarely approached was the electric vehicle's lack of performance in cold weather. This 1902 Studebaker ad claims the car "can be run any day in the year by any member of the family." The same ad claims a range of 40 miles on one charge and the ability to climb hills successfully, even when the grade is "not only steep, but covered with sand and mud."

Automobile shows provided potential customers with glimpses of the new electrics and free advertising in the newspapers. The Cycle and Automobile Show at Madison Square Garden in 1900 featured an electric Foster & Co. runabout weighing about 950 pounds and having a capability of being

MODEL 50 SPECIAL

A New National Electric

with a record of over 100 miles on one charge of battery.

Complete information and description of our ten models, and price on application.

NATIONAL VEHICLE CO., 900 E. 22d St., Indianapolis, Ind., U. S. A.

National Electric ad, 1902[49]

charged in forty-five minutes.[51] The same show featured entries by the American Electric Company, the Indian Bicycle Company and the Riker Electric Company (eight entries). In 1906 major EV manufacturers formed the Association of Electric Vehicle Manufacturers. Their prime objective was to raise awareness of their product lines. To accomplish this they made efforts to secure better exhibition space at auto shows and to show their potential buyers refinements in their cars and their usefulness for both pleasure and commerce.[52] The electric automobile show held in 1909 at Madison Square Garden was another high-profile event. Coverage written by H. A. Harper (Babcock) for the *New York Times* spoke of the delicate design and mechanism of electric vehicles, and their usefulness for the theater, calls in the afternoon, or a ride in the park. He claimed they were excellent vehicles for ladies and physicians as the cars were economical, simple to operate and required no mechanical aptitude to run. Advances in the storage batteries had also added speed and mileage, and garages "will now charge batteries for a small expense to the owner."[53] Such events and articles introduced the public to the EV's style and potential.

Advertisers also turned their attention to accessories that the new vehicles needed. By the mid teens, many ads were appearing for batteries, tires, etc. Some products were successful and others were not. To combat the inconvenience of relying on charger stations, companies offered home battery chargers. The auto recharging plugs were not standardized, so owners purchased these according to the car and model they drove. For people without electric power to their homes in 1900, Baker offered an optional accessory—a Merriman 500-watt electric charger powered by a water-cooled gasoline engine. Women were depicted plugging in their automobiles for charging in the ease of their own homes. The Lincoln electric battery charger consisted of a motor-generator set and steel cabinet with a knife switch and special connectors. The chargers were notoriously inefficient and did not enjoy widespread success.

By 1909 Studebaker's advertising had moved on to recognize the competition from the ICE touring cars. Their answer? Buy both, the cars are not rivals. "Where the one is, there also should the other be—in every garage where there is a high priced gasoline touring car, there ought also to be an electric for city

Riker ad, August 1900[50]

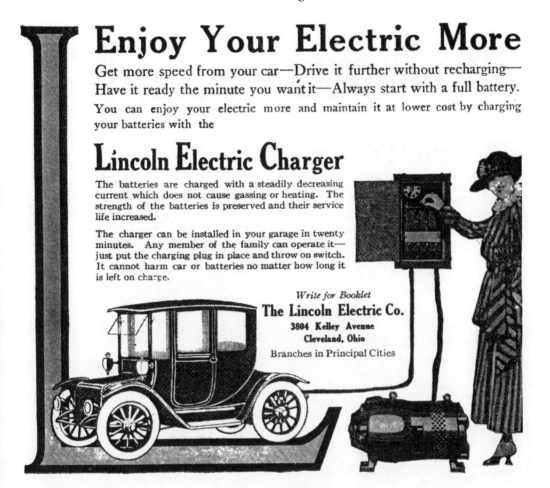

Enjoy Your Electric More

Get more speed from your car—Drive it further without recharging—
Have it ready the minute you want it—Always start with a full battery.

You can enjoy your electric more and maintain it at lower cost by charging
your batteries with the

Lincoln Electric Charger

The batteries are charged with a steadily decreasing
current which does not cause gassing or heating. The
strength of the batteries is preserved and their service
life increased.

The charger can be installed in your garage in twenty
minutes. Any member of the family can operate it—
just put the charging plug in place and throw on switch.
It cannot harm car or batteries no matter how long it
is left on charge.

Write for Booklet
The Lincoln Electric Co.
3804 Kelley Avenue
Cleveland, Ohio
Branches in Principal Cities

Lincoln Electric Charger[54]

service—Studebaker preferred, of course, since we are considered high class equipment
... YOU MAKE YOURSELF RIDICULOUS, you see, when you compare the gasoline with the electric as if they were rivals—just as ridiculous as if you were to say you preferred a Tuxedo
to a traveling suit, without specifying for what occasion."[55]

Columbia and Studebaker, in addition to aiming at the woman's market, appealed
to the "rational" man by showing the logic of using the practical electrics in town.

The Columbus Buggy Company was advertising heavily in 1909. Its town car was
promoted as having the ability to make "99 short trips in one tour," and was meant to
"supplant the big gasoline touring and limousine cars *for city service.*" It asks, "It is true
that no electric will serve the purpose of a touring car but is it *rational* to use a big high-
powered machine about town when an electric will carry you quickly and cheaper and
you can drive yourself?" Its ads were also directed toward women, emphasizing ease of
operation—"Takes no strength. The control is easy, simple. A delicate woman can practically live in her car and never tire"—and toward the modern man who supported a
woman's right to greater freedom: "It makes the women of your family independent of
chauffeur and coachman." "The Columbus Electric has one lever, no foot pedals, except
for one emergency brake."

Studebaker ad, January 1909[56]

This Is the Car Which Has Rendered Other Electric Types Obsolete

Let us recapitulate briefly some of the points which have won first place for the *Detroit* Electric—the carriage which, by its remarkable 1060-mile trip from Detroit to Atlantic City without a broken part, established the world's record for electric vehicles.

Here in Detroit—the automobile center of America — the *Detroit* has displaced all other models.

Here, and in every community of consequence, it is the chosen car of the electrical engineer, the builder of gas cars—the men of technical and practical experience.

How has this come to pass ?

The picture practically answers this question.

It shows a car of surpassing elegance and dignity—

It shows that the *Detroit* door opens to the front instead of the rear—

The step pads are oval instead of having sharp, square corners—

The cushions are more luxurious ; the rear one 20 inches deep ; the front one 15 inches (the deepest you have ever seen in an electric are 18 and 19, 13 and 14 inches).

The curved front windows are larger ; there is nothing whatever to obscure the operator's vision at any angle—

The grab handles on the doors—and all trimmings—are silver finished.

So much—although these are only the more important points—that make for perfect ease and luxury in the *Detroit*.

Let us look over the mechanical and operating details.

The battery is larger and more powerful—

You get more mileage and greater speed—many a *Detroit* owner in continuous, every-day service, is getting a consistent average of 85 miles ; and 100 miles is easily possible.

You have five speeds forward and three reverse. You had thought three forward and one reverse the ultimate limit.

Speed control, the alarm, and motor brake are concentrated in one lever—simplest and easiest control.

Mounting the motor under the body in the center of the frame removes undue weight and strain from the rear axle and tires.

We could go on enumerating full fifty distinctive *Detroit* features, improvements which make for efficiency and economy of operation.

As it is, haven't we told you enough to show you conclusively what a splendid carriage the *Detroit* is — how much better than the finest and best you have seen in other makes.

So write for the complete catalogue and for the booklet which pictures and describes the Detroit-Atlantic City tour referred to above.

The Detroit plant of the Anderson Carriage Company —the largest in the world devoted to electric carriages— represents years of successful vehicle manufacturing.

Anderson Carriage Company, Dept. F., Detroit, Mich.

Detroit ad, 1909[57]

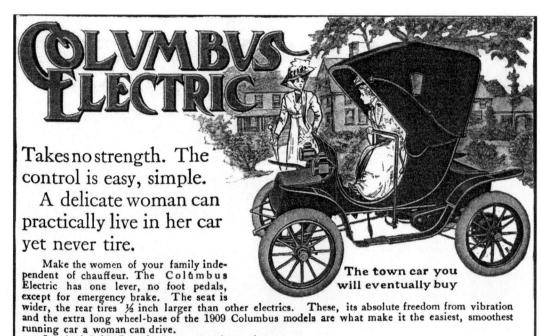

Columbus ad, April 1909[58]

The Hupp-Yeats Corporation presented its enclosed vehicle with a sloping front end in 1911. Promoted as having a "French design of the very latest fashion…. With its low-hung body, its curve of roof, and slope of hood — radical changes from accepted design — it presents rare beauty," it was giving the public a "new" design.

An article in a 1912 *New York Times* stated that the National Electric Light Association estimated over $10,000,000 was invested in electric trucks and over $30,000,000 in electric pleasure vehicles. The figure was predicted to climb to $80,000,000 by 1913. The Association planned to introduce "an ingenious method of determining the real efficiency of an electric vehicle" at its upcoming convention in Seattle. The method recorded actual hours of use and rates of charging and the expected miles left to be used. One of the difficulties faced by the EV manufacturers was improper battery charging, causing shorter battery life and less than expected mileage per charge. The Association intended to use this new recording method to minimize the improper charging by educating the owner in the proper recharging sequence as shown by the information gathered. The Association wanted to keep the buying public interested in the electric vehicles as a solid investment.

The Electric Vehicle Association of America began an extensive national advertising campaign in 1910 to promote the electric vehicle as a "perfected device." By 1912 they were struggling against the popularity of the gasoline car. The Association planned an

Opposite: Top — Columbus ad, March 1909[59] and Columbus ad, 1909[60]

The town car
you will eventually buy

2-passenger Stanhope with Victoria top—a model you
can use for years without fear of its going out of style.

In New York, the Electric

continues to supplant the big gasoline touring and limousine cars *for city
service*. It is clean, odorless, noiseless. It takes no strength to run it.
It makes the women of your family independent of chauffeur and coachman.

All electrics are simple, but the Columbus Electric is conspicuous for its simplicity
of construction. Complete control with one lever; no foot pedals to confuse you; no
complicated parts. The Columbus Electric costs less than a horse to maintain. The
famous Exide Batteries are our standard equipment.

Write today for catalogue showing our 1909 models of four and two-passenger Coupés
Stanhopes and other styles. Let us refer you to *users*.

THE COLUMBUS BUGGY CO.

Established 1870   382-450 Dublin Ave.   COLUMBUS, O.

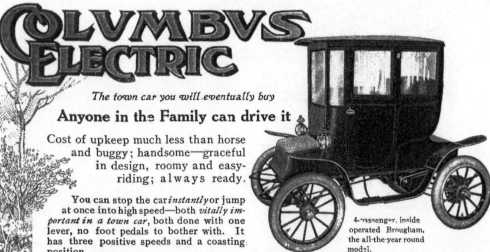

The town car you will.eventually buy

Anyone in the Family can drive it

Cost of upkeep much less than horse
and buggy; handsome—graceful
in design, roomy and easy-
riding; always ready.

You can stop the car *instantly* or jump
at once into high speed—both *vitally important in a town car*, both done with one
lever, no foot pedals to bother with. It
has three positive speeds and a coasting
position.

The Columbus Electric is lighter than
any other electric—from 100 to 500 pounds
lighter. This means greater mileage on a
charge, less wear on tires. Extra large tires
—3½ inch front and 4 inch rear—also greatly reduces tire expense. The famous Exide
batteries are our standard equipment.

Unusually comfortable and easy-riding,
due to its luxurious upholstering, long
wheel-base and carefully graded springs.

4-passenger, inside
operated Brougham,
the all-the-year round
model.

Just the car for calling, shopping and the theater..
You can learn to drive it in 15 minutes; can care for
and charge it yourself. No complicated machinery.
All moving parts enclosed and run in oil—*dust proof*.

We have agents in almost every city. Our cars are being run
by owners in every state. Let us refer you to *users*. Write us
for 1909 catalogue showing 4 passenger and 2 passenger styles open
and closed and stanhopes with Victoria tops, and name of agent
in your locality.

Established 1870.

The Columbus Buggy Co.   382-450 Dublin Ave.   Columbus, O.

educational campaign to boost the acceptance of electric vehicles. They decided to take the high road and promote the electric vehicle's simplicity, economy and serviceability. "The committee felt also that in the preparation of the advertising matter it should be borne in mind that the electric has its own very broad field, and that while the electric in many instances came in direct competition with the gasoline car, the publicity should not include a 'knock,' if you will pardon that expression, aimed at the gas-engine-propelled vehicle."[61] The horse, however, was in a different field: "It was further determined that the criticism of the horse and the indication of its being the passing victim of an age of higher efficiency whose elimination was demanded by present-day economy and sanitation would be wise and justifiable." The committee hired the advertising agency of Wm. D. McJunkin, who came up with the slogans "Before you buy any car—consider the electric" for pleasure and passenger vehicles, and "Public interest and private advantage both favor the electric" for commercial vehicle advertising. It was decided to advertise in six media aimed at different groups. "First, those reached by general publications; second, those reached by publications appealing to the wealthy and fashionable; third, those

reached by central-station publications; fourth, those reached by auto trade papers; fifth, those reached by medical publications; sixth, those reached by purely trade publications, subdivided into light and heavy delivery service."[62] Thomas A. Edison commented that "I think the advertising campaign which has been conducted by the Electric Vehicle Association of America will be productive of absolute results in the electric vehicle advancement.... Mr. Edison has expressed himself as being very well pleased with the manner in which the campaign has been handled." The committee decided to place the address of the Association under the name in the advertising and welcomed inquiries to the "Information Bureau." Within a few months, they had received 702 inquiries and found they were not in a position to answer the questions of operations and cost data, especially the most frequently asked questions—"How far will it run?" and "Will it climb a hill?" It was decided to change the phrase soliciting inquiries from the term "Information Bureau" to "Interesting Literature about Electric

Detroit ad, December 1919[64]

Vehicles Gladly Sent. Write To-day" for later advertisements. The committee also decided that the advertising campaign was worthy of continuing and "that by persistent and proper educational publicity the mind of the purchasing public may be diverted from 'some vehicle' to that of the 'electric vehicle.'"[63]

A 1912 Detroit Electric ad claimed the vehicle had "dependability built into it ... and electrical principles are inborn." It was also aimed at higher-income individuals, or those aspiring to be wealthy, by proclaiming the purchase of a Detroit Electric would be a "foundation of your investment and will yield inestimable dividends of pleasure for yourself and friends." By 1919 interest in EVs was dwindling, and to prop up sales designers began emulating the design of the more powerful ICEs. Detroit Electric changed the design of the front end of its enclosed car to resemble the shape of an automobile with a gasoline engine. The advertising proclaimed, "A perfect harmony of line — graceful, distinctive, yet dignified" and focused on appealing to the wealthy by promoting "an artistic selection in upholstery and interior fittings which combines beauty, luxury and comfort."

The heyday of the electric vehicle's existence featured advertising directed to women. Women appeared in ads more than men at a ratio of about three to one. The advertising strategy was formulated by L. D. Gibbs of the Boston Edison Company in 1911 as: "In advertising the electric pleasure vehicle the use of illustrations showing a handsomely dressed and attractive lady operating her own car is far more convincing than a bald admonition to use such a vehicle. Such a picture at once conveys a notion of comfort, luxury, cleanliness, elegance and that identifiable element denominated 'class.'"[68] Women were shown in ads taking their children on picnics, attending club meetings and generally enjoying social events and their independence. Electric vehicles were advertised for their reliability, comfort, convenience and luxury, ignoring the technical appeal thought to interest most men. A 1913 Woods advertisement proclaimed "The Woods Electric, with all its beauty, its ease, its convenience, typifies the civilization of our times, bearing testimony to man's conquest of the elements and to the constantly advancing status of the American woman, and the desire and intention upon the part of man to supply her with all the luxurious attributes of a real queen."

Hupp-Yeats ad, 1911[65]

Utility

Your Rauch & Lang or Baker Electric will carry you in style
to the social function or serve as a cheerful conveyance for a day
outdoors.

   The wonderful ease of control—the silent, efficient, dependable motor—and the genuine Coach Work—all these unite in
making your Rauch & Lang or Baker Electric a Car of Utility and
Enjoyment.

THE BAKER R & L COMPANY
Cleveland, Ohio

Baker Electric ad, 1916[66]

The Owen Magnetic Company, acquired by Baker, Rauch & Lang in 1915, made a hybrid vehicle with a gasoline engine driving an electric transmission that eliminated the clutch and gear system. It was advertised as the "Car of a Thousand Speeds."

EV ads reflected trends in language as well as living styles. During the early 1900s "reliability" was the term most often given to the electric vehicle to indicate a stable mechanical performance. "Dependability" is a word that did not appear in very many advertisements until the 1930s; it was first widely promoted by Horace Dodge and used sparingly in early Detroit Electric ads. Dodge also included power and rugged construction as attributes of his automobiles.

After World War II, EVs had few supporters. Automobiles were reflecting a different life style. The 1940s, and '50s and '60s advertising brought hot rods and muscle cars and the "Put a Tiger in Your Tank" slogan from Exxon. The roar of the engine and power were emphasized. Popular singing groups like the Beach Boys praised ICEs with lyrics that extolled the virtues of the Chevy V-8. Artists in the early 1950s captured the spirit of that era's image of cars. They were not interested in painting the car by itself. Instead, they used it as symbols for speed and motion.[69] The electric vehicle did not have the power, range or rumbling noise appeal to compete with this market.

Automobile Racing

From the earliest days of the automobile, racing has been used to demonstrate the superiority of one make or feature over another and to illustrate the potential of a particular machine. Electric vehicles were no exception. They also used racing and setting land speed records as important methods for putting themselves into the public eye. Race coverage was popular in the newspapers of the early 1900s. In November 1901 A. L. Riker ran his electric carriage on a one-mile straightaway in a time of 1:08 at the Long Island Automobile Club races. The cars in this race were stripped down to the frame and seat. Having an EV competing in a race increased awareness of the electric's potential. On one occasion, it was also a reminder to spectators of the inherent dangers of auto racing. In 1902 a Baker Electric racer attempted a new land speed record at Staten Island, New York. W. C. Baker designed the vehicle along the lines of an earlier Riker racing car. The machine's aerodynamics were ahead of its time, with a torpedo-shaped body tapered at both ends, constructed of an iron frame and covered with wood and fabric. The wheels had wooden rims with three-inch pneumatic tires and were also covered with a canvas fabric. The auto weighed 3,000 pounds, a hefty machine for a racer. The weight was primarily due to the batteries and controlling apparatus, consisting of forty cells of "light-weight" Gould lead-zinc accumulators, assembled around the vehicle in a U-shape on each side of the operator's seats.

Two people were required to operate the racer and the driver peered through a small isinglass window. The test became a disaster when the car reached about 60 mph, swerved to the right and struck some trolley tracks. The vehicle left the ground and when it touched down, the hand brakes had been applied with an uneven distribution and the car smashed broadside into a crowd of spectators. The drivers were unhurt, but two onlookers were killed and a half dozen others were injured. This caused the sponsor, the Automobile Club of America, to cancel all further road speed tests and concentrate the energies of its members on the "development of the pleasure of commercial automobiles."[71] A 1917 run sponsored by the Electric Vehicle Association set a new record for an intercity run in an EV. The run from Atlantic City, New Jersey, to New York City was made in 5 hours 48 minutes with an average speed of 20.5 mph over a 123-mile stretch.[72] These auto races showcased the EVs and reminded the public of their viability, but the ICE performance overshadowed the small strides made by EVs in distance and speed. The race coverage was more likely to point out the electric's inability to match performance with the ICEs.

The Arizona Public Service utility company sponsored the "APS Solar & Electric 500" race at the Phoenix International Raceway in 1992. It included fifty cars and four events, featuring a Saturn SC electric with nickel/cadmium batteries. The Saturn ran about eighty-four miles per hour for 125 miles without a pit stop.

Hupp-Yeats ad, 1911[67]

Baker Electric racing car 1902[70]

At the Bibendum Challenge race in November 2001, Carroll Shelby introduced a Cobra CSX powered by a V8 fueled by hydrogen. It generated 180 hp and went 108 mph. The event showcased more than fifty entries powered by natural gas, diesel and hybrid engines.

Challenges for the EV market

EVs have always held the trophy in environmental points against their gasoline engine competitors. It has been their major competitive lead. With the advances being made in fuel efficiency, this lead is growing smaller. Which technology will have the competitive edge with tomorrow's consumers? Who is interested in buying an EV? People who are concerned about the environment and want to help keep it clean and quiet. People who want leading-edge technology such as fuel cell and hybrid technology in their lives. People who want fuel-efficient cars with good mileage and households with a combined income of over $120,000. Will consumers who want environmentally friendly autos support the EV in the marketplace?

By 1993 General Motors' electric vehicle marketing department was exploring ways to attract buyers. The major problem in marketing EVs is that the product is not market-driven but mandated by law. A *Ward's Electric Vehicle Study* in 1993 showed that two-thirds of the respondents doubted that EVs would be sold in significant numbers in any state that does not require them by law.[73] GM's marketing director John Dabels said, "Introducing electric vehicles is a lot like convincing consumers to try other technologically advanced products. The major difference is that no government body ever passed legislation requiring marketers of microwave ovens and compact discs to meet certain sales goals."[74] They decided the best approach was to join in a consortium with Ford Motor Company and Chrysler to develop technology and manufacturing techniques. The companies began building prototypes to be used in fleets for utility companies and government entities. These could be used as tests to gather information about consumer reactions in real-world use. Mr. Dabels said, "We want to put people in the vehicles and ask them what they really think after they sit in it, drive it, go shopping and take the kids places."[75] During the same time, the Japanese formed the Japan Electric Vehicle Association to research, develop and popularize electric vehicles in Japan. GM's marketing department identified price, range and infrastructure as the major areas to address. A study showed that most people in Boston and Los Angeles were driving about seventy-five miles per day, well within the range of the electric vehicles available. The infrastructure needed would be charging stations at work, shopping centers and restaurants along with homes. They proposed small charging stations similar to parking meters that would accept credit cards. GM has formed partnerships with companies like the Los Angeles Department of Water and Power, Southern California Edison, San Diego Gas & Electric, Pacific Gas & Electric, Sacramento Municipal Utility District, Arizona Public Service, and Tucson Electric Power Company to build an electric car charging infrastructure. So far, more than 1,100 chargers have been installed and are in use by EV1 customers in California and Arizona. Nearly 500 public charging stations are located at shopping malls, restaurants, beaches, airports, Saturn retail facilities, and key workplaces. For the near future, most of them are free.[76] As in the past, multiple-car–owning families could use an electric car for short shopping trips and still have a traditional ICE vehicle for longer tips. The prevailing thought of the day was to get the message out to the public and then find out what they want and what is important to the consumer.

Honda began its experiments with a battery-only vehicle in the late 1990s with the EV Plus. It was designed from the ground up, not a conversion based on an existing platform. Honda marketed the car heavily in the southern California area with newspaper advertising. This resulted in sales of only 300 vehicles in two and a half years. The problems again were lack of public demand due to the inconvenience of "plugging in" and the cost of the batteries. The battery pack weighed in at about a thousand pounds, cost forty thousand dollars and would last for only about five years. Cold weather climates reduced the range and hot weather climates resulted in battery failures. Steve Ellis, the American Honda Manager of Alternative Fuel Vehicle Sales and Marketing, noted in an interview that even if the cost of the battery pack was reduced by half, to twenty thousand dollars, that would equal the price of a new Honda Civic Hybrid or a Natural Gas Civic.[77] The Natural Gas Civic came on the market in 1998 and had a range of two hundred miles and carried an SULEV rating. Honda sells about one thousand Natural Gas Civics a year primarily for fleet use. They have not been marketed to the general retail consumer because of infrastructure challenges. Honda's all electric EV Plus did not find a market.

In 1996 France was thought be a good market for electric vehicles partly because nuclear generating stations were producing most of the electricity. The French government was also subsidizing electric vehicles to keep costs in line with conventional ICEs. But sales were only about one-third of what was expected in 1996 and most of the units were going to fleet use. Gut Sarre, an engineer for SAFT SA, a French battery company, said, "I don't think we can develop a market by regulation and restraint. We develop a market by having a good product at a low cost."[78] Even with abundant power available, the French preferred the ICEs.

A *Business Week* analysis and commentary article in 1997 stated, "Motown insists the public doesn't want them [EVs]. With gasoline cheaper than bottled water, American consumers seem unable — or unwilling — to curtail their addiction to gas-guzzlers. Chrysler Corporation claims fuel economy ranks 19th among buyers' criteria in picking cars — right after 'quality of air conditioning.'"[79] With Japan's Toyota Prius newly on the horizon, Stephen Girsky, Morgan Stanley Group's auto analyst says, "Eventually the Big Three will be forced to field a car like this."

By 1998 the Big Three automakers were spending about 10 percent of their budgets on research and development on alternative fueled vehicles. Fuel cell technology was becoming less of a dream and looking more like a real solution for new cars, a solution that might be available within ten years. With no infrastructure for hydrogen filling stations to fuel the cells, researchers looked to gasoline for a hydrogen supply source. Extracting hydrogen from gasoline still produces carbon dioxide at levels not acceptable to those supporting zero emissions. David E. Cole, director of the University of Michigan's Office for the Study of Automotive Transportation, says, "The fuel cell has great potential, but it's certainly not the solution to global warming."[80]

By 1999 polls indicated that the public was not so much enamored with the ICE, but by the concept of a private automobile. Many would be willing to buy an electric vehicle if, and this is the big IF, the performance and price were comparable to the ICE. Range is the performance issue most often mentioned. Consumers want to travel several hundred miles on a single charge at a comparable price. The electric is also at a disadvantage because the designers had not found an alternative to using the battery for powering the federally required heating. The energy must come from the battery, reducing power and range. Other factors include the fact that consumers want luxury extras, like air conditioning, power steering, power windows, etc. All of those add-ons deplete the batteries and shorten range considerably. The trade-off is not one the buying public is interested in making. A third reaction of those polled named battery replacement and driving around in a vehicle filled with acid as contributing factors to the resistance of buying EVs. These perceptions make marketing an EV challenging, but still give promise that buyers will come if the product meets the buyers' expectations.

As stated by the *ACEEE's Green Book* car guide, "Perhaps the best green consumer news is that most of this year's (2001) Greenest Vehicles list is comprised of gasoline-powered cars."[81] The list is topped by the hybrids, Honda Insight and Toyota Prius, which use standard gasoline and do not need to be plugged in. They are alternatives to ICEs that can be treated "like a regular car," with no special plug, cords or charging stations. This remarkable recommendation by a "green" (environmentally friendly) publication emphasizes the fact that EVs are not in demand by the general public and that battery technology alone has not progressed as expected, but the technology for hybrid electrics is moving forward. The results are catching consumers' attention. New hybrid vehicles are priced at about $20,000 and in 2000 involved a waiting period of three to four months for delivery. There is also a growing market of used hybrids, primarily the Toyota Prius and the Honda Insight. A used 2001 Toyota Prius ranges in price from $17,000 to $21,000. The price for a used 2000 Honda Insight ranges from $14,000 to $15,000.

Consumers have reacted positively to the limited variety of hybrid-gasoline vehicles currently available and adjusted to their little quirks. The Honda Insight has two doors and strong aerodynamic lines, while the Toyota Prius has four doors and a trunk. When either car stops at a light, the engine is shut off and the driver must fight the initial response to reach for the key and start the car. Owners report actual mileage well over 50 mpg and have a good feeling about driving an environmentally friendly car that gets good gas mileage. The Prius has a gasoline engine on one side of the engine bay and an electric motor on the other, connected by a planetary gear transmission. Five microprocessors determine which engine will drive the car. The NiMH batteries are behind the back seat and are charged by the gasoline engine. Hard acceleration engages both power sources. The Honda's electric motor/generator and gasoline engine are also balanced using computers. Their configuration provides the buyer the option of either a manual 5-speed or continuously variable automatic transmission. Each uses regenerative braking and has proven to be environmentally friendly, with Insight having slightly higher efficiency in producing less carbon dioxide. Each vehicle also meets California's SULEV (super ultra low emission vehicle) standards, positioning at 75 percent cleaner than the ULEV (ultra low emission vehicle). Both the Toyota Prius and the Honda Insight enjoyed higher-than-expected sales in 2000, the Prius with 5,562 sales in 2000 and the Insight with 4,099 sales through February 2001. The Insight's success prompted Honda to advance plans for the Insight technology, and it is currently implemented in its highly successful Civic models. Both manufacturers have attracted consumer attention with the technical advances of combining electric motors with convenient gasoline engines.

EV Testing

The Department of Energy (DOE) is in charge of testing EVs. Its Field Operations Program uses four testing methods to produce repeatable results. The first is called Baseline Performance and involves testing on closed tracks or with dynamometers. The test parameters include acceleration, range, handling, charging, maximum speed and braking. The second is called Accelerated Reliability Testing and includes driving the vehicles at high mileage, up to 25,000 to 30,000 miles per year. The testing includes energy use, maintenance requirements and the effect of mileage on range. The third is EV Fleet Testing where Qualified Vehicle Testers (QVTs) collect data on electric vehicles within commercial fleets. This includes energy use, maintenance requirements, mileage, range and reliability. The fourth is Urban and Neighborhood Electric Vehicle Testing. This involves small pure-electric vehicles much the size of golf carts, and has a slightly different set of performance goals from the full-size electric vehicle.

The DOE has also been involved with hybrid electric vehicles since 1993 in a partnership with the PNGV. The official name is National Renewable Energy Laboratory (NREL). The NREL uses the assistance of the Big Three automakers, Ford, General Motors and Daimler/Chrysler, for technical work. They test vehicle performance, battery thermal management and auxiliary loads reduction.

The Fleets Market

The conventional EV manufacturers have struggled to find a technology breakthrough that will provide a product to meet the buyer's expectations. Since individual consumer acceptance has not materialized, retail markets will develop only when there is value for the customer. The auto dealers expanded sales efforts to public agencies and private industry in an attempt to put their product in the public eye, and meet ZEV obligations. In 1998 over 90 percent of all EVs sold were for fleet use. This included the Ford Ranger Electric, GM EV1 and the Toyota RAV4 EV.

GM's EV1, an all-electric zero emission vehicle developed by their Saturn division, originally leased for $480 a month after government incentives, but in 1996, GM had to cut the payment by 25 percent due to disappointing sales. GM offered a nickel metal-hydride battery that doubles the seventy-to-ninety mile range of the lead acid battery.

In 1997 GM spent $10 million for advertising in Los Angeles, San Diego and Sacramento, California; and Phoenix and Tucson, Arizona. By 1998, with little response to the special effects television ads, GM switched to print advertising and direct mail to increase public awareness of their product. GM discontinued building the EV1 in 1999, but production facilities remain in place.

Honda began selling its ultra-low emission (ULEV) Accord in 1998 and promised to have a ZLEV engine in production in a few years.

Ford introduced its Ford Ranger Electric Vehicle in 1998. It uses NiMH batteries and advertises a range of ninety to one hundred miles between charges. It will take a full charge at six to eight hours, but have an 80 percent recovery after four hours.

Better batteries, convenient refueling/recharging, and competitive price continue to challenge the EV industry as it strains to be competitive against the advances made in the ICE's lower tailpipe emissions and increased fuel efficiency. In the early 1900s moguls in the electric vehicle industry believed that any substantial increased use of electric vehicles would naturally be followed by an increase in charging stations. Even with the ad campaigns sponsored by the associations and support from manufacturers and EV enthusiasts, sales were disappointing.

From the beginning of the motor age, the touring motorist needed both good roads and refueling or recharging stations. Roads improved through the efforts of pioneers like Colonel Albert A. Pope, the "father of good roads." In the mid–1890s he rose as a leader of the League of American Wheelmen (LAW), a national organization of bicycle enthusiasts at MIT, which promoted research and design centered around road construction. The U.S. Post Office started rural free delivery (RFD) in 1896 and politicians followed the public demand for good roads by increasing the monies to be spent.[82] Better roads spurred more auto travel. Gas stations soon dotted the landscape at convenient locations. Gasoline suppliers saw an opportunity and quickly took advantage of the interest in ICEs. The oil and ICE auto industries were able to combine resources to build the infrastructure needed to support the needs of the touring motorist. Electricity suppliers did not emerge and give coverage in large enough numbers for the electrics to have the same convenient fuel stations. Electric grids existed mainly in towns and most of the rural areas had cars before light bulbs.[83]

A century later, electric vehicles and, more recently, the HEV fuel cell electrics, have not experienced the good fortune to have an infrastructure develop to provide widespread service for their automobiles. Today, electrics continue to operate in a Catch-22. Although the sale of gasoline hybrid electrics looks promising, the volume of sales for other alternate fuel vehicles is too low to make offering recharging or alternate fuel stations for hydrogen, natural gas or methanol attractive to suppliers. This is partly due to vehicle cost. In order to increase sales and lower costs, the refueling stations must be in place. Utility deregulation for natural gas looked like it might have possibilities for AFVs. As an alternative to a natural gas refueling station, deregulation has allowed an individual who owns a home that is piped for natural gas to install a refueling station next to the driveway (it must be outside the residence). The installation cost is about $5,000 to provide refueling for a vehicle overnight. It is an expensive investment. The buying public did not find the option appealing. The possibility did not spark interest from consumers. To make the electric vehicles interesting to potential car owners, both competitive cost and fuel availability have to be in place.

Marketing Obstacles and Strategies

Companies at the beginning of the 21st century are weighing the viability of the battery versus the fuel cell, or the ICE and hybrids. Which technology will become a standard and be attractive to the public? Where are the dollars for research and development best spent? In 1880 Edison demonstrated the use of electricity by stringing wires for a central electric grid. This marketing was used to create public demand. But Edison was adamant about retaining DC (short range) over changing to AC (long range), which he said was dangerous. He locked into the wrong technology, was forced out of the scene, and lost his company. Ford won market share by knowing what the customer was able to understand and afford. What direction will this century take?

At the 1914 convention of the Electric Vehicle Association, members supported an advertising campaign for electrics. Conventioneers expressed concern about producing low-priced cars and whether electrics should be marketed as touring cars. A paper was presented by George H. Kelly titled "The Cost of Electric Vehicles." He pointed out that the demand for electric cars fluctuated widely from month to month and this made it impossible for the manufacturer to anticipate production. At the time, the use of high-grade materials and expert workmanship also increased the price of the electric passenger cars. Kelly proposed creating a demand for the electrics by implementing an extensive advertising campaign involving all factors interested in the electric vehicle. Part of this campaign would be to educate the public in what the electric was, what it could do and show how it could do more to reduce the price over other choices. It was suggested that an advertising plan should use printed materials, such as booklets, charts, etc., sending them to potential customers with the view of interesting the prospect and creating a desire. This should be followed by personal letters and other forms of communication. Trained salesmen should answer every inquiry that was received and women demonstrators should be employed to demonstrate passenger cars to prospective buyers.[84] The convention was divided on two issues: production of large heavy vehicles versus the lighter models of earlier years, and touring cars versus city-use cars. Mr. Kelly presented the arguments that the public would not accept an electric car for touring purposes until the speed could be increased and the batteries could be perfected to last an entire day or could be recharged or exchanged in less time than it would take to fill a gasoline tank. J. M. Skinner, of the Philadelphia Storage Battery Company, claimed it was possible for the electric cars to be used in touring throughout the entire eastern states, and relayed that he frequently made the trip from Washington, D.C., to Boston without difficulty, averaging fifty miles per charge. The general consensus of the convention, however, was to recommend that people not go touring in the country with the ordinary electric vehicle, "as trouble will surely be encountered."[85]

The HEV industry today is facing a marketing issue similar to the problems confronted by the EVs of the early 20th century. Internal combustion engines are entrenched in our culture. We are familiar with their maintenance, enjoy their power and speed, and rely on the freedom they provide. To be successful, the HEV industry will have to show their cars' strengths over both the ICEs and the conventional battery-powered EVs. They are making progress. One key advantage for the fuel cell is its capacity to be refueled. Unlike batteries, which must be recharged or discarded, fuel cells can mimic ICEs in convenient "fill-ups." This aspect alone, if used in a customer-awareness campaign, presents the potential for taking market share from the "other environmentally sound" automobiles, as the HEV has convenience, economy and technological advances in fuel cell development.

Convincing the public to buy the alternate fuel products is not easy. Although both EVs and HEVs have many positive environmental aspects, they each have perception problems with potential customers. Where EVs must overcome consumers' dislike for battery replacement and driving in a vehicle filled with acid, fuel cell technology must overcome the public perception that hydrogen is dangerous. Many people still remember the *Hindenburg* airship disaster and connect it with the dangers of having hydrogen on board. This continues to haunt advocates of the fuel cell.

Paralleling the environmental interest, many people consider buying an EV or hybrid as a patriotic issue. The price of patriotism comes high. It may take up to ten years before the owner sees cost savings over the fuel, maintenance and purchase costs of an ICE, but they are contributing to help reduce the dependence on foreign oil. Another consideration is that the successful hybrids today are manufactured only in Japan and therefore contribute to the U.S. trade deficit.[86]

The fuel cell industry and HEV manufacturers are aware of the obstacles in moving their product to the marketplace. Firoz Rasul, Chairman and CEO of Ballard Systems Fuel Cell Company, said in 2000 that they were taking on some major market forces, the automotive industry, oil industry, utilities and the government. Ballard is concentrating on obtaining patents and intellectual property now, while investing in research and product development with the help of consumers, then will focus on mass production three to five years down the road.[87]

"People have to want to buy fuel efficient vehicles," says Chrysler vice-president Robert Libaeratore. "We will go wherever customers go." The price remains high in part because the volume of sales is just not there, and the volume remains low because the initial price is too high.

Hybrid cars have the advantage of being more flexible in design; they can have a variety of combinations. There are two basic types of hybrid vehicles, series and parallel. In the series, a gasoline engine generates power to drive the electric motor. In parallel, the two systems are separate, being able to propel the vehicle independently or together. The hybrid can consist of gasoline-electric, fuel cell-electric, diesel-electric, CNG/LNG-electric, methanol/ethanol-electric, etc. Hybrids are competitive, even while being sold at a loss. This loss should change as technological advances improve the vehicles and production is increased in the United States. CARB has indicated it is willing to create a separate emission category for hybrid vehicles. This may lead to a competitive advantage in the marketplace. Buyers seem ready to view this new technology as an option to consider seriously, if the price is right.

Fleet Testing

Fleets are a main market niche for electric vehicles. Although there have been some difficulties with cost and supply, from the onset their reliability and usefulness as commercial and government transport was touted. Between 1905 and 1917 EVs were used as ambulances, patrol wagons and delivery vehicles. By 1917 some units had been in service for close to eighteen years. The New York Edison Company had a fleet of 105 electric vehicles in 1912. The General Inspector of the company conducted a study of its fleet and determined the vehicles could be run practically twenty-four hours a day with a number of shifts in drivers. In comparison, no one could get more than eight hours of work out of a horse. Two-thirds of the orders for electric vehicles for commercial use were re-orders. Once again, however, their usefulness decreased with better roads and wider territories to cover. Limited range became the downfall of the electric vehicle in all but a limited fleet market.

Both small and large manufacturing companies supplied EVs for fleet service, some with more satisfactory results than others. In 1975 American Motors Corporation supplied the U.S. Postal Service with a fleet of 352 jeep-size electric vans. The initial cost was twice as much as an ICE and the expected life of the EV was only eight years.[88] But, two years of fleet testing revealed the EVs were about 30 percent less expensive to operate than comparable internal combustion vans. This type of vehicle is perfectly suited for Postal Service needs, using them to travel only eight to fifteen miles a day making 100 to 300 stops. When stopped to deliver mail, the motor is turned off and expends no energy. The Batronic Truck Corporation of England provided 107 trucks to over fifty U.S. utility companies in 1975. The trucks cost about $10,000 and carried about five-hundred-pound loads. Unfortunately, the small manufacturer could not supply replacement parts readily and many of the trucks sat idle for months at a time.[89] Generally, companies wanting electric vehicle fleets find suppliers for these needs.

Today, government agencies, utilities and corporations are dabbling in the more environmentally accepted alternate fuel vehicles for their fleets, while keeping an eye on the "bottom line." By 1992 electric vehicles were seen as playing a major part in the reduction of air quality problems, such as those addressed by CARB in 1990. Marketing strategists thought that if utilities and government agencies would participate in fleet ownership and testing, it would go a long way to promoting the general acceptance of electric vehicles. By using electrics, government agencies could show support for air quality programs. In 1992 the Electric Vehicle Coalition predicted an EV fleet market of 5,000 vehicles by 1997, with about half being ordered by utilities and the other half by government agencies. The actual figure was about five hundred vehicles due to competition and cost-cutting by state governments and the high price of the EVs. In 1999 Daimler/Chrysler and Ford announced a test fleet of fuel cell powered vehicles to be used in Los Angeles. In 2000, of the 17,000 EVs sold in the United States, approximately 10 percent went into fleet use. This was an acceptable showing, but the same tell-tale problems continue to hound the marketing of these vehicles even in this specialized market. The most commonly reported problem in the acceptance of Alternative Fuel Vehicles in fleet use is the lack of infrastructure, including a lack of fueling stations and the cost to build these stations. This is followed by high initial purchase cost, maintenance costs, range, availability and performance.[90] Most fleet operators show a dichotomy in their approach to the economics of Hybrid Electric Vehicles, citing economics both as a reason to use HEVs and also as an obstacle to obtaining them. Fleet use surveys show a strong interest in performance and costs with little regard for emissions information. Products were selected based on information gathered from a variety of sources by the fleet operators. The sources included the Internet, government publications, trade publications and direct mail.[91] Trade publications were the preferred source of information. Hybrid vehicles are gaining the interest of fleet operators. The advancing technology meets the public's environmental concerns without the agency's having to go to a completely electric vehicle.

Natural gas, a major competitor of EVs and HEVs in the fleet market, is another fuel option. The mixture is primarily methane with propane and ethane and is environmentally friendly. It produces 85 percent less nitrogen oxide and 74 percent less carbon

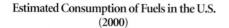

Estimated Consumption of Fuels in the U.S. (2000)

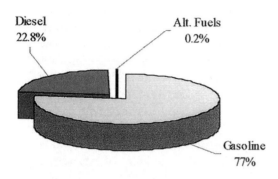

Figure 1[92]

Estimated Consumption of Alternative Fuels in the U.S. (2000)

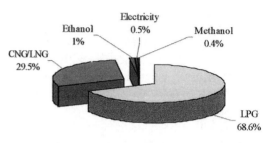

Figure 2[93]

monoxide. Natural gas must be compressed (CNG) or liquefied (LNG) to be convenient and useful. Most heavy-duty vehicle fleets like trucks and buses use the LNG, while fleet cars use CNG. To the benefit of EVs, natural-gas–powered vehicles have the same drawbacks as EVs. The conversion of a vehicle to natural gas adds about $5,000 to the cost. The infrastructure is a problem for both location and billing. There are about 1,300 high-pressure refueling natural gas stations in the United States. However, more than 40 percent of these are privately owned, or owned by local governments for their fleet cars, and are not open to the public. This greatly decreases their availability and accessibility for shared fleet use. Many stations require a special key card to use the pump. Each utility company provides its own unique charge card causing a major problem with the CNG infrastructure. The deregulation laws in 2000, stipulating that the industry cannot pass on the cost of infrastructure building to consumers, has also hampered infrastructure development and makes the natural gas alternative less competitive. Some manufacturers claim a range of over 300 miles, but actual road tests show a range of about 120 miles. Some of the vehicles equipped for natural gas fueled engines are the Volvo V70 (dual-fuel), Honda Civic GX, Toyota Camry CNG and a variety of Ford products including the Contour and Crown Victoria. In 2001, there were 28 stations in the Phoenix, Arizona, area, 44 stations in the British Columbia, Canada, 191 stations in California and 89 in Texas.

Table 1. Number of Fueling Stations by Census Region and Fuel Type — 2/8/01[94]

Region	LPG	CNG	Methanol	Ethanol	EVs	Total
Northeast	376	162	0	0	19	577
South	1,222	407	0	3	129	1,761
Midwest	760	204	0	103	10	1,077
West	924	468	3	5	399	1,799
Total	3,282	1,261	3	111	557	5,214

Although these fleet alternate fuel vehicles and EVs are in competition, they have similar issues. It is easy to buy a natural gas vehicle, but the infrastructure is not in place, and it is easy to use the electric grid infrastructure, but the vehicles are too expensive.

For over a century, the auto industry has used many methods for providing convenience to their customers and finding ways to attract the buyer's attention. In 1896 Morris and Salom began an electric cab company instead of selling the autos to individuals because they believed the EV needed to be under a regular maintenance schedule and the electric vehicle was too complicated and unreliable for lay operators. Electric cabs caught on and a market opened. Electric cab drivers in the Boston area in 1900 were earning about $14 a week for twelve hours of work and remarked, "...the people they served were more agreeable than the ordinary street car passenger."[95] In today's market, automakers are looking for that competitive edge as marketing strategies evolve. In 1993, Nissan created its first advertising slogan for its FEV concept car: "Gentle to People, Gentle to Society, Gentle to Earth."[96] GM's strategy mirrored the Morris and Salom philosophy. The EV1 was leased exclusively to customers and not sold. The Saturn Division offered to send a representative to help consumers with an EV1 selection to help choose the right person for the right car. Automakers Ford and Daimler/Chrysler are working in conjunction with the Ballard Fuel Cell Company to develop a vehicle that is "better than conventional vehicles." It would offer enough electricity to operate electric A/C, electric brakes, electric steering, Internet dashboard, drive-by-wire capability and a video screen in the back for the kids. Even with the new approaches, attracting buyers continues to be a problem for updated century-old concepts, but attitudes may be changing in favor of the EVs and HEVs.

Business Economics, in October 2000, projected global sales of more than one million electric vehicles by the year 2007. This would represent 1.5 percent of the total global motor vehicle production and 0.5 percent of the motor vehicles on the road. "Clearly, we are looking at a narrow, albeit fast-growing market."[97] They also predicted that most of the electric vehicles would be battery-powered. Hybrids and fuel-cell-powered cars will be increasing faster in the second half of this decade. Electric vehicles will appear in volume in the large densely populated cities of the world first. The consensus remains that air pollution is easier to control at central power generating plants than from individual vehicles. This leads to the promotion of greater use of electric vehicles while controlling emissions from electric generating plants. Disposal and recycling of lead-acid batteries has been partially resolved. New types of batteries are being developed, with thought to environmental concerns. Fleet sales continue to be a major portion of overall EV sales.[98] The recharging infrastructure will continue to grow, albeit slowly. General acceptance of the EV is here, but consumers are still slow to open their wallets. Consumers are willing to consider alternatives to the ICEs if the new auto power plants and design fit the image and reflect the owner's lifestyle. Markets open when products meet buyers' expectations and catch their fancy.

6 Conclusion

Publications of the day chronicle the electric vehicle's roller-coaster existence. Their prose captures the early optimism of EV dominance in the 1890s, and today's more practical approach to the market's attitude about electrics. The following pages highlight the EV's story — optimism to realism. It is obvious, based on the limited progress over one hundred years, that a new battery technology that would increase range and decrease costs dramatically will not take place overnight or in the near future, if ever. This may leave the battery-only powered vehicles in a niche market. There is, however, a great deal of genuine optimism concerning the hybrid vehicles already on the road — the Toyota Prius and Honda Insight and Civic — and the nascent fuel cell technology. These developments, combined with the more-fuel-efficient ICE engines being developed, appear to be the obvious next steps in reducing our dependence on foreign oil and eventually replacing the traditional internal combustion engine with one more environmentally friendly. The EVs have, and continue to provide, balance and incentive to improve our means of transportation. Writers throughout this last century have captured the sentiments of the acceptance, flaws and development cycles of the electric vehicle. As each generation rediscovers the EV, we see the same points recur.

As early as 1897 comments about electric vehicles were showing up in print. One of the earliest reports on the new electric taxicabs in New York City strikes a slightly negative note. The *New York Journal* penned a column titled *A Chappie and a Horseman Try the New Horseless Carriage.* In it, pseudonymous columnist "Cholly Knickerbocker" chronicles an outing in an electric cab taken by him and his new bride as a diversion on their honeymoon. He noted,

> There is a sense of incompleteness about it. You seemed to be sitting on the end of a huge pushcart, propelled by an invisible force and guided by a hidden hand. Gradually, I felt I did not need the protection of a horse in front of me. I congratulate myself that I survived the ordeal. The horseless carriage will have to be improved before it becomes popular in chappiedom.[1]

On another ride with a portly friend, the two of them weighing approximately 425 pounds, Morris and Salom's cab was put out of balance. Knickerbocker's friend, Francis Trevelyan, said:

> I do not think the [electric] motor cab will be anything more than a fad. The horses, especially when they are well-bred trotters, regard it rather curiously, but on the whole contemptuously; but in the bosom of the average cyclist it seems to arouse derision, scorn and contempt. It gives the occupant a hopeless sensation of being perpetually shot through a chute, with the pleasing possibility of being utilized as a battering ram in a collision with a cable car or a runaway team.[2]

Fortunately for the future of EVs, not everyone considered them just a passing fad. Some periodicals predicted a rosy future for the electrics. *Scientific American* proclaimed in its May 13, 1899, issue:

> Electricity, too, has made its "debut" in locomotion. An almost perfect electric motor has been found. Backward and forward motion, and excellent brake arrangement, absence of noise, smell or vibration, are only a few of the qualities of this wonderful motor. It has only one fault, an immense quantity of electricity is wanted. Then they have to be refilled at the works [recharging station]. Accordingly, electric carriages can only be employed within a small radius of these works, from which the supply of energy is obtained. Still, they seem to be destined for a great future in town locomotion by reason of the ease with which accumulators [batteries] may be obtained.[3]

The optimism of the enthusiasts showed dreams of a new era of companionship and travel. An article in *McClure's Magazine* in 1899 declared,

> It is not hard to imagine what a country touring station will be like on a summer afternoon some five or ten years hence. Long rows of vehicles will stand backed up comfortably to the charging bars each with its electric plug filling the battery with power. The owners will be lolling at the tables on the verandas of the nearby road house. Men with repair kits will bustle about tightening up a nut here, oiling this bearing and regulating that gear. The new electric cabs are unquestionable immensely popular as fashionable conveyances.[4]

Fashion was not the only vision the EV supporters saw. They realized the problems that were already plaguing cities: the use of horses had long caused one environmental problem, and the early ICEs had brought another. The electric automobile was considered the perfect solution for city use at the turn of the century. That new era would mean quieter streets and cleaner air. In 1899 *Scientific American* said,

> There seems to be a general impression that for passenger transportation in and around our cities the electric automobile is the best. It has the great advantage of being silent, free from odor, simple in construction and gearing, capable of ready control, and having a considerable range of speed.[5]

Some manufacturers saw the electric's potential and were eager to get into the business of designing a product that would grab the customer's attention. Colonel Albert A. Pope in 1900 was one of these entrepreneurs.

> Fifteen thousand of his bicycle agents throughout the country were "fairly howling" for automobiles to meet an enormous demand. Pope knew the need was for a reliable automobile that would sell for less than $1,000. Although he recognized that the current automobiles fell far short of this standard, he confidently hoped that "next year we will currently have a machine near perfection."[6]

Marketing on fuel economy alone did not seem to interest the early adapters. In the 1900 Paris-Dijon road race, one electric car traveled 164 miles at an average speed of ten miles per hour on a single charge.

> In energy equivalence, this electric car traveled 183 miles per gallon. At the time, steam vehicles were achieving six miles per gallon, over atrocious roads, and gasoline powered cars 12 miles per gallon. Fuel costs have had little impact on the choice of the motive power of cars, indicating there have been other subjective and objective reasons.[7]

Around the same time, the motoring magazine *Horseless Age* noted that during the period from July 1 to December 31, 1902, the issues "had five articles listing new electric cars, 67 announcing gasoline-powered cars and 19 introducing steam cars."[8]

By 1905 there had been several experiments with hybrid gasoline-electric vehicles. The *Automobile* devoted an entire chapter to these gasoline-electric vehicles and observed that the combination of the two motors could have the advantage of balancing the disadvantages of each separately. It noted,

> The greatest inconvenience of the petrol motor, as has been shown, is its want of elasticity [efficiency], as it must have an excess of power which there is no use for in ordinary circumstances where the petrol spirit yields only a part of its theoretical heat energy. To obtain variable speeds with a petrol motor there has to be a complicated system of spur gears or of pulleys and belts, which, of course, wastes much power. On the other hand, a large amount of energy can be carried on a petrol car, and further supplies can be easily obtained on the road. Opposite in every way to this is the electric motor; this has remarkable elasticity being able to bring the requisite amount of energy into play at each moment and to dispense with [a] mechanical speed changing gear, but its great disadvantage is that frequent new supplies are essential. This balancing of advantages and disadvantages naturally has led to the idea of associating two motors, one of each type, in the same car. The weight of the petrol-electric car is a consideration ... as the whole mechanism is essentially heavier... [This] type of vehicle is proving itself highly successful for lurries [trucks] and omnibuses, where actual weight is comparatively unimportant. How far it can be adapted for passenger vehicles and pleasure cars of the lighter kind remains to be seen.[9]

By 1907 "the electric vehicle has taken its logical position as a means of freight and passenger traffic in cities and for short tours out of town; while the gasoline machine is rapidly gaining recognition as the automobile *par excellence*."[10]

In 1910, a Technical Society publication pronounced great promise in using electrics for touring. The article proclaimed that,

> [T]hese have not been trips around a circle or through a certain territory but have been right across the country. They show it is perfectly feasible to tour in an electric where the driver is sufficiently familiar with his machine and the methods by which it may be charged to take advantage of the current supply where the ordinary facilities for charging are lacking. North of the Ohio and east of the Mississippi, cities and towns where electric current may be obtained are so numerous and so close together that there is practically no part of this large territory in which a car would have to be driven much beyond its ordinary mileage in order to reach a charging current. In view of the number of garages that are equipped with the necessary facilities for taking care of electric cars to be found in every town and city, it is possible to lay out extended touring routes anywhere in the territory in question. Runs of 50 to 80 miles per day may be averaged and while touring is not recommended by its builders, these performances have shown in a very striking manner of what it is capable.[11]

In that same year, while he sold an electric car battery of his own commercially, Thomas Edison predicted widespread popularity for electric cars. He told Walter Baker of the Baker Electric Company, "If you continue to make your present caliber of automobile, and I my present quality of battery, the gasoline buggies will be out of existence in no time."[12] To promote their transportation concept, the Electric Vehicle Association of America partnered with electric utility companies for a joint EV advertising campaign:

> An advertising fund of large proportions we are about to solicit and secure. Our idea is, by means of this fund [for a publicity campaign], to advertise all over the land that the electric vehicle is a perfect device, and that it can and does perform certain services better and cheaper than any other agency. We are to *sing the praises* [italics added] of the electric vehicle as such, and to get the public to adopt and use the electric vehicle.[13]

In 1911, the *Scientific American* noted,

> The electric pleasure car is coming into its own. For certain kinds of service it is ideal. Its simple and responsive control will always be its most remarkable feature. The gasoline car has perhaps obscured the development which the electric has been undergoing in recent years. [In the following article] will be found a summary of those mechanical and electrical perfections which have been introduced in recent cars, and which have elevated the pleasure vehicle to a remarkable pitch of perfection. Popular misconceptions are corrected, so far as the function and energy of the storage battery are concerned, and the remarkable luxurious furnishing of the electric carriage is illustrated. The many mechanical expedients devised to make the electric carriage a comfortable and easily operated vehicle, are set forth.[14]

A 1911 *Electrical World* article reiterated a theme seen from the EV's earliest design and through the century, "If charging stations could readily be found in every town where there is electric service, the use of electric pleasure cars on fairly long runs would become much more common than it is now."[15]

The October 1912 Report to the Electric Vehicle Association of America was presented by the publicity committee complete with illustrations. The presentation included lantern slides of the images. The report covered the progress of the previous two years of their national cooperative advertising campaign. The campaign was fairly well supported by the members and subscribers and various editorial comments reflected this consensus of opinion. Some remarks were,

> We are very well satisfied with the results of our campaign last year, and the writer has been so well pleased with the efforts and beauty of the E.V.A. matter that we are very desirous of again going on into our local campaign and of co-operating with the E.V.A. so as to use their copy concurrently in our newspapers.
> …There can be no question whatever that such extensive and excellent promotion must have the effect of popularizing the electric vehicle. We are, of course, conducting local campaigns with this same object in view.[16]

There is a sense however, reading between the lines, that the electrics were losing the battle. The president stated,

> The aim of the Electrical Association of America is to promote the use of the electric vehicle for business and pleasure purposes. One of our first duties, we believe, is

to educate the public as to the advantages of electric propulsion. It is *hoped* [italics added] that the national advertising will be supplemented by consistent and continuous local advertising, both on the part of vehicle manufacturers and the central stations.[17]

A 1912 article in the *Horseless Age* claimed charging stations had been established to the limited extent that an electric car owner could travel between New York and Buffalo, and from Philadelphia to New York, this representing "touring." "This development was an infrastructure that enhanced the value of an electric car, an omission which today limits the value of the modern electric automobile. The gasoline station, in contrast, is everywhere present."[18] A 1912 *Scientific American* article noted optimistically,

> It is remarkable to note the extraordinary favor with which the electric vehicle is being accepted in the commercial world to-day. But, popular as the electric vehicle is at present it is bound to find far greater favor as its advantages become more appreciated. In fact the mechanism of an electric car is so simple that there are only two things upon which there can be any extensive improvement, i.e. the battery and the motor.[19]

Nineteen fifteen saw electrics promoted as an auto of perfection that manufacturers kept improving. The *Automobile* carried especially glowing comments about the beautiful electrics.

> Although many people are apparently settled in the belief that the electric passenger car has reached perfection and no further improvement is possible without some radical departure from accepted construction, the car makers themselves are far from sharing this view of the matter, each year surpassing themselves in the improved appearance and in luxurious fittings, finish and equipment. These features, developed to the extent that they might be referred to as boudoirs on wheels, render the electric passenger car, as built today, especially attractive to women, and at the same time not too ornate for the every-day use of even the most conservative business man....
>
> Chassis have been simplified, lightened and made more accessible wherever possible without impairing the solidity of construction. The increased use of worm, spiral-bevel and herringbone gears in the final drive has done much to promote efficiency. Weight reductions due to chassis simplification and the use of aluminum for bodies, together with the elimination of resistance from the presence of dirt and grit in the working parts by the provision of improved protection, and the more thorough utilization of battery equipment have done much towards increasing mileage per charge, and at the same time towards cutting down operating expense for the owner.[20]

A 1921 article for *Electrical World* indicated that the electrics had not had the success expected in 1915, but supporters remained optimistic. It stated, "A new day has dawned for the electric vehicle after a period of sub-normal appreciation of its economic capabilities.... The line of new installations is rapidly lengthening and many of the foremost men in the industry are standing up to be counted as believers in the electric vehicle opportunity."[21] Thomas A. Edison noted, "I am pleased to hear that the electric vehicle for city traffic is receiving more attention lately from the electric lighting companies. Any merchant who keeps accurate costs will buy electrics."[22] "Those who have cast their lot with the transportation side of the great electrical industry will realize they have not labored in vain."[23]

In 1922, in response to an assertion that the price of electric vehicles was too high and may include an inordinate amount of profit, a *London Electric Review* article noted, "As an answer to this totally erroneous view, it may be stated, as an incontrovertible fact, that, in this post-war period, no British firm building electric vehicles has made any profit worth speaking of—indeed, it would be safe to say that most, if not all of them, have made losses on the business done."[24] The article went on to list three justifications for the high initial cost of the electric: (1) lack of demand, (2) initial high costs could be offset by the fact that the useful life of the electric is twice that of a comparable gasoline vehicle, and (3) it is the best long-term investment for short-distance haulage. Businessmen generally accepted using electrics for delivery vehicles after an opening trial period. This position was still not accepted by the general public of the day. The lack of a convenient number of charging stations, even in a country like England where the distances between towns were relatively short, continued to be problematic for the average consumer. The *London Electric Review* was still optimistic, stating,

> There are good reasons for predicting the employment of electric vehicles upon a considerable scale in the near future. It will, no doubt, be mainly in urban areas, but any improvement upon the present type of battery in the direction of increased capacity per unit of weight will widen the field of utility, and if, concomitantly with such improvement, we come to the establishment of the battery exchange system and sufficiently numerous exchange stations, it will undoubtedly lead to electrics being employed in rural or long-distance transport. With the improvement, which is continuously in progress in road construction, we may very likely see the electric entering this wider field of employment at no very distant date.[25]

Little was written about electric vehicles again until World War II. By 1940, gasoline was needed for war. Electrics came back into service to keep people and products moving without sapping precious fuel from the military effort. The electrics' use was encouraged, while their limitations were acknowledged.

> From the national and patriotic standpoint, too, every gallon of petrol saved improves our position for waging the war and it is estimated that if electric vehicles were given their rightful place in the transport services of this country no fewer than 70,000,000 gallons of petrol would be saved every year.... The long life of the electric vehicle is a further point that would appeal to those responsible for conserving our national resources. In this connection it must be remembered that practically all the lead in an old battery is recoverable and can be used again....[26]

As in the early years, the dream of improved technology was also a consideration in 1940.

> When a lighter or standard battery appears on the scene, a new vista will be opened for electric vehicles for private purposes. Even now they have a limited market as town runabouts for doctors, lady shoppers, business men, etc., and, as in the case of a vehicle just purchased by Ferguson, Pailin, Ltd., for running between a factory and a station, etc. With a maximum range of about 50 miles and a maximum speed of 30 MPH, the vehicle for private use will necessarily be favoured only by people who possess another car.[27]

The *Saturday Evening Post*, in 1960, saw renewed interest in electrics creeping into society.

Production of "the old square jobs" ceased thirty years ago, and no one expects their return. Like the Stanley Steamer, they lost out to the gasoline engine. The steamers are gone for good, but electrics are coming back, in a variety of forms. With stream lined bodies and updated innards, new electric trucks and passenger cars are rolling now in Atlantic City, Lansing, Detroit, Cleveland and Spokane, and in several towns in France and England.

Most of the experimental electrics are good-looking on the outside, pretty crude inside. I have driven two experimental models. They were silent, of course, and they handled well. My wife tried them too—and got an I'd-like-one look in her eye. If we lived in a city or suburb, instead of far out in the country, she'd have a case. Trouble is, these cars run only eighty miles or so on a fresh battery charge, so they won't do for long trips. But for in-town use by a two-car family they are unbeatable on several counts....[28]

Environmental concerns became prevalent in the 1960s with optimism for solutions running high. A *Scientific American* article in 1966 proclaimed,

Some engineers have never lost faith in the electric car, and the basic arguments for its revival are cogent and becoming stronger year by year. Chief among these is the increasingly dangerous pollution of our air by the millions of gasoline burning vehicles invading our cities and countryside. We also face the inescapable fact that the supply of cheap gasoline will not last many decades longer at the present rate of consumption of fossil fuels. And while the cost of gasoline is rising, electricity is becoming more plentiful and cheaper. Only technical problems have stood in the way of producing an electric car that could replace the internal combustion one. Solutions for these problems are now definitely in sight.[29]

Distance and battery technology continued to be discussed as a drawback for the EVs. In 1967,

An automobile, even a small car, cannot have a range of 150 miles with any presently available storage battery systems. It may be five to ten years before more advanced systems now being studied are ready for road testing.[30]

Jim Williams, according to his colleague Steve Thompson of *Car and Driver*, had a different take on the environmentalist concerns.

...the real social force behind what B. Bruce-Briggs aptly called *The War Against the Automobile* in his '70s book with that title was not environmentalism, safety consciousness or the national-security concerns of dependence on foreign oil. Instead, Williams concluded that a new Puritanism was abroad in the land, in the form of what he called "The Alliance Against Fun."

It has taken the ensuing decades to show how right I think Williams was in his judgment that it wasn't really what the cars of the era actually did (or didn't do) that made so many in his theoretical Alliance hate them. It was what cars *are*: expressions of individual choice and freedom of action.

If Williams' hypothesis about car haters is correct, it means that moving from an oil economy to a hydrogen economy via hybrids, NGVs and other interim solutions will have no effect on these New Puritans, who will continue not only to be haunted by the fear that someone, somewhere is happy in an automobile, but is actually using it.[31]

The 1970 Clean Air Car Race, a cross-country race from Pasadena, California, to Cambridge, Massachusetts, was covered by the *New York Times*, likely in response to the growth of interest at the time in pollution control. It reported that the race was not "…a stunt, is neither a campus caper, nor a far-out demonstration. The more such activity and awareness [of alternative fuel vehicles] spreads, the less automakers can expect to put-off that change at their pleasure."[32] General Motors had two internal factions concerning the concept of electric vehicle production. "Yes, an electric vehicle can really perform… At what cost?"[33]

The 1973–4 energy crisis provided a long-awaited reawakening in the interest in electric vehicles. The "just around the corner" theme surfaced again.

> Today's fuel shortage and tomorrow's projected per-gallon costs for gasoline appear to create the correct timing for the fledgling electric car industry.[34]

Later in the year, *Industry Week* approached the continual problem of limited range of electric cars by stating,

> In defense, they would also point out that high-density batteries are surely just around the corner, which would swing all logic to electrics. We look to the battery industry for a technology breakthrough.[35]

In a 1989 article A. F. Burke found the advancement of battery technology for electrics lacking. He stated,

> Methods for accurately including the effects of changes in battery temperature and age must be developed and demonstrated before any battery state-of-charge unit can be used with confidence in a vehicle. None of the battery management systems tested established sufficiently accurate and reliable operation in both the charge and discharge modes that they could be used in the test programs to control the cycling of the batteries…. [While] considerable progress has been made in battery management systems for electric vehicles in recent years the available systems are insufficiently dependable for unattended use.[36]

Ernest Wakefield expressed an historical perspective in comparing early discoveries to today's product.

> It is interesting to note that after a century of effort, the most commercially suitable battery in 1990 for electric vehicle propulsion is a derivation of Plante's lead-acid battery of 1859. Also, the modern version is less than twice the delivered energy per unit weight of Julien's 1888 lead-acid battery.[37]

The Department of Energy, with the Idaho National Engineering and Environmental Laboratory (INEEL) and other partnerships, has been working on developing advanced batteries, such as nickel/iron, lithium-ion, nickel/zinc, etc.

> Although these advanced batteries show exciting promise, the problems of solving the associated research problems and of producing a practical battery at low cost is a great challenge. These advanced batteries may hold out the best hope for a substantial replacement of gasoline cars with electric cars.[38]

In 1996 increased pollution caused by generating the additional power needed for electric vehicles was examined.

The debate about electric vehicles often revolves around whether increased smokestack emissions—from power plants generating the electricity needed to recharge all those EV batteries—will offset the reduction in pollution from tailpipes.[39]

The adverse effects of increasing lead-acid batteries needed to power zero emission electrics was also an environmental concern. An abstract from *Environmental Science and Technology* predicted that the CARB mandate requiring that 10 percent of motor vehicles must be Zero Emission Vehicles by 2003 would add 500,000 batteries for disposal.

> In contrast to the small ozone-related benefits from BPVs, the potential environmental problems are considerable. Mining, smelting, and recycling more than 500kg of lead batteries per vehicle would result in environmental lead releases 80 times greater per vehicle mile than those of a gasoline-powered vehicle with a current starter battery. Half a million lead-acid BPVs would increase national lead discharges to the environment by about 20%.[40]

In 1997, *Scientific American* again brought hybrids back for a look.

> …There are actually hundreds of engineers around the world who are working on hybrid electric vehicles. But almost a century after the hybrid was first conceived, more than 25 years after development work began on them in earnest, and after more than $1 billion has been spent world wide, in recent years on development, not a single hybrid vehicle is being offered to the public by a large automaker. In fact, not a single design is anywhere near volume production. In the U.S., where the government has spent about $750 million since 1994 on almost frenzied efforts to advance the technology of hybrid electric vehicles [HEVs], the concept is still a political football rather than a commercial reality.[41]

Revisiting hybrids included reviewing the fuel cell as a possible energy source. In 1998, reviews on fuel cells were mixed. *Business Week*'s Science and Technology section stated,

> Other pieces of the fuel-cell puzzle are falling into place. Impressive progress has been made in developing transmissions, for instance. While consumers haven't flocked to battery-powered cars, the R&D that went into them helped Detroit cut the cost and improve the reliability of the motors and generators. Insiders say that GM, thanks to its EV1 electric car, has an edge in electronic controllers, which coordinates all high-voltage operations of the drive system. By 2000, these sources expect GM to have an electric transmission equal in cost to a traditional automatic transmission.
>
> Still. Researchers may have trouble keeping up with the public-relations machine. Already, engineers are looking for wiggle room in the pronouncements by senior managers. Even Ford's Bates has a hard time accepting the newfound optimism. "We really have no confidence these things will completely deliver on their promise," he admits. "But the promise is so great, you just have to give it a go." Or risk seeing more German and Japanese cars in the driveways.[42]

The fuel cell powered vehicle had its skeptics at the turn of the 21st century. In response to the NECAR 4 and P2000, *Car and Driver* featured these comments.

> In Sacramento, California, Daimler-Chrysler and Ford scored first in the headline wars with a press intro of their NECAR 4 and P2000 fuel-cell-powered machines as part of the widely ignored Earth Day festivities. These vehicles were the opening salvo in a test fleet of 45 cars and busses to be powered by the magic cells in Los Angeles basin over the next four years.

Yes, fuel-cell cars powered by hydrogen are zero-emission units, but several issues have been conveniently ignored by the press during its euphoric announcements, including the "total energy" process required to produce, deliver and consume fuel in any vehicle. In this context, a gasoline-powered engine is radically more efficient than any fuel-celled alternative.[43]

Environmentalists of the 1990s stressed the impact ICEs had on an international issue of the day, global warming. Discussions on global warming included the need to find ways of coping with the problem ICEs cause with their exhaust. The Sierra Club in 1999 and an article in *Time* in 2002 earmark the problem and a possible solution in the not-too-distant future.

Motor vehicles consume half the world's oil and account for a quarter of its greenhouse gas emissions. The biggest source of air pollution in a majority of the world's cities is auto exhaust.[44]

Hybrids are the first viable alternative to the gasoline engine. Cars that run on fuel cells—widely expected to be the next technological advance in automotive power—are at least ten years off.[45]

In the early 21st century's market, carmakers continually maintain that EVs cost about $20,000 more to manufacture than a gasoline vehicle. Manufacturers met government mandates for zero emission vehicles with varying degrees of enthusiasm, but the demand was not there.

[The] oil industry acted aggressively against both the CARB mandate and the electric car. General Motors worked against the mandate only, and has been fairly enthusiastic about having an advanced electric car for sale. Ford and Chrysler have not to the same degree been enthusiastic about electric cars, and certainly not about the mandate. Toyota is taking a more active role in Japan.[46]

The Honda Insight and Toyota Prius hybrids began to get consumers' attention soon after their U.S. arrival. Well-known talk-radio hosts Tom and Ray Magliozzi, from *Car Talk*, test-drove the cars in 2001 and concluded:

The Honda Insight is currently the second best hybrid vehicle on sale in the United States. We should also mention that there are only two hybrids in that category. The other is the Toyota Prius. We can sum up the differences between the Insight and Prius this way: The Insight is a vehicle for people whose first and foremost goal in life is to get the best possible gasoline mileage, everything else be damned. And the Prius is a great little car that happens to get outstanding gas mileage.[47]

In 2003 General Motors' vice president for research and development, Larry Burns, has a novel approach to the AFV concept.

"The stone age didn't end because we ran out of stones." This Larry Burns aphorism is one you hear from his acolytes at General Motors' facilities around the world. He means it to suggest that a superior technology can replace a proven one by offering advantages, rather than by waiting for a resource to run out. We didn't stop heating our homes with logs because the trees were all gone, and we didn't put ourselves on wheels because there was a global shortage of horses.

Burns doesn't aim to replace stones or trees or even wheels, but internal combustion engines. He is passionate about this, and he has GM chairman and CEO

Richard Wagoner backing him up. They're driven, you might say, to push the transition away from internal combustion of petroleum derivatives and into fuel cells running on hydrogen. And by repeating his "Stone Age" line, what his minions mean to convey is they share Burns' conviction that fuel cells can be made into a superior alternative, one that can attract consumers on its own merits rather than being foisted on them by force of government decree or onerous taxation.[48]

The history and future of the electric, hybrid and alternative fuel vehicles has vacillated over the last one hundred years. Optimism prevailed in the early years when many projected the dominance of the electrics, but battery cost and performance could not compete with the distance and speed the ICEs could deliver without major advances in battery technology. After a century of research and development and commercial availability, battery technology, lack of infrastructure, and sluggish consumer support continue to be stumbling blocks for electric vehicles. The logic that if there were more cars, charging stations would be more prevalent has been repeated time and again, through five wars, energy crises and whenever concerns about environmental issues arise.

The major auto industry manufacturers readily finance research and development in the 21st century to develop new technologies. Since gasoline is still the most widely available fuel, the current infrastructure still relies on gasoline. Consumer acceptance varies widely with small pockets of enthusiasts scattered throughout the continents, and many more poised to revisit EVs. The consumer's view of electrics has not varied much over the last one hundred years. The concept of an environmentally friendly machine continues to grab their attention, and if the electric meets their expectation of convenience, performance and cost, many will buy it by choice. The most promising development to replace the ICE and dependence on foreign oil supplies seems to be the hybrid engine, with fuel cell vehicles possibly emerging as a viable alternative in about ten years.

Will this prediction come any closer to fulfillment than so many other predictions of the last hundred years? We will all just have to wait and see.

Appendix: Historical Highlights

1771 — Nicolas Cugnot invents a steam-driven vehicle in Paris.
1802 — Sir Humphey Davy builds a fuel cell of carbon and nitric acid.
1839 — Principle of the hydrogen fuel cell established.
1859 — E. L. Drake brings in the first oil well in Titusville, PA.
1860 — Gaston Plante invents the lead-acid storage battery.
1876 — Nikolaus Otto invents the four-stroke internal combustion engine.
1881 — First electric vehicle is a tricycle in Paris.
1889 — Thomas Edison builds a nickel-alkaline battery powered vehicle.
1891 — Wm. Morrison, Des Moines, Iowa, devises the first American electric car.
1892 — The first production electric car is shown in Chicago.
1893 — Charles Duryea produces America's first gasoline-powered car.
1895 — One-third of all cars in Michigan are battery operated.
1895 — The word *automobile* is first used by the *Pall Mall Gazette*, London.
1897 — The Olds Motor Works is founded by Ransom E. Olds.
1899 — Jenatzy's electric car *Jamais Contente* sets a world speed record of 68.8 mph in an electric car.
1900 — Gasoline cars beat electric cars for the first time in a Chicago race.
1901 — Oil is discovered in Beaumont, Texas.
1902 — The Cadillac Motor Company is founded.
1903 — The first patent for a windshield wiper is awarded to Mary Anderson.
1904 — One-third of all powered vehicles in New York, Chicago and Boston are electric.
1907 — Peking-to-Paris race.
1907 — A steam-powered vehicle sets a land speed record of 127 mph.
1908 — Henry Ford's Model T sells 10,000 units.
1910 — A neon sign is used to advertise automobiles at the Paris Automobile Show.
1911 — The Electric Vehicle Association is formed.
1912 — Kettering introduces the electric starter.
1912 — The high point for electrics, with 20 manufacturers and 30,000 cars.
1913 — Henry Ford introduces the moving assembly line.

1915 — Ford produces one million vehicles.

1917 — France stops all private motoring to conserve gasoline for war interests.

1919 — Oregon enacts the first state gasoline tax.

1921 — Almost all steam and electric cars have disappeared from the market.

1923 — The last national automobile show for a new electric vehicle.

1928 — Ford introduces the Model A.

1929 — The stock market crash and Great Depression cause many companies to fail.

1935 — Over 3 million cars are equipped with radios.

1940 — Germany has over 27,000 EVs in service.

1955 — Air Pollution Control Act of 1955.

1958 — Seat belts are introduced.

1963 — Clean Air Act of 1963.

1966 — Electric Hybrid Vehicle Development Act of 1966.

1968 — The Electric Vehicle Council is formed.

1973 — The Arab oil cartel embargoes crude oil to the United States.

1975 — CAFE standards are established.

1976 — Electric Hybrid Vehicle Act of 1976.

1990 — CARB regulations established.

1992 — Energy Policy Act of 1992.

1992 — Clean Cities Program established.

1996 — CARB updates ZEV regulations due to lack of buyers' interest.

1999 — Canadian government allots $30 million to support fuel cell research.

2000 — CARB revises regulations to include hybrids and other alternate fuels.

2001 — United Kingdom passes regulation allowing busses to control traffic signals.

2001 — Switzerland subsidizes EV purchases by individuals.

2001 — California experiences severe electric power shortages.

2001 — Over 1,100 charging stations installed in California and Arizona for EVs.

2002 — British Parliament approves largest wind farm.

2002 — Ford discontinues Th!nk car production.

2002 — Honda Civic hybrid is introduced.

2002 — President Bush supports hydrogen fuel cell development.

2003 — Controversy over building a turbine wind farm off Cape Cod.

Chapter Notes

Preface

1. Ernest H. Wakefield, *History of the Electric Vehicle* (Warrendale, Pa.: Society of Automotive Engineers, 1994).

Introduction

1. *Scientific American*, October 18, 1902, Vol. 87, No. 16, p. 266.
2. *Horseless Carriage*, September 1896, Vol. 1, No. 11, p. 18.
3. *Business & Economic History*, Winter 1997, Vol. 26, Iss. 2, pp. 304–10.
4. *Horseless Age*, March 1897, Vol. 2, No. 5, p. 5.
5. *Cyclopedia of Automobile Engineering* (Chicago: American Technical Society, 1910), Vol. 3, p. 11.
6. Michael B. Schiffer, Tamara C. Butts, and Kimberly K. Grimm, *Taking Charge* (Washington: Smithsonian Institution Press, 1994), p. 70.
7. *Scientific American*, January 7, 1899, Vol. 80, No. 1, p. 4.
8. David A. Kirsch, *The Electric Vehicle and the Burden of History* (New Brunswick, N.J.: Rutgers University Press, 1964), p. 93.
9. *New York Times*, December 21, 1906, 10:1.
10. *Scientific American*, May 13, 1899, Vol. 80, No. 19, p. 304.
11. Matt Villano, "Plug in a Car, and Give It Juice," http://future.newsday.com/4/fbak0430.htm accessed April 5, 2001.
12. *Horseless Age*, December 12, 1902, Vol. 7, No. 11, p. 22.
13. *Cyclopedia of Automobile Engineering*, 1910, Chicago: American Technical Society, Vol. 3, p. 12.
14. *Electrical World*, June 22, 1911, Vol. 57, No. 25, p. 1590.
15. *Ibid.*
16. *Electrical World*, June 11, 1911, Vol. 57, No. 22, p. 1437.

17. *Electrical World*, June 22, 1911, Vol. 57, No. 25, p. 1590.
18. *Automobile*, October 22, 1914, Vol. 31, pp. 753–4.
19. *Country Life in America*, January 1913, v. 23, p. 23–6.
20. *Ibid.*
21. *Automobile*, January 20, 1916, Vol. 35, pp. 122–9.
22. Hans Fogelberg, *The Electric Car Controversy* (Göteborg, Sweden: Dept. of History and Technology and Industry, Chalmers University of Technology, 1998), p. i.
23. Mark De Luchi, Quanlu Wang & Daniel Sperling, *Transportation*, 1989, Res. A Vol. 23A, No.3.
24. *Scientific American*, October 18, 1902, Vol. 87, No. 16, p. 266.
25. Bill Vance, "Stanley and the Steam-powered Automobiles," http://www.canadiandriver.com/articles/bv/stanley.htm accessed May 21, 2001.
26. Robert Pool, *Beyond Engineering: How Society Shapes Technology* (New York: Oxford University Press, 1997), pp. 152–4.
27. *Scientific American*, May 13, 1899, Vol. 80, No. 19, p. 300.
28. "Electric Cars; The Drive Toward Fresh Air," *Humanist*, May/June 1994, Vol. 54, Iss. 3, p. 43.
29. *Scientific American Supplement*, February 2, 1918, Vol. 25, no. 2196, p. 70.

Chapter 1

1. *Anon.*
2. Hans Fogelberg, *The Electric Car Controversy* (Göteborg, Sweden: Dept. of History and Technology and Industry, Chalmers University of Technology, 1998), p. 31.
3. James J. Flink, *America Adopts the Automobile, 1895–1910* (Cambridge, Massachusetts: MIT Press, 1970), p. 238. (Original source "Automobile Motors," *Scientific American*, August 5, 1899, Vol. 81, No. 82.)
4. *The Automobile* (New York: Cassell and Company, Ltd., 1905), Vol. 1, p. 347.

5. *Ibid.*

6. *Scientific American*, September 2, 1899, Vol. 81, No. 9, p. 153.

7. *Scientific American*, January 9, 1892, Vol. 66, No. 1, p. 18.

8. Michael B. Schiffer, Tamara C. Butts, and Kimberly K. Grimm, *Taking Charge* (Washington, D.C.: Smithsonian Institution Press, 1994), p. 36.

9. *Scientific American*, January 9, 1892, Vol. 66, No. 1, p. 18.

10. *Scientific American*, March 23, 1895, Vol. 72, No. 12, p. 177.

11. *Ibid.*

12. *Scientific American*, November 18, 1899, Vol. 81, No. 81, p. 324.

13. Ian Ward, *The World of Automobiles* (Milwaukee: Purnell Reference Books, 1977), v. 5, p. 693.

14. *Ibid.*

15. Ernest H. Wakefield, *History of the Electric Automobile: Hybrid Electric Vehicles* (Warrendale, PA.: Society of Automotive Engineers, 1998), p. v.

16. Mark Olama, "*Ferdinand Porsche,*" http://www.foi.hr/~molama/History.htm accessed July 15, 2002.

17. *Scientific American Supplement*, October 24, 1903, No. 1451, p. 23253.

18. *Scientific American*, May 13, 1899, Vol. 80, No. 18, p. 294.

19. *Scientific American Supplement*, January 6, 1900, Vol. 49, No. 1253, p. 20088.

20. *Horseless Age*, August 1897, Vol. 2, No. 9, p. 12.

21. *Scientific American*, May 22, 1897, Vol. 76, No. 21, p. 331.

22. Schiffer, p. 58.

23. *Scientific American*, May 22, 1897, Vol. 76, No. 21, p. 331.

24. *Scientific American*, December 13, 1902, Vol. 87, No. 24, p. 427.

25. Gérard Lavergne, *The Automobile* (New York: Cassell and Company, Ltd., 1905), Vol. 2, p. 697.

26. *Ibid.*

27. *Ibid.*

28. *Ibid.*

29. Nick Georgano, *The Beaulieu Encyclopedia of the Automobile* (Chicago: Fitzroy Dearborn Publishers, 2000), Vol. 1, p. 160.

30. *Scientific American*, October 14, 1899, Vol. 81, p. 244.

31. *Ibid.*

32. Clay McShane, *The Automobile* (Westport, Connecticut: Greenwood Press, 1997), p. 24.

33. Georgano, p. 1334.

34. *Scientific American*, May 13, 1899, Vol. 80, No. 18, p. 294.

35. *Scientific American*, December 22, 1900 p. 389.

36. Ward, v. 10, p. 1237.

37. *Automobile*, September 24, 1914, Vol. 31, p. 567.

38. *Ibid.*

39. Georgano, p. 489.

40. *Motor World*, August 7, 1902, Vol. 60, No. 4, p. 540.

41. *Electrical World*, March 16, 1911, Vol. 57, No. 11, p. 679.

42. *Ibid.*

43. http://www.econogics.com/ev/babcock.jpg accessed March 10, 2001.

44. Ward, v. 5, p. 93.

45. *Electrical World*, June 1, 1911, Vol. 57, No. 22, p. 1436.

46. http://www.econogics.com/ev/raulangl.jpg accessed March 10, 2001.

47. Georgano, p. 326.

48. *Electrical World*, September 19, 1914, Vol. 64, p. 573.

49. *Illustrated World*, October 1916, Vol. 26, No. 2 p. 229.

50. Georgano, p. 1037.

51. *Electrical World*, March 6, 1911, Vol. 57, No. 11, p. 678.

52. http://www.econogics.com/ev/bkr1908.jpg accessed March 10, 2001.

53. Ward, v. 5, p. 154.

54. *Ibid.*

55. *Automobile*, January 21, 1915, Vol. 32, p. 138.

56. Georgano, p. 258.

57. http://www.econogics.com/ev/century.jpg accessed March 10, 2001.

58. Ward, v. 5, p. 96.

59. *Electrical Review*, October 2, 1915, Vol. 67, pp. 641–3.

60. Georgano, p. 430.

61. http://www.econogics.com/ev/model46.jpg accessed March 10, 2001.

62. Georgano, p. 430.

63. http://www.econogics.com/ev/rlmilbu2.jpg accessed April 2, 2001.

64. *Literary Digest*, March 25, 1916, Vol. 52, No. 13, p. 857.

65. *New York Times*, January 7, 1917, III, 15:1.

66. *Electrical World*, June 15, 1918, Vol. 71, p. 1264.

67. Georgano, p. 1557.

68. *Ibid.*, p. 490.

69. http://www.econogics.com/ev/enfield.jpg accessed February 20, 2000.

70. Georgano, p. 488.

71. Bob Gritzinger, "1966 GMC Electrovan," *AutoWeek*, January 1, 2001, Vol. 51, Iss. 1, p. 27.

72. *Automotive News*, December 5, 1994, Vol. 69, No. 5581, p. 2i (supp.).

73. Don Schroeder, "General Motors EV1," *Car & Driver*, October 1996, Vol. 42, pp. 77–8+.

74. *Ibid.*

75. Supplied by Corbin Motors 2001.

76. http://www.familycar.com/Future/gm_precept.htm accessed July 30, 2003.

77. http://www.ott.doe.gov/hev/concept.html accessed June 22, 2003.

78. *Economist*, July 1, 2000, v. 356, iss. 8177, p. 83.

79. Interview with Bob Kelly, Budget Supervisor, Customer Service, Budget Rent-a-Car System, Inc., Phoenix, Arizona, April 16, 2001.

Chapter 2

1. "Why Detroit's Going Green," *Sierra*, July/ August 1999, Vol. 84, No. 4, p. 38.

2. Daniel Sperling, *Future Drive* (Washington, D.C.: Island Press, 1995), pp. 10–11.

3. Bill Moore, "Shell's H2 Future," http://evworld. com/databases/printit.cfm?storyid=396 accessed August 20, 2001.

4. "Selden Patent Plaque," http://vintagecars. about.com/library/weekly/aa110799.htm?terms=seld en accessed January 5, 2000.

5. James J. Flink, *America Adopts the Automobile, 1895–1910* (Cambridge, Massachusetts: MIT Press, 1970), p. 327.

6. *North American Review*, August 1904, pp. 168–77.

7. *Ibid.*

8. *Ibid.*

9. *Scientific American*, December 21, 1901, Vol. 85, No. 407, p. 407.

10. *New York Times*, November 11, 1899, 6:2.

11. *Ibid.*

12. *Horseless Age*, January 24, 1900, Vol. V, No. 17, p. 17.

13. *Scientific American*, May 6, 1899, Vol. 80, No. 18, p. 278.

14. *North American Review*, August 1904, pp. 168–77.

15. *New York Times*, March 11,1906, 10:5.

16. *New York Times*, March 11,1906, 11:2.

17. *New York Times*, July 8, 1906, 18:4.

18. *Outlook*, January 1906, Vol. 47, pp. 502–4.

19. *Ibid.*

20. *Ibid.*

21. *Outlook*, August 7, 1909, Vol. 92, pp. 859–60.

22. *Outlook*, December 15, 1906, Vol. 84, pp. 903–4.

23. *Harper's Weekly*, March 30, 1907, Vol. 51, p. 470.

24. *Ibid.*

25. *Nation*, September 3, 1908, Vol. 87, No. 2283, pp. 199–200.

26. *Outlook*, June 12, 1909, Vol. 92, pp. 342–3.

27. *New York Times*, June 24, 1917, 2, 4:1.

28. *Literary Digest*, November 6, 1920, Vol. 67, pp. 80–88.

29. *Scientific American Supplement*, April 1924, Vol. 130, p. 252.

30. *Literary Digest*, March 24, 1923, Vol., 76, p. 25.

31. "The Civil Shaping of Technology: California's Electric Vehicle Program," *Science, Technology & Human Values*, Winter 2001, Vol. 26, Iss. 1, pp. 56–82.

32. *Wall Street Journal*, January 18, 1974, 30:1.

33. *Ibid.*

34. *Wall Street Journal*, February 21, 1974, 32:1.

35. *Ibid.*

36. Ernest H. Wakefield, *History of the Electric Automobile: Battery-Only Powered Cars* (Warrendale, PA.: Society of Automotive Engineers, 1994), p. 284.

37. *WARD'S Auto World*, June 1992, Vol. 28, p. 32.

38. *Ibid.*

39. *Ibid.*

40. Bob McCool, "Are Oil Companies Trying to Kill the Electric Auto?" *Oil & Gas Journal*, September 11, 1995, v. 93, issue 37, p. 21.

41. William Baumgartner and Andrew Gross, "Global Market for Electric Vehicles," *Business Economics*, October 2000, Vol. 35, Iss. 4, p. 51.

42. *Oregonian*, Dec. 9,1996, p. B02.

43. "Campaigns Against Electric Cars Gaining Strength," *National Petroleum News*, July 1995, Vol. 87, pp. 18+.

44. *Ibid.*

45. "Basement Mandarins," *Newsweek*, March 22, 1999, Vol. 133, Iss. 12, p. 50.

46. David Welch, "The Eco-Cars," *Business Week*, August 14, 2000, No. 3694, pp. 62–8.

47. Hanssen, Greg, "Is CARB Getting Real, or Caving In?" November, 30, 2002, http://www.evworld. com/databases/storybuilder.cfm?storyid=458 accessed December 30, 2002.

48. F. T. Surber, et al., "Hybrid Vehicle Potential Assessment," #5030–345 (California Institute of Technology, Pasadena: Jet Propulsion Laboratory, 1980).

49. "Hybrid Electric Vehicles," *Scientific American*, October 1997, Vol. 277, Iss. 4, p. 71.

50. "Why Detroit's Going Green."

51. *Ibid.*

52. Sperling, p. 144.

53. J. Francfort and M., Carroll, *Field Operations Program Incremental Funding Activities Status Report*, March 2001.

54. *Ibid.*

55. Bill Moore, "California's Line in the Sand," http://www.evworld.com/databases/printit.cfm?storyid=388 accessed October 12, 2002.

Chapter 3

1. Ernest H. Wakefield, *The Consumer's Electric Car* (Ann Arbor, Michigan: Ann Arbor Science Publishers, Inc., 1977), p. vi.

2. *Economist*, June 22, 1996, Vol. 339, Iss. 7971, p. 3.

3. *Globe and Mail*, September 16, 1999, p. 17.

4. Transportation Research Board, National Research Council, *Toward a Sustainable Future: Addressing the Long-Term Effects of Motor Vehicle Transportation on Climate and Ecology* (Washington, D.C.: National Academy Press, 1997).

5. *Ibid.*

6. Bill Moore, "Can Wind Compete with Coal?" http://evworld.com/databases/storybuilder.cfm?storyid=250&first=3052&end=3051 accessed June 2, 2002.

7. Gwynne Dyer, *Spectator*, Final Edition, November 17, 1998, A10.

8. *New York Times*, July 4, 1899, 6:4.

9. Ernest H. Wakefield, *History of the Electric Automobile* (Warrendale, PA.: Society of Automotive Engineers, 1994), p. 127.

10. *Scientific American*, February 18, 1899, Vol. 80, p. 98.

11. *Scientific American*, December 21, 1901, Vol. 85, No. 407, p. 407.

12. *Scientific American*, October 18, 1904, Vol. 80, No. 1, p. 5.

13. *Ibid.*, p 4.

14. Kevin A. Wilson, *AutoWeek*, September 2, 2002, Vol. 52, Iss. 36, p. 9.

15. *Outing*, January 1906, Vol. 47, pp. 502–4.

16. *Scientific American*, March 27, 1909, Vol. 100, p. 238.

17. "Danger in Gas Exhaust Fumes," *New York Times*, December 16, 1917, sec. 2, 11:4.

18. Patrick Bedard, "Filling Up with Clean, Free Wind, and Other EV Fantasies," *Car & Driver*, January 1999, Vol. 44, No. 7, p. 19.

19. Alisyn Camerota, "Wind Farms Fan Flames of Controversy," Fox News, August 21, 2003, accessed August 22, 2003 http://www.foxnews.com/story/0,2933,95273,00.html.

20. L. B. Lave, et.al., "Battery Powered Vehicles: Ozone Reduction Versus Lead Discharges," *Environmental Science and Technology,* 1996, Vol. 30, No. 9, p. 402A–407A.

21. John DeCicco and James Kliesch, *ACEEE's Green Book, The Environmental Guide to Cars and Trucks, Model Year 2001* (Washington, D.C.: American Council for an Energy Efficient Economy, 2001), p. 26.

22. *Economist*, April 1, 2000, v. 355, iss. 8164, p. 74.

23. D. Leung, "How the Ballard Fuel Cell Works," *Ottawa Citizen*, May 24, 2001, http://www.tcp.com/~ether/articles/fuel-cells.html accessed September 2, 2001.

24. Jim Motavalli, "Your Next Car?" *Sierra*, July/August 1999, Vol. 84, No. 4, p. 41.

25. Online Fuel Cell Information Center, "Frequently Asked Questions," http://www.fuelcells.org/fcfaqs.html#invest accessed January 22, 2002.

26. *Mass Transit*, July 1998, v. 24, no. 4, p. 32.

27. Carl Pope, Executive Director of the Sierra Club, March 6, 2002, http://newyork.sierraclub.org/rochester/hybrid.htm accessed December 14, 2002.

28. Bill Moore, "Can Wind Compete with Coal?" October 20, 2001, http://evworld.com/databases/storybuilder.cfm?storyid=250 accessed June 2, 2002.

29. Don Ryan, Associated Press 3/26/2002, image number 6207733 (3P1X1).

30. "The Wind Powered Automobile," *Scientific American*, September 1923, Vol. 129, p. 171.

31. Kathleen O'Mara, with assistance from Phillip Jennings, "Wave Energy," Australian Renewable Energy Website, http://www.acre.murdoch.edu.au/ago/ocean/wave.html accessed June 6, 2002.

32. U.S. CAR (Council for Automotive Research), http://www.uscar.org/techno/vrp1.htm accessed April 20, 2000.

33. "Why Detroit's Going Green," *Sierra*, July/August 1999, Vol. 84, No. 4, p. 40.

34. "Toyota's Fuel Cell Vehicles," http://www.toyota.com/html/about/environment/partner_tech/fuelcell_hybrid.html#fchv-5 accessed January 22, 2001.

35. Daniel Becker, Director of the Sierra Club's Global Warming and Energy program, September 19, 2002, http://newyork.sierraclub.org/rochester/hybrid.htm accessed December 14, 2002.

36. David Willett, "Sierra Club Welcomes Honda's New Civic Hybrid," http://lists.sierraclub.org/SCRIPTS/WA.EXE?A2=ind0112&L=ce-scnews-releases&D=1&T=0&H=1&O=D&F=&S=&P=825 December 20, 2001 accessed February 15, 2002.

37. "Hybrid Cars Try Merging into the Mainstream," http://www.thenewenvironmentalist.com/articles_0702/transport1.html#2008 accessed February 15, 2002.

38. "Hybrid Electric Vehicles," Scientific American, October 1997, Vol. 277, Iss. 4, p. 71.

Chapter 4

1. Helmut Weule, head of Daimler-Benz research and technology at their fuel-cell-vehicle unveiling in April 1994.

2. "Recent Improvements in Electric Vehicles," *Scientific American*, September 7, 1912, Vol. 107, No. 10, p. 194.

3. Bob Gritzinger, "Beta vs. VHS?" *AutoWeek*, May 20, 2002, Vol. 52, Issue 21, p. 6.

4. *U.S. News and World Report*, April 29, 2002, Vol. 132, No. 14, p. 59.

5. *Ibid.*

6. Interview with Hugh Holman, Technology Analyst, CIBC, 3/29/00.

7. David A. Kirsch, *The Electric Vehicle and the Burden of History* (New Brunswick, N.J.: Rutgers University Press, 1964), p. 89.

8. *Ibid.*, p. 88.

9. Cy A. Adler and Gary G. Reibsamen, *Electric Vehicles at a Glance* (New York: McGraw-Hill, 1978), p. 12.

10. Kirsch, p. 93.

11. *Scientific American*, December 22, 1900, Vol. 83, No. 25, p. 389.

12. *Ibid.*

13. *Scientific American*, September 7, 1912, Vol. 107, p. 194.

14. *Scientific American*, January 14, 1911, Vol. 104, No. 2, p. 31.

15. *Country Life in America*, January 1913, Vol. 23, pp. 23–6.

16. Hawker Energy Products, Inc., "An Introduction to Batteries," http://www.hepi.com/basics/history.htm accessed April 10, 2000.

17. *Scientific American,* January 14, 1911, Vol. 104, No. 2, p. 30.

18. *Scientific American*, May 13, 1899, Vol. 80, p. 295.

19. *Scientific American*, June 8, 1901, Vol. 84, No. 23 p. 357.

20. *Ibid.* p. 356.

21. *Scientific American*, December 22, 1900, Vol. 83, No. 25, p. 389.

22. *Iron Age*, September 24, 1978, Vol. 221, p. 21.

23. "EV Batteries," http://www.radix.net/~futurev/battery.html accessed October 11, 2000.

24. J. Byron McCormick and James R. Huff, "The Case for Fuel-Cell-Powered Vehicles," *Technology Review* 82 (Aug/Sep 1980), p. 56.

25. *Ibid.*

26. "The Fuel Cell's Bumpy Ride," *Economist*, March 24, 2001, Vol. 358, No. 8214, p. 39.

27. http://www.ballard.com/ accessed February 12, 2000.

28. Interview with Hugh Holman, Technology Analyst, CIBC 3/29/00.

29. Daniel Sperling, *Future Drive* (Washington D.C.: Island Press, 1995), p. 144.

30. http://dealer.vw.com/vwpress/fullStoryA.html?release_id=4904 accessed April 12, 2000.

31. *Scientific American Supplement*, October 24, 1903, Vol. 56, No. 1451, p. 23253.

32. *Ibid.*

33. *Scientific American*, September 20, 1902, Vol. 87, No. 12, p. 196.

34. http://prius.toyota.com/interior/index.html accessed January 12, 2000.

35. http://prius.toyota.com/ accessed March 15, 2000.

36. http://www.honda2001.com/models/insight/customize.html accessed March 12, 2000.

37. Pope, Bryon, "Honda Insight," *AutoWeek*, January 15, 2001, Vol. 51, No. 3, p. 15.

38. http://www.corbinmotors.com/about.htm accessed March 15, 2000.

39. "GM Energy And Environment Strategy," http://www.gm.com/company/environment/products/chart/index.html accessed February 12, 2000.

40. Ford Motor Company, Technical Information Division, Dearborn, MI.

41. P. Bedard, "Why EVs Are No-Shows," *Car & Driver*, March 2000, p. 137.

42. http://www.evrental.com/cars.shtml accessed March 15, 2000.

43. "Aerovironment Electric Vehicle Travels 777 Miles In 24 Hours" http://www.aerovironment.com/news/news-archive/news-fastchrgrecord.html accessed March 12, 2000.

Chapter 5

1. Victor Appleton, *Tom Swift and His Electric Runabout, or the Speediest Car on the Road* (New York: Grosset & Dunlap, 1910).

2. Charles J. Lynch, "Emerging Power Sources," *Science and Technology*, October 1967, p. 36–48.

3. *Ibid.*

4. Hans Fogelberg, *The Electric Car Controversy* (Göteborg, Sweden: Dept. of History and Technology and Industry, Chalmers University of Technology, 1998), p.3.

5. Michael B. Schiffer, Tamara C. Butts, and Kimberly K. Grimm, *Taking Charge: The Electric Automobile in America* (Washington, D.C.: Smithsonian Institution Press, 1994); David A. Kirsch, *The Electric Vehicle and the Burden of History* (New Brunswick, N.J.: Rutgers University Press, 2000); Rudi Volti, "Why Internal Combustion?" *American Heritage of Invention and Technology*, Vol. 6, No. 2 (Fall 1990), 42–47.

6. Michael Schrage, "Toys for Big Boys," *Across the Board*, April 1995, Vol. 32, Iss. 4, p. 47.

7. *Ibid.*

8. *New York Times*, March 9, 1971, 42:1.

9. *House Beautiful*, January 1914, Vol. 35, pp. 56–7.

10. *House Beautiful*, January 1914, Vol. 35, p. 56–7.

11. *Life*, March 11, 1909, Vol. 53, No. 1376, p. 330.

12. *Literary Digest*, July 20, 1912, Vol. 45, No. 1, p. 115.

13. *Life*, March 11, 1909, Vol. 53, No. 1376, p. 331.

14. *New York Times*, March 4, 1906, 12:1.

15. *Scientific American*, November 9, 1907, Vol. 97, p. 330.

16. *New York Times*, January 24, 1909, 4, 4:1.

17. *Ibid.*

18. *Literary Digest*, February 8, 1913, Vol. 46, p. 299.

19. *Literary Digest*, May 10, 1913, Vol. 46, p. 1068.

20. *Ibid.*

21. *Electrical World*, June 6, 1914, Vol. 63, p. 1318.

22. *Ibid.*, p. 1319.

23. *Automobile*, January 21, 1915, Vol. 32, p. 127.

24. *Electrical World*, August 4, 1917, Vol. 70, pp. 212–13.

25. The *New York Times*, January 7, 1917, III, 18:1.

26. *Electrical World*, January 6, 1917, Vol. 69, p. 29.

27. *Ibid.*

28. *Literary Digest*, February 3, 1923, Vol. 76 pp. 60–4.

29. *Life*, May 27, 1909, Vol. 53, No. 1387, p. 744.

30. *Life*, April 20, 1916, Vol. 57, No. 1747, p. 777.

31. *Ibid.*

32. *Life*, May 27, 1909, Vol. 53, No. 1387, p. 744.

33. *Ladies' Home Journal*, June 1912, Vol. 29, No. 11, p. 79.

34. *New York Times*, February 23, 1931, VIII, 6:1.

35. *Outing*, May 1904, Vol. 44, pp. 154–9.

36. *Ibid.*

37. *New York Times*, January 7, 1917, 3, 11:1.

38. *Life*, May 27, 1909, Vol. 53, No. 1387, p. 542.

39. *Ladies' Home Journal*, March 1912, Vol. 29, No. 3, p. 69.

40. *Life*, March 9, 1916, Vol. 57, No. 1741, p. 744.

41. *Walt Disney's Donald Duck Beach Party*, A Giant Comic (New York: Dell Publishing Co., No. 5, 1958).

42. Laura Dent Crane, *The Automobile Girls Along the Hudson or Fighting Fire in Sleepy Hollow* (Philadelphia: Henry Altemus Company 1910).

43. *Ibid.*, p. 19.

44. *Ibid.*, p. 33.

45. *New York Times*, January 7, 1917, 3, 11:1.

46. *Ibid.*

47. *New York Times*, June 24, 1917, II, 4:4.

48. *Scientific American*, December 13, 1902, Vol. 87, No. 24, p. 422.

49. *Scientific American*, December 13, 1902, Vol. 87, No. 24, p. 422.

50. *Cosmopolitan,* August 1900, Vol. 29, No. 4, p. 5.

51. *Horseless Age,* January 24, 1900, Vol. 5, No. 17, p. 12.

52. *New York Times,* December 21, 1906, 10:1.

53. *New York Times,* January 24, 1909, pt.4. 4:1.

54. *Literary Digest,* April 15, 1916, Vol. 52, No. 16, p. 1121.

55. *Life,* January 7, 1909, Vol. 53, no. 1367, p. 37.

56. *Ibid.*

57. *Life,* June 3, 1909, Vol. 53, No. 1388, p. 783.

58. *Life,* April 15, 1909, Vol. 53, No. 1381, p. 533.

59. *Life,* March 18, 1909, Vol. 53, No. 1377, p. 375.

60. *Life,* February 4, 1909, Vol. 52, No. 1386, p. 148.

61. Electric Vehicle Association of America, *Report of the Publicity Committee on the National Co-operative Advertising Campaign of the Electric Vehicle Association of America* (New York: J. Kempster Print. Co., 1912), p. 6.

62. *Ibid.,* p. 9.

63. *Ibid.,* p. 19.

64. *Literary Digest,* December 20, 1919, Vol. 63, No. 12, p. 107.

65. *Harper's Weekly,* August 5, 1911, Vol. 55, No. 2850, p. 29.

66. *Life,* March 9, 1916, Vol. 57, No. 1741, p. 744.

67. *Harper's Weekly,* July 1, 1911, Vol. 55, No. 2845, p. 24.

68. *Electrical World,* June 1, 1911, Vol. 57, No. 22, p. 1374.

69. *New York Times,* September 20, 1953, II, 11:3.

70. *Scientific American,* June 11, 1902, Vol. 86, No. 24, p. 419.

71. *Ibid.*

72. *New York Times,* June 24, 1917, II, 4:4.

73. *WARD'S Auto World,* January 1993, v. 29, p. 51.

74. Raymond Sarafin, "How to Plug Electric Cars," *Advertising Age,* January 11, 1993, Vol. 64, Iss. 2, p. 12.

75. *Ibid.*

76. General Motors Corporation, "Charging toward the Future," http://www.gmev.com/charging/charging.htm accessed October 22, 2002.

77. Josh Landis, "Honda Insight — Part 3," *EV World,* August 09, 2003, http://evworld.com/databases/storybuilder.cfm?storyid=453&first=5687&end=5686 accessed October 23, 2002.

78. *Automotive News,* October 21, 1996, Vol. 71, No. 5683, p. 34i.

79. *Business Week,* December 29, 1997, Iss. 3559, p. 50.

80. *Business Week,* March 2, 1998, Iss. 3567, p. 66.

81. John DeCicco and James Kliesch, *ACEEE's Green Book, The Environmental Guide to Cars and Trucks, Model Year 2001* (Washington, D.C. : American Council for an Energy Efficient Economy, 2001), p. 25.

82. David A. Kirsch, *The Electric Vehicle and the Burden of History* (New Brunswick, N.J.: Rutgers University Press 1964), p. 170.

83. *Ibid.,* p. 174.

84. *Electrical Review and Western Electrician,* October 31, 1914, Vol. 65, pp. 868–74.

85. *Automobile,* October 22, 1914, Vol. 31, pp. 753–4.

86. Bill Moore, "California Cruising by Civic Hybrid — Part 3," *EV World,* August 09, 2003, http://evworld.com/databases/storybuilder.cfm?storyid=419&first=3960&end=3959&subcookie=1.

87. Interview with Hugh Holman, Technology Analyst, CIBC 3/29/00.

88. *Barron's,* June 13, 1977, 57:11+.

89. *Ibid.*

90. M. V. Whalen, *HEV Information Needs Study — Summary of Results* (Golden, Colorado: NREL, U.S. Dept. of Energy, July 2000).

91. *Ibid.*

92. Leslie Eudy, *Field Operations Program — Overview of Advanced Technology Transportation, Update for CY 2001* (Golden, CO: NREL National Renewable Energy Laboratory, April 2001), p. 5.

93. *Ibid.*

94. *Ibid.,* p. 7.

95. *Horseless Age,* January 24, 1900, Vol. 5, No. 37, p. 13.

96. William McWhirter, "Off and Humming," *Time,* April 26, 1993, Vol. 141, Iss. 17, p. 53.

97. William Baumgartner and Andrew Gross, "The Global Market for Electric Vehicles," *Business Economics,* October 2000, v. 35, iss. 4, p. 51.

98. *Ibid.*

Chapter 6

1. *Horseless Age,* March 1897, Vol. 2, No. 5, p. 15–16.

2. Ernest H.Wakefield, *History of the Electric Automobile: Battery-Only powered Cars* (Warrendale, PA: Society of Automotive Engineers, 1994), p. 50.

3. *Scientific American,* May 13, 1899, Vol. 80, No. 19, p. 293.

4. Wakefield, p. 127.

5. *Scientific American,* September 2, 1899, Vol. 81, No. 81, p. 153.

6. James J. Flink, *America Adopts the Automobile, 1895–1910* (Cambridge, Massachusetts: MIT Press, 1970), p. 238 p. 35. (Original source, "Fairly Howling," *Motor World,* October 11, 1900, Vol. 1, No. 17.)

7. Wakefield, p. 213.

8. *Ibid.*

9. *The Automobile* (New York: Cassell and Company, Ltd., 1905), Vol. II, p. 730–3.

10. Hans Fogelberg, *The Electric Car Controversy* (Goteborg, Sweden: Dept. of History and Technology and Industry, Chalmers University of Technology, 1998), p. 71.

11. *Cyclopedia of Automobile Engineering* (Chicago: American Technical Society, 1910), Vol. 3, pp. 101–3.

12. Wakefield, p. 219.

13. Electric Vehicle Association of America, *Report of the Publicity Committee on the National Co-operative Advertising Campaign of the Electric Vehicle Association of America* (New York: J. Kempster Print. Co., 1912), p. 1.

14. *Scientific American,* January 14, 1911, Vol. 104, No. 2, p. 31.

15. *Electrical World*, June 22, 1911, Vol. 57, No. 25, p. 1590.

16. Electric Vehicle Association of America, *Report of the Publicity Committee*, p. 15.

17. *Ibid.*

18. Wakefield, p. 247.

19. *Scientific American*, September 7, 1912, Vol. 107, No. 10, p. 194.

20. "Electric Cars," *The Automobile*, January 21, 1915, Vol. 32, p.132.

21. *Electrical World*, June 11, 1921, Vol. 77, p. 1357.

22. *Ibid.*

23. *Ibid.*, p. 1358.

24. *Electrical Review*, November 17, 1922, Vol. 91, pp. 740–1.

25. *Ibid.*

26. *Electric Review*, February 16, 1940, pp. 177–180.

27. *Ibid.*

28. *Saturday Evening Post*, March 12, 1960 accessed 04/17/2001 through http://www.econogics.com/ev/se6000312.htm.

29. *Scientific American*, October 1966, Vol. 215, No. 4, pp. 34–40.

30. *Science News*, March 11, 1967, Vol. 91, p. 232.

31. *Auto Week*, November 11, 2002, Vol. 52, No. 46, p. 15.

32. *New York Times Index*, August 30, 1970, IV, 10:1.

33. Wakefield, p. 278.

34. *Industry Week*, January 28, 1974, Vol. 180, p. 24+.

35. *Industry Week*, June 3, 1974, Vol. 181, p. 42.

36. A.F. Burke, *Evaluation of State-of-Charge Indicator Approaches for EVs*, SAE 8990816 (Warrendale, PA: Society of Automotive Engineers, 1989).

37. Wakefield, p. 155.

38. Jeff Zodronik, *Eighth International Electric Vehicle Symposium*, Washington, D.C., 1986

39. *Technology Review*, August 1996, p. 50.

40. Lester B. Lave, et al., "Battery-powered Vehicles: Ozone Reductions Versus Discharges," *Environmental Science and Technology*, Vol. 30, Iss. 9, p. 402A.

41. *Scientific American*, October 1997, Vol. 277, Iss. 4, p. 70.

42. *Business Week*, March 2, 1998, Iss. 3567, p. 68.

43. "Fuel-cell Miracles and Urban Sprawl," *Car and Driver*, August 1999, Vol. 45, No. 2, p. 30.

44. *Sierra*, July 1999, Vol. 84, No. 4, p. 34.

45. *Time*, April 29, 2002, Vol. 159, No. 17, p. 52.

46. Fogelberg, p.95.

47. "Honda Insight 2001," http://cartalk.cars.com/Info/Testdrive/Reviews/honda-insight-2001.html accessed August 3, 2003.

48. Kevin A. Wilson, "Green Machines and Politics," *AutoWeek*, January 13, 2003, Vol. 53, Iss. 2, p. 16.

Select Bibliography

Bedard, Patrick. "Filling Up with Clean, Free Wind, and Other EV Fantasies." *Car & Driver*, January 1999, 19.

Good list of why environmentalists object to every form of power plant. Hydroelectric power depletes salmon runs in the Northwest. Wind turbines kill birds. Solar power takes up too much space and doesn't work at night. Geothermal sites are located in protected areas. Nuclear energy has waste storage problems. "EVs, in the real world, don't pass the laugh test."

_____. "Why EVs Are No-Shows." *Car & Driver*, March 2000, 137.

The article gives five reasons why ZEV technology is not important in Y2K. It includes an interesting observation from Daniel Sperling that the "new" gasoline cars with RFG are "for all practical purposes, zero emitting." It remarks that EV advocates are giving up and CARB is backpedaling. It notes that the U.S. Advanced Battery Consortium (USABC), an industry/government partnership formed in1991 to produce a practical EV battery, has not been successful, finding itself in a Catch-22 situation. The battery technology cannot deliver the performance and range expected by consumers and the vehicles must be sold at a loss. Consumers are not willing to spend more money for less-than-average performance.

Brown, Mark B. "The Civil Shaping of Technology: California's Electric Vehicle Program." *Science, Technology and Human Values* 26(1): 56 (Winter 2001).

Lengthy technical and political discussion of how government shapes technology policy for people and how people shape civic policies. Points out that while government has a role to play in shaping new technologies, its policies are also shaped by citizens. CARB is an example in its setting regulations and later revising them. Initial CARB policy (1990) was designed to promote a "participatory [citizen] conception of citizenship." When it realized in 1996 that the public was not particularly interested in buying EVs, it began changing factors involving technical criteria and postponed initial sales mandates. This shift in policy recognized a "consumer conception of citizenship." Citizens and consumers may play different roles. While a citizen may favor a regulation promoting EVs, the consumer does not act on it by purchasing an EV.

Brown, Stuart F. "It's the Battery, Stupid." *Popular Science*, February 1995, 62.

Considers the situation of government's issuing policies when the technology is not yet ready. CARB's mandate that 2 percent of all vehicles sold in California by 1998 must be ZEVs is questioned. The price of an electric vehicle was too high, requiring subsidies and tax credits. Even with that stimulus, EVs were not a marketable alternative. Also mentions that the mandate of the time was to require manufacturers to build electric cars, but not necessarily to sell them.

Crane, Laura Dent. *The Automobile Girls Along the Hudson or Fighting Fire in Sleepy Hollow.* Philadelphia: Henry Altemus Co., 1910.

The Automobile Girls series was advertised, with a number of other young adult series, as

"The Best and Least Expensive Books for Real Boys and Girls. These fascinating volumes will interest boys and girls of every age under sixty." The price was 50 cents per volume. This series followed the adventures of four young women and their aunt as they motored outside New York City. Although they were motoring in an automobile they had to start by cranking, the clothing and sentiments about driving reflect those of both electric and gasoline motorist enthusiasts of the era.

"An Interesting Automobile Damage Case." *Scientific American*. December 21, 1901, 85(407): 407. Describes a case in Bridgeport, Connecticut, in 1901 that involved a silent electric vehicle approaching a horse-drawn carriage from behind. The horse was spooked and the carriage driver was thrown down and dragged. Part of the complaint argued that the electric vehicle was so noiseless in its running that it was dangerous. The driver lost his case, but the important part historically was not the case itself but the judge's instructions to the jury. The growing realization was that motoring interest was expanding and that all must recognize a personal responsibility and show a respect for the right-of-way of fellow motorists, and that carriage riders must accommodate the faster motorized transports.

"Maryland Favors Auto Reciprocity." *New York Times*, March 3, 1912, sec. 4, 10:1. Examines early state laws concerning the use of roadways by automobiles licensed in various states. New Jersey had passed a bill allowing non-resident tourists to use the highways for a period of fifteen days. The new Maryland law would repeal the current law requiring non-residents to obtain a tag to be affixed to the rear of the vehicle before using the Maryland roads. It also included a provision that would require motorists to display at least one bright light during the period from one hour after sunset to one hour before sunrise.

McCormick, J. Byron, and James R. Huff. "The Case for Fuel-Cell-Powered Vehicles." *Technology Review*. 82:54 (1980). Good brief history of fuel-cell development from 1839 through 1970s. Mentions that Wilhelm Ostwald, in 1894, foresaw the pollution problems with the internal combustion engine, but his electrochemical strategy was not understood and so not implemented. Touches on research by Allis-Chalmers Manufacturing Company into hydrogen/propane oxygen fuel cell, the predecessor of the cells used in *Apollo*'s backup system, cells using phosphoric acid electrolyte, potassium hydroxide electrolyte, the six-kilowatt alkaline fuel-cell built by Karl Kordesch of Union Carbide, and briefly on the feasibility studies in 1978 for economic potential of fuel cells. Result of the study: the technology was there, but the economics were still out of reach.

Neil, Dan. "Pump This!" *Car & Driver*, April 1999, 110. Amusing tale of a journey across country in 1999 by two reporters using a natural-gas-fired car. They run into a few problems. Although they had been told the car would have a range of about 300 miles, it actually was more like 120 miles. Their bible was the *Directory of U.S. Natural Gas Vehicle Fueling Stations*, which they found was loaded with "out-of-date and erroneous information that has been painstakingly tabulated by chimps." Many of the stations required a unique charge card for that particular station. They discover that due to recent industry deregulation, natural gas companies cannot pass on the price of infrastructure-building to consumers, resulting in more CNG outlets closing instead of opening. They gave up the trip in Colorado after eighty hours of travel averaging 26 miles per hour.

Perrin, Noel. *Solo: Life with an Electric Car*. New York: W. W. Norton & Co., 1992. A fun story about an adventure of a cross-country trip with an electric car. Noel Perrin drove his new electric car in 1991 from California to Vermont and describes his experiences on his journey. The car was a converted solar-electric Ford Escort with a cruising speed of 65 mph and a range of 45–60 miles. Hills, mountains and finding a place to plug in to recharge make for an entertaining adventure. He arrived in Vermont after three weeks and put the car to use as a daily commuter.

Raynal, Wes. "Honda Insight — The Smart Car." *AutoWeek*, July 31, 2000, 13. Positive report about the beginning of a year-long test drive of the Honda Insight. The

AutoWeek test driver will use the car under normal driving conditions for one year; initially the car is getting 55 mpg. The only negatives to date are: a lousy stereo system and noise at freeway speeds.

Schiffer, Michael Brian. *Taking Charge: The Electric Automobile in America.* Washington, D.C., and London: Smithsonian Institution Press, 1994.
Very good history. Emphasizes Ford and Edison working together. Places demise of electric cars on social factors. Women wanted them, but didn't have the financial influence to affect the market.

Schrage, Michael. "Toys for Big Boys." *Across the Board*, April 1995, 22.
Points out perceived differences between men and women in their preferences in vehicles: men want cars as toys for power, touring, racing and adventure; women want reliability, comfort, safety and cleanliness. "The patriarchal family structure [of the early 1900s] and the economic nature of the middle class is what doomed the electric car." Points out that EVs are a good idea, but that doesn't necessarily make them a viable innovation.

Sperling, Daniel. *Future Drive.* Washington, D.C.: Island Press, 1995.
Takes an assertive stance promoting environmental and economic transportation ASAP. Looks at the history of electric vehicles and has a sprinkling of the politics of CARB. Explains a variety of possible non-conventional solutions. Feels the government is best equipped to guide consumers and encourage experimentation with vehicles and fuels in a benign way.

Wakefield, Ernest H. *History of the Electric Automobile: Battery-Only Powered Cars.* Warrendale, PA: Society of Automotive Engineers, Inc., 1994.
Definitive and thorough history of battery-powered vehicles. Includes many photographs and technical charts concerning batteries.

_____. *History of the Electric Automobile: Hybrid Electric Vehicles.* Warrendale, PA: Society of Automotive Engineers, Inc., 1998.
Comprehensive coverage and historical account of hybrid automobiles involving electricity, flywheels, gasoline and solar power. Includes many photographs and technical drawings. Briefly mentions the Toyota Prius introduced in Japan in 1997. About half the book is dedicated to solar power. It is extensively documented with about 30–40 references per chapter.

Zittel, John D. "Electric Vehicles from Letters to the Editor." *Issues in Science and Technology* 11:14 (Spring 1995).
In response to Sperling's article "Gearing Up for Electric Cars," Zittel argues that consumers will respond to EVs only if they can be a competitive option to conventional vehicles. Sperling's suggestion that EV government mandates are the only way is quietly challenged. Zittel suggests that the USABC shows promise in delivering on a suitable battery. It may be that flexibility for manufacturers is a better means for meeting the environmental problems as EV mandates may indicate that electric is better than internal combustion, but the environmental costs of exotic materials for the auto and auto battery components is less clear.

Index

Index